Her Name ......

My Daughter, Her Transition and Why We Must Remember Her

CAROLINE LITMAN

Caroline Litman is a writer, campaigner and former psychiatrist based in Surrey. She is on X as @alicemydaughter.

Alice Litman died by suicide in May 2022, aged just twenty years old, having already waited almost three years for her first appointment at a gender identity clinic.

In stunningly beautiful prose, Caroline Litman captures the realities of an often-messy journey navigating both her daughter's transition and the days, weeks and months after Alice's untimely death.

Searing, urgent and utterly unique, *Her Name is Alice* is the raw, human story of a mother's love and grief for her child – and of a young trans woman who is impossible to forget and who *must* be remembered.

FOR PR ENQUIRIES PLEASE CONTACT:
alex.layt@harpercollins.co.uk

HB: 9780008667931 | EB: 9780008667948 | EA: 9780008667955

Some trans readers may find discussions of suicide, self harm, body dysmorphic disorder and genital mutilation distressing. Names and identifying characteristics have been changed in order to protect people's privacy.

Mudlark
An imprint of HarperCollins*Publishers*
1 London Bridge Street
London SE1 9GF

www.harpercollins.co.uk

HarperCollins*Publishers*
Macken House, 39/40 Mayor Street Upper
Dublin 1, D01 C9W8, Ireland

First published by Mudlark 2024

1 3 5 7 9 10 8 6 4 2

A catalogue record of this book is
available from the British Library

ISBN 978-0-00-866793-1

Printed and bound in the UK using 100%
renewable electricity at CPI Group (UK) Ltd

For Alice ...
... and for Kate, Harvey and Peter,
who must live without her.

Prologue

When my third child was born, I was told I had a boy. The baby was given a boy's name and raised in that gender. But when she died, twenty years later, she died as my daughter, and will forever be remembered that way.

Throughout this memoir, Alice is referred to as Alice, whether I'm writing about her before, or after, her transition. She had a different name for many years, but this is commonly referred to as a 'dead-name' and I choose not to use it.

I also use she and her pronouns to talk about her throughout. In this way, I acknowledge what I believe Alice wanted: to have been seen as a girl from the start. I use the word trans to describe any individual who was assumed one gender at birth but lives as a different one. Very occasionally, I use the word cis to describe anyone who is not trans, anyone whose internal sense of gender aligns with their sex assigned at birth. I do this where required to make it clear I'm talking about people who are not trans. Some people consider the word cis a slur. I use it as a descriptor, for clarity.

A trans woman is assigned male at birth but identifies as female. By 'assigned male at birth', I mean the midwife announcing proudly, 'It's a boy', due to the presence of the typical male genitalia of a penis and testes. This is what happened with Alice.

———

And what is this, my story? A story of joy, fear, regret, anger, shame, love, confusion, hope and almost unbearable sadness. My story is this: that for a long time, Alice had a different name, was raised with all the expectations that her earlier name bestowed. She was a more vulnerable and precious child than I could ever have imagined having the privilege to know. A child for whom living as she deserved to live is all too often a subject for political, religious and journalistic debate, and dinner-table entertainment. A child who taught me humility, tolerance and compassion; yet a child born into a society that struggles to understand her and her kin, and seems to offer little tolerance or compassion in return.

This is the story of her childhood – of our special bond that felt sublime, almost supernatural, as though nothing would ever break it. It is the story of a breakage – how in one profound way I was not connected to Alice at all. For a long time, there was something deep and fundamental in her make-up that she did not know herself, so how could I? It is the story of her first tentative steps along the rocky path towards transition, and how, at first, I was not much better than those dinner-party guests I scorn, I am afraid. In my desperate attempts to maintain the status quo, I would at first put her at considerable risk. And I'm not particularly unusual or unique in this response; I'm fairly typical of many of my peers, with my fears, doubts and misunderstandings. And when life seemed at last to be running smoothly, being kind to me, I would cry: why, Alice? Why her? Why me? Why this?

It is a story that tells how fear – both hers and mine – that might so easily have destroyed her before she had the chance to embrace her true self turned to acceptance and the embracing of difference. It is a story about change, for both of us, and the hope that blossomed that final spring. It is the story of my grief; for when all the signs pointed to the path levelling off, and the possibility of a future seemed within her reach, she chose to die. It is her legacy.

25–26 May 2022

A knock at the door, a trip to accident and emergency

On the morning of Thursday, 26 May 2022, at around 8.30 a.m. there's a ring at the door. I don't hear it. I'm in a deep sleep, having spent the night in accident and emergency with my ninety-five-year-old mother. Mum is registered blind, due to a triple whammy of glaucoma, cataracts and macular degeneration, but this doesn't stop her living a full and independent life. She's a keen gardener and loves nothing more than spending time pottering in her garden, pruning, weeding and watering.

This was how she'd spent the previous morning until a stubborn weed that would not budge caused her to tumble backwards, sustaining a nasty cut to her elbow. Mum's skin is tissue-paper thin and peels off her flesh like the skin from an overripe peach. Typically, she didn't want to bother me, so she sought the help of a neighbour, a one-time district nurse, who Steri-Stripped her wound. Suffice to say, at eighty-three herself, the neighbour's patching skills weren't what they used to be. So, some eight hours after Mum's fall, around 7 p.m., I received a call: I'm in a bit of a mess, can you pop over?

Mum still lives in my childhood home, and it's just fifteen minutes away. I arrive to find her in a bad way. As I remove the loose bandage from around her wound, a congealed Steri-Strip bundle slides down her arm, in a lava-like flow. There is a large skin flap, with embedded soil and debris. It is beyond my repair skills, so we head to the local hospital, where we wait nine hours for Mum to be seen. Which is why, after seeing her safely into bed, I don't return home to slip under my own duvet until almost 7 a.m. the following day and why I am

3

dead to the world when the doorbell rings one and a half hours later. Instead, I'm woken by my husband, Peter, shaking me gently on the shoulder. There's a policeman at the door, he says.

29 November 1971

An earlier knock at the door, an unfortunate incident by the bread van, the seeding of shame and anger

I've experienced a policeman at the door before. Not a policeman exactly, a man in uniform, army uniform. And on this occasion, he hadn't come to speak to me.

My father was a major in the Royal Artillery and we were on a posting in Germany. My brother, then aged ten (six years older than me), was away at boarding school in England. So, on the day in question, it was just me and my parents living together in army quarters, with other army families all around.

Writing now, it strikes me that this is the first time I've ever referred to myself as having parents, in the plural. I've never spoken of two parents, together, have never had a conscious sense of my mother and father existing simultaneously. My life has had two distinct eras: 'when Daddy was alive' (an abstract concept for me, as I've no memory of it at all) and 'after Daddy died', mostly just me and Mum. This was the way my mother defined our lives, so it was the way I framed it, too. All the stories I know of 'when Daddy was alive' have been told to me, almost entirely, by my mum. What I'm about to tell you now was told to me by her first, some forty years after it happened, over a cup of tea in her garden.

———

I was upstairs playing. My father was out on military exercise, only for the morning, due back for lunch – tuna spaghetti casserole (Oooh, good, I like that, he'd said, as he left).

Around the time he was due back to eat, there was a knock at the door. I wasn't called down, not this time. My mother answered. It was a colleague of my father's. There's been an accident, he said. Mike is dead. His jeep was driven off the road by a lorry. It hit a tree. The only tree for miles around, he continued, as if to rub the bad luck in a little bit harder. He would have died instantly, he added, as some sort of consolation.

Later that day, my mother, in shock, told me there'd been an accident, that Daddy was in hospital, that he was very ill. So I went to bed that night thinking Daddy was still alive.

In the morning, I asked to go out to play. There were lots of children on the base and it was a Saturday. The local baker was doing his rounds, selling fresh bread and pastries from his van. But he also had trays of sweets, and on Saturdays, all the children would swarm around to buy them. That morning was no different. My mother gave me a few pfennigs and let me go.

The next thing my mother knew, there was a loud knocking on the door, and one of the other army wives was asking her, breathlessly, What have you told Caroline about Mike?

Nothing, said my mother. Only that he's ill.

The neighbour went on, You've got to tell her. The children are telling her.

I have to imagine my experience that day because imagination is all I have.

The other children had been told my father was dead. Your dad's dead, they must have said. No, he's not, I would have retaliated. Yes, he is, they would have gone on. He's not, I would have said again. Is … isn't … is … isn't … That's how I imagine it. Me standing my ground and defending myself, because I knew the truth. I had it from the most reliable source: my mother.

But after the neighbour left, my mother called me in. She sat in the hall, on the bottom step, and patted the space next to her for me to sit by her side.

The lies the children had been telling me were confirmed as truths. It was I, not them, who was wrong. I must have been flooded with feelings, feelings adults at the time thought too complicated for a four-year-old to experience. Sadness, of course, fear and anger, but this other thing, too – shame and embarrassment. I was wrong.

As my mother told it, I turned and pummelled her with both fists, kicked her, too, shouting, Not my daddy, not my daddy. She tried to comfort me, but I wriggled free and ran upstairs, shut myself in my room, behind a slammed door, threw myself on my bed and howled.

As my mother recounted this story to me – and I say this because it felt like a story and not something that happened to me – she said she was so surprised.

What? That I was angry? I asked.

Yes. You were so cross, with me and I didn't know why.

I can guess, I replied. But in the moment, Mum seemed not to hear me, couldn't really grasp it, acknowledge any kind of mistake in the telling.

I've lived with the fallout from that day my whole life. A tripwire set deep inside of me that gets tripped more times than I care to recall. Growing up, and into adulthood, I've struggled to believe in myself, to speak up, unless I'm absolutely certain I am right. And even then, I harbour a constant nagging fear of being proved wrong. I have always been this way.

And it's left me with one other scar. I expect bad things to happen to me. And they often do. Mine is a life lived in expectation, waiting for the next knock at the door.

Late May 2022

A momentary suspension of belief

When it comes, I don't feel a massive rush of fear or panic. I walk calmly downstairs, merely thinking, it can't be Mum. I only put her to bed a few hours ago; what possible trouble could she have got into in that time, and how would the police even know?

Our house is almost entirely open-plan downstairs. I descend our spiral staircase to find the policeman hovering sheepishly inside the front door. Is there somewhere we could sit? he asks.

I'm about to be told bad news, for sure. I gesture to the clearly visible sofa and chairs in the sunken living area, thinking, haven't you got eyes in your head? You're clearly not much of a detective. My brain allows me to scorn the policeman for using a stock phrase he must have used many times before delivering bad news – even lets me be a little amused with myself. But it won't let me think anything bad has happened to my immediate family; it's protecting me. Who's dead? I wonder. I move on from my mother to my brother, to one of his children: Rosie, Michael or Grace? How odd, I think, that they should send a policeman here, at this time, to tell me this. How sad. And even when the penny does begin to drop – because who has ever been woken by a knock on the door from a nervous policeman to tell them their niece is dead? – I think first of Kate and Harvey. Kate has been assaulted in Leeds, Harvey has been in an accident in Central America, that's it. Until my thoughts finally settle on my youngest child, Alice. It's Alice, I say. It's Alice. Because of course it is Alice. What's happened to Alice?

1996–2002

From careless shag to family of five

Alice was born in Epsom General Hospital on 23 February 2002. I was thirty-four. She was my third child, a child I wanted more than anything else in the world.

For a medic, family planning hadn't been my forte. Peter and I conceived Kate after a giggly, rash moment of unprotected sex in the spring of 1996. Six weeks later, immediately before my first set of exams for Part-1 membership of the Royal College of Psychiatrists, I began to feel sick. I put it down to nerves. When my nausea didn't subside with the exams over, I took a pregnancy test. It was positive and I was happy, but it wasn't planned.

In my first antenatal class I sat next to Jane. We made some small talk and soon became, if not quite friends at first, then allies. We were sarcastic and unkind about some of the other women in the group who appeared to be wholesome 1950s' caricatures of mothers in this affluent, leafy village we called home. They would give up work and dedicate themselves to motherhood, whilst Jane and I planned to return to our jobs and pursue our careers. Joining forces gave us something intangible that we didn't possess as individuals, a security that came with a recognition of some sort between us. Initially at least, our relationship was perhaps built more on shared fear – of ourselves, each other, the outside world – than affection. It was complicated. But we made each other laugh and that was a start.

Once Peter and I had embarked on having a family, I imagined a large one, an abundance of babies, who would be better respected and understood than I had ever been. But our family, like most, began with one, then grew from there.

I secretly hoped for a boy. Despite her solid love and support, and some spectacular triumphs at certain points, my relationship with my mum growing up had been tricky. My experiential view of mother–daughter relationships was that they were unpredictable and often quite unpleasant. So, I preferred to think of myself as the mother of a boy first, then a girl, once I was more accomplished. But Kate came out, a daughter. Jane had a boy, Archie. I regularly dressed Kate in navy and red, but with maybe a little nod to her gender (a bow detail, or pink socks), then felt irritated when strangers thought she was a boy, because they didn't look closely enough and made assumptions.

We took our babies to the rounds of postnatal coffee mornings, but we felt separate, somehow, from these other mums who seemed to be getting on just fine with themselves and each other, so we attended less and less. Jane out of necessity, as she quickly returned to work, and me because I felt like an outsider without my ally. Kate was an easy baby, during daylight hours, so – without Jane's eye to catch and illicit plans for a trip to the pub to be made – sitting in endless coffee mornings, with other people whose babies bawled and retched, held little appeal. Jane was my aqualung and without her I couldn't breathe. Instead, when the opportunity arose, we took our babies to the pub that summer, pushed them in their buggies and drank a little more than we should. We moaned about our own mothers much of the time, yet didn't think we were very good at mothering ourselves. We pretended not to care; we were above all this – more than mothers. But really, we were sinking.

After Kate was born, I had complications of an infected episiotomy. The pain made sex impossible. Six months later, I had surgery to repair an open wound that hadn't healed. Post surgery, things felt no better. I was still breastfeeding, so wasn't on the pill. I wanted to be intimate with Peter, but our first attempt at post-surgery sex, using a condom, reduced me to tears. I began to catastrophise that our sex life was ruined and desperately missed the special bond that came from good sex. We tried again, and as pain arrived once more, in teeth-clenching waves, I told Peter to abandon the condom. I didn't care; I couldn't do it any other way.

He was at work when I peed on a pregnancy test for the second time in my life. I pushed nine-month-old Kate to the pond and we sat watching the 'duckdars' (Kate's first word). I held the positive test in one hand, rocked the pram with the other and sobbed. I hadn't had one period since having Kate. I couldn't have another baby, I wailed silently to myself. I couldn't cope with the one I had. And I'd more exams to do, to climb the career ladder: registrar, senior reg, consultant. It was way too soon. How would we manage the childcare? When would I study? All the usual questions. But I wasn't about to have an abortion – this was something I felt very strongly about. Other people could do it, but not me. Babies were not for terminating, or worse still, giving away. As an adopted person, both were anathema to me.

I loved Kate so much that now I was pregnant again I wanted another girl – what I knew – but this time, I had a son, Harvey. As far as Peter was concerned, we were done. A neat little nuclear family: mother, daughter, father, son. It was hard, working as a junior doctor with night shifts and weekends and a husband who commuted to a London office job. It was what I'd always wanted, a family of my own, but it wasn't working out quite as anticipated. After a couple of years of peace and harmony between Kate and Harvey, probably around the time Harvey learned to speak, they decided they didn't really care for each other that much and the he-said-she-said tittle-tattle began. I had no instinct for how to deal with it. I didn't feel like a very good mother, certainly not the ideal I had pictured for myself, righting all the wrongs of a previous generation. Our social circle narrowed, as it became increasingly difficult to take our children anywhere when they fought at the slightest thing, and they – and I – were met with disapproving stares. We employed a series of au pairs to help me with childcare, but they rarely stayed long, for either I did not like them or they did not like us.

The instinct I did have was that another child would help. Perhaps not the large family I'd imagined, but just one more. Peter was appalled. No! he said, regularly reminding me of the lunacy of my plan when I was reduced to tears by yet another physical wound or war of words between our warring infants. I pleaded and pleaded but he wouldn't budge. I wouldn't let it go. I wanted to change our family dynamic, not just between Kate and Harvey, but intergenerationally. I didn't want the one-boy-one-girl structure of the jinxed family I grew up in. A third child would break my family curse. I pressed on and on with my need, though I knew I couldn't expect it. I was afraid of running out of time. Kate turned four in December 2000, Harvey would be three the following June, I feared that the older they got, the weaker my argument would become.

Then one night, in the late spring of 2001, Peter rolled over to me in bed and said, with a broad grin, Shall we try for that third baby, then? I can feel the thrill of it as if it was last night. (If he was hoping for a ramping up of our sex life, he had a short memory – it had become a private joke that we could probably conceive a baby over the phone.)

We went to a wedding that June, the day after I'd peed on a stick for the third time. There's a picture of Peter and me on that day, which is my absolute favourite photo of us together, ever. During the speeches, I'd knotted all the pale pink ribbons from the dainty bags of wedding-favour almonds into bows in his short black hair. The picture is so full of joy and contentment. Pleasure radiates from me; I have never looked so beautiful. I was expecting Alice.

26 May 2022

Bad news, the first sign of difference, a marriage put to the test

Twenty years later, I am sitting in my living room, hearing my daughter is dead.

The policeman is kind. He attempts to soften an unsoftenable blow. His sister-in-law killed herself the previous year, he says, so he has some understanding of how we are feeling. This is well intentioned, but I dismiss him. I've just been told that a body has been found on the undercliff path at Rottingdean. There's reason to believe it's Alice. I do not know myself how I'm feeling, so how can he? I'm thinking, here we are, this is it, this is what it is like, this thing I have been quietly expecting all my mothering life, it has arrived. I feel quite composed, as if what's happening isn't happening to me. I don't seem to mind that much. I well up a little, as if I'm listening to a radio drama, experiencing some fictional loss.

There is a moment, when the policeman has to check Alice's gender, just to clarify. She is trans, I say. He nods in understanding and continues his duties as he should, never misgendering her, mindful that she is our child and she is dead. Though at this stage he is repeatedly at pains to say he – the police – are not certain it's Alice, there's reason to believe it could be her, but it isn't confirmed. There have been mistakes in the past, it seems, but I have no doubt. The policeman talks but I'm not really listening. I just say, 'It's Alice, it's Alice, I know it's her'. Over and over.

He's explaining how they've traced us from a mobile phone found at the scene. I don't really care for the police procedural part of how they've come to be here, in my living room, telling me my child is, probably (definitely) dead. He goes on. Can he show us a photo of a distinctive jacket found at the scene? Yes, that's hers. Can we describe a tattoo on her upper arm. Yes, again. Could we clarify: left or right? We're not sure, it was fairly new. We've only seen it once. There is a tattoo on her torso, too; no, we don't know about that.

For me these checks feel pointless. I'm convinced that it's my daughter who's been found, by a passer-by, around 5.30 a.m. on that clear late May morning. Poor chap, minding his own business, on his way to work in Brighton. Alice has ruined his day. I'm certain and oddly detached.

Peter's in bits, sobbing uncontrollably, making wounded animal noises, groaning and moaning: no, no, no. He's sat on the far end of the sofa, as far away from me and the policeman as possible, as if putting distance between us somehow separates him from the fact of Alice's death. I sit on an armchair and remain composed. If this is what bereavement looks like, it turns out I'm rather good at it. This time, anyway. It doesn't feel that bad; in this moment, I have it nailed. How odd that the poets and the playwrights have it all wrong, I think.

And then somehow, we're together and hugging and Peter is asking, begging, please don't turn me into the man in your story. I won't, I won't, I reply. But it has already crossed my mind, that weeping and snotty as he is, he's rather like Bob. Bob is the fictional husband in a short story I wrote about fifteen years previously for an Open University creative writing course, back in the brief period when I'd thought I might turn my hand to writing and never did. A story that began with a policeman knocking at the door – a remarkably prescient story as it now turns out. And in that story the husband and wife split up after the death of their daughter. A process that begins when Bob reaches for his wife's hand and she, repulsed by the pudgy, wet, raw-sausage sliminess of his grip, pulls away. I hold on to

Peter, repeat that he isn't Bob, but his snot-smeared cheek rubbing against mine does not reassure me.

The policeman wants a picture of Alice, so we'll be spared having to make a formal identification of her body. In these times of social media, with cameras on almost every phone, you'd think we would be able to lay our hands on a picture of her with the utmost ease, but we can't. Alice has been camera-shy over the past few years. Not many photos have been taken, and those that were have never been printed off – a task for a rainy day with some spare time, a day that's never come. So, we sit, separately again now, and scroll through thousands of photos in unsorted albums and WhatsApp threads. We swipe and curse, swipe and apologise, swipe and joke: I have this one of her sister, where they look very alike – you can have that, I quip. Of course, it will not do. I can feel my heart quickening, a restlessness vibrating through my body, as I scroll and scroll. Alice is gone and I don't have a single picture. I'm a bad mother. Not a single picture as she is now, not one. And then I find one and I feel relief that I'm not such a bad mother, after all. And it's perfect, the picture. She looks so beautiful and happy and she's back with me, though it's just a picture, which I show to the policeman on my phone. She's wearing the jacket – that would seal it. Yes, the policeman says, this one will do. I feel almost pleased, that the photo is suitable. Until, abruptly, I don't.

I don't suppose it takes much more than an hour, this visit that veers my life off on yet another tangent, and then he's gone, and we're on our own and must make plans. The real and very practical business of bereavement is about to begin. People have to be told. Kate and Harvey need to know. There is not a moment to lose. They must not find out any other way.

2002–2010

Bottom shuffling, mirror writing and bedwetting, amongst other things

Once we were expecting our third child, we decided to find out the sex of the baby in advance. Kate was five years old and insisting on a sister. We wanted to prepare her for any disappointment. But when Alice was born, we didn't have to worry. She was a delight and adored by everyone. I asked Jane to be Alice's godmother. We had grown close over the intervening years. Jane, like me, marvelled at this new little baby who was so at peace in her world, when we were so at sea in ours.

Our tendency to drink to numb some of the terror of parenting had, in Jane, developed into alcohol dependence, which I discovered one sunny summer afternoon in 2002, when Alice was just six months old, and all seemed ok with the world. I'd dropped in on Jane with a bottle of wine, on my way to take Harvey to a swimming party. We enjoyed a glass each, before I left with Harvey for the party. When I returned, around half an hour later and suggested another glass, there was an awkward moment. Jane had finished the bottle whilst I was gone. I remember our mutual discomfort, the vast silence, as I dug deep to say something to her. I was working in the drug-and-alcohol dependency unit at the time; I couldn't ignore it. That Christmas, she was booked into the Priory for five weeks of rehab and has been sober ever since.

I sometimes wonder if I could have gone the same way, too, if I'd also been on my own, if being Alice's mother had been anything less than effortless. She slept through the night from six weeks. Not the meagre five hours from midnight to 5 a.m. that many new mums would reasonably claim as a huge victory, but a full twelve hours from 7 p.m. to 7 a.m. Her older siblings had been terrible sleepers; this baby who slept so long was a gift from the gods. She never seemed to whinge and cry the way her siblings had, or other babies did, I always seemed to know what was needed, be it food, warmth or a nappy change, and she was content. If Alice had been my first, I'd have been an unbearably smug new mother. But she was my third and I was simply happy that I seemed to have found my maternal instinct.

And Alice had these little things about her that connected me to her in a way that was so deeply gratifying. As an adopted person, I felt outside of my family, by way of looks and personality, and in other ethereal ways. Growing up, I felt very alone, different, misunderstood. Now I was a mother, I had biological connections to my children, but people would keep telling me how like their father Kate and Harvey looked. Then Alice came along and everything changed. She had a slightly misshapen left ear: a pink penny shrimp of an ear, with the helix – the rolled-over bit at the top and around the edge – stuck down to the main part of the ear, so you couldn't run your thumb tip into the gap. I have the same minor deformity on my ear, too, but on the right-hand side.

When I traced my birth mother later, she wrote me a letter, describing a little defect on her left ear. Like Alice! I gasped. For the first time I had a family thread that connected me, by a little zig-zag stitch through time, to my world. I felt secure.

When Alice reached three months old, I became suddenly irritable, impatient and snappy – not with her, but with her siblings and Peter. I'd felt like this when the initial joy of having Kate and Harvey had worn off. This was mothering, I'd thought: exhausting, demoralising, impossibly hard. I had undiagnosed postnatal depression, of course, but I only picked it up this time because there was no logical reason for it. I was getting plenty of sleep, and Alice was so easy to care for, but I was tetchy and tearful none the less. I started antidepressants and within four days, I was doing better. The science couldn't really explain it. SSRIs are supposed to take two to four weeks to work, not four days, but within a week, I was well and felt safe again. The tablets had worked their magic and the science, or lack of it, did not matter to me.

Whilst Kate and Harvey still struggled to find common ground to unite them, they both bonded with Alice and she with them. I remember holding her in my arms in the kitchen, when she was still too young to join in with their play, with her pointing through the window to be with them. When she started to speak, her first words were 'garden' and 'outside'.

Alice was a bottom shuffler. I was delighted she got around on her backside like this, just the way I had at that age. Instead of bringing on concerns about possible developmental delay, as I might have experienced with Kate, this idiosyncrasy simply served to connect us more deeply.

By the time Alice was old enough to enjoy being read to, Kate was a fluent reader and spent hours reading to her or making up stories where they had their own personal adventures. Kate could make Alice laugh so much she often broke wind and sometimes more. Then more laughter ensued. Harvey and Alice used to spend hours together, too, playing Power Rangers and Lego. In her easy, relaxed way of being in her relationships with us all, Alice filled the house with light.

When Alice started to write, she adopted mirror writing: ɘɔilA. It was so cool, so amazing and weird. How does she do that? I'd ask, enchanted. Why is Alice doing it and not the others?

I'd never heard of it before. It was a little freaky. Google said not to worry – it was a fairly common phenomenon which would spontaneously resolve. Which it did. I found this progress rather sad. It had been magical, special and very, very different.

Not everything about Alice's early years was entirely straightforward. She was a bedwetter, not dry at night until well after her seventh birthday. But this was just who she was, though it meant bed-sheet changes in the middle of the night when we tried her without a nappy. I mentioned it during a routine check with the school health visitor and treatment with an enuresis alarm was undertaken. The alarm consisted of a pad fitted inside her pants at bedtime. It was designed to go off and wake her as soon as she began to wet herself, but unfortunately, although the alarm was so loud it woke up everyone else in the household, with much noisy complaining from her siblings, Alice did not stir. It was bloody annoying, but also amusing, and in a few weeks she was dry.

Even things that should have felt difficult felt easy. Too easy, I said. It will come back to bite me.

26 May 2022

The bloody dog, a series of tellings, panic rising and driving north

At the time of Alice's death, neither of her siblings is living at home. Kate, aged twenty-five, is in Leeds doing her history master's and Harvey, aged twenty-three, is travelling with his girlfriend, Shin Ah, in Guatemala. They are our immediate priority. We'll drive to Leeds to tell Kate in person and then, together, we'll tell Harvey. That's the plan.

Then we remember Pippin. The bloody dog. Should we take him with us? A quick decision is required. I need to be in Leeds now. Every second wasted seems a failure. I need my surviving children to know. I cannot bear that Alice is Schrödinger's cat – dead in my world, but still alive in Kate's and Harvey's. A friend, Ian, who lives down the road, is called and muddled plans are cobbled together. Pippin will be left behind and cared for by others, so we can focus our efforts where they'll be needed most: the children, the rest of the family – someone must tell my mum. The tables are turned. In an echo from fifty years ago, I find this time it's me who doesn't have the courage to tell her. I cannot tell her because whilst Alice was walking from Hanover towards Rottingdean, whilst she was standing on the edge of a cliff and looking out to sea and into the void, I was in accident and emergency getting my mother's wound dealt with, caring for my mother. And in this moment, I hate her. I hate her for preventing me from caring for Alice. I hate that she's alive and Alice is dead. If it weren't for my mother's obsession with gardening, Alice would still be alive because I could have been there to stop her. Although, of course, I would have just been in bed sleeping if I hadn't been with Mum, which would have just been a different way of not being there for Alice, of letting her down.

If I can't tell my mother, someone else must do it. I ring my brother. Alice has killed herself, I say.

You're joking, he replies.

No, I say and immediately regret telling him. I hate that already Ian and my brother know Alice is dead, whilst Kate and Harvey do not.

I am coming undone, the first signs of panic rising. We've asked the policeman to arrange for Alice's housemate, Keith, to be informed. I must stop them. I'm terrified the news of Alice's death might spread, get out on social media, her siblings finding out about her death on Twitter/X or Facebook. A raft of remedial action is required. Ian is called again; he mustn't tell his son who was in Alice's year at school. I call my brother back, ask him not to tell the cousins. My children must not find out by accident.

Finally, with a few random articles of clothing stuffed in a holdall, a key under the mat for Ian, we're ready to leave for Leeds. I will drive. Although I've had less than two hours' sleep, I feel wide awake, wired – there's no way I could sleep now. I'll drive first, then we'll stop halfway and Peter will take over.

It's surprisingly easy to drive whilst talking about the suicide of our daughter hours before. Already, I start to make plans for the funeral. We cannot have it in a stuffy hotel with finger sandwiches and cups of tea in fine bone china. I'm very clear. It needs to be young. A barbecue, beers, Krispy Kremes for pudding – the last thing she and I ever ate together. We'll ask the rugby club if we can have it there, just like when the kids were little and we hosted festivals. But it will be better than that. It will be June, we'll have deckchairs and picnic blankets, the sun will shine. In these first few hours of the drive, I have it all planned.

We pull in at Northampton services to take a break and change places. Peter is hungry, maybe he'll get a burger. How he can think of eating baffles me. We dither by WH Smith. I have a headache and need to wee, so I leave Peter buying me paracetamol and head to the loos.

I feel the unravelling beginning as soon as I step away from him. A kind of fizzing inside, like the bubbles gathering on the surface of a pan of milk, steadily coming to a simmer. The crying starts in the cubicle. The bubbling over.

2003–2005

Another mother, good Mum/bad Mum, a touch of paranoia, a resignation

When Alice was a toddler, I didn't cope well with the pressures of medicine, raising three children close in age, a husband who left for work before nursery opened and got back after it closed, the logistics of childcare almost entirely mine. My career faltered. Whilst pregnant with Kate I'd passed Part 1 MRCPsych at the first attempt and was doing well, but after she was born, I went part-time, choosing jobs for their nearby location or lack of pressure, rather than their intellectual appeal. I then had Harvey seventeen months later. I made two attempts at Part 2 of my professional exams, both of which ended in failure. I passed my written exams each time, but when I had to speak in front of an authority figure, my knowledge failed me. I decided to take a step off the traditional career ladder to become a staff-grade doctor. I could go back to a psychiatric training post anytime, once child rearing got a little easier. It never did.

I complained to Peter that young children had something of the dementor about them: they demanded more and more of me, until I felt sucked dry. Harvey was such a whirling dervish of exuberance and mischief; I could never keep on top of him. Kate had a will of iron. Sometimes I hated being a mother, wished the children had never been born, wanted to undo the cascade of events that dominoed on from that careless, carefree shag on the living-room floor. Oh, to go back to easier childless times, to be responsible for only myself. But these were only fragmentary fantasies. I would never give up on any of them. I had made my choices. I loved them

23

fiercely. I started to think more and more about the woman who gave me away.

I'd always known of my adoption. My mother told me I was special, chosen, but I didn't feel special. I felt like a victim and I painted my birth mother as one, too. Probably only a child herself, and persuaded, perhaps forced, to abandon me; if not entirely abandoned by her own family, at least abandoned as a mother.

Adopted children are prone to an unconscious psychological process whereby they split their two mothers into good and bad. This was not widely recognised in the 1970s, but looking back, I clearly assigned my birth mother the role of good mother and Mum, the one who raised me, became the baddy. She didn't look like me for a start. She was short, whilst I was tall; she had brown hair, whereas mine was white-blonde. When I entered puberty, I remained flat-chested, whereas Mum had an ample bosom. And our temperaments were so different. She rarely cried, but I was sensitive, blubbing at the slightest thing. I lost my temper often, whilst Mum was calm and quiet for the most part, apart from when she 'lost her patience' and I fled to my bedroom, terrified of the hairbrush. She'd end up in bed, then, too, curled up under the covers, and I'd hear her cry, so that eventually, I'd tiptoe to her room, kneel beside her bed and say sorry, over and over, for this was the only time I ever saw her tears – whenever I'd been bad. I'd pray to God to please make me into a well-behaved child, so I can stop upsetting Mummy, but it never worked. And the one thing I wanted, more than anything, was something parents weren't inclined to proffer back then: a 'sorry' in return.

So, for complex, unrecognised reasons, I was bad, Mum was bad, but my birth mother, a woman who had given me up, and whom I'd never met, was good. In the way of fairytales, my birth mother was a fantasy figure who might still, at any point, have saved me from this intensely complicated relationship with this other mother I'd been lumbered with.

But when I became a mother myself, the story I used to tell myself as a child began to shift. My birth mother wasn't good, for if she was, why would she have given her baby away? The feeling intensified with each child I birthed. There were days I felt utterly lost in this dark place I'd created for myself, a dense forest of parenting, partnering, doctoring, studying. I had barely enough energy to look after myself, let alone the three children who depended on me, but to be without them was unthinkable. My birth mother and Mum began to trade places. Despite the hardship and battles my adoptive mother faced, she never gave up on me, never gave me away.

I understood intellectually what had happened to me. I was born in 1967, a peak period for adoption in the UK. I realised it was the social norm then to give up a baby if you were unmarried; to have kept me would have been unconventional. But some other mothers did keep their babies, I argued to myself. My birth mother was weak, easily led, lazy. Who was this heartless woman who gave me away? I embarked on finding out. In September 2003, when I was thirty-six and Alice was eighteen months old, my birth mother and I met for the first time since I'd been taken from her, at ten days old.

Our reconnecting was a period full of optimism and joy, pessimism and misery. I liked her, and superficially we got on well. But these things aren't superficial. I was overwhelmed with complex, challenging emotions to navigate. We both were. I was not good at seeing things from her point of view, nor she from mine. We were both, in our own ways, damaged.

She visited me at home, met Peter and the children. Kate and Harvey were not particularly taken with this new grandmother, who sometimes intervened to tell them off, but Alice accepted her readily.

Then one day, about a year into our tentative relationship, we had a row. We were talking over the phone (the details escape me now) and she hung up on me. She rang back quite quickly and left a voicemail. She apologised, but I was hurt and didn't reply. Weeks, then months passed. I gradually began to feel consistently calm. Not having a relationship with her seemed to be better for my mental health. A card came occasionally, for one or other of the children's birthdays or for Christmas. Just 'Dear', and 'Love from', nothing more. I found it upsetting and it set me back. It was a connection, but such a bland one. What did it mean?

I can see now I was setting my birth mother a test, giving her an opportunity to fight for me, to show a passion and a determination that she had not shown when she gave me away. But she didn't fight, though she soldiered on. Cards continued to come for a year or so, and each time, they unsettled me. This ongoing relationship that wasn't a relationship, utterly lacking in intimacy. In the end, I wrote and asked her to stop sending them. My mental health was continuing to improve and I thought it would be better if we stopped communicating, I said. I hope my letter was kind (I didn't keep a copy). And she obliged. At the time it felt empowering. *I* had turned *her* away.

―――――――

Though when Alice dies, my thoughts turn to my birth mother again, as they have done and will continue to do throughout my life. One loss reactivates another. Opportunities missed. Different paths for the taking. Ifs and buts occupy so many of my waking hours.

―――――――

This was the backdrop against which I would sit all day in my outpatient clinic, within the community mental-health team, listening to everyone's personal difficulties that I couldn't fix; because you can't fix the adverse outcomes of poverty, abuse and neglect in a twenty-minute session. And sometimes their stories weren't even all that bad. I had to fight the urge to say, 'Here, take my seat, listen to this'.

Growing up during the IRA conflict, a fear of terrorism had pervaded my childhood, and 9/11 in New York had slowly reawakened that fear. In August 2004, a large-scale terrorist plot was foiled in the UK, but surely more were planned, I reasoned. The nation grew a little paranoid and so did I. I had to pick Peter up from Gatwick after a weekend away. The children wanted to come, had been promised a burger whilst we waited. As the time approached, I didn't want to go, specifically to McDonald's, where I imagined a bomb planted underneath our seat. The children were eight, seven and two and a half. I didn't want them to die in an explosion, whilst I popped to the counter to order their Happy Meals.

My paranoia escalated over the ensuing months, culminating in an episode driving home from work, where I dropped back from a white van in front of me out of fear that it was carrying explosives and I was about to be blown up, leaving my children motherless. In clinic, I'd been treating patients for mania, schizophrenia, suicidal thoughts, yet here I was, their doctor, worried that terrorists lurked on the Mickleham Bends. And not just thinking it, but acting differently, slowing down, taking a different turning at the roundabout. I wasn't quite delusional, but I wasn't well. I didn't tell a soul.

I cried more and more, in the car, at work, in the toilets between patients. Just before Christmas 2004, my psychotherapist, who I did tell, persuaded me I needed time off. My GP issued a sick note for six weeks. Immediately, the anxiety and crying stopped. I went back in February 2005, as Alice turned three. The crying started again. I had nothing left for my family at the end of the working day. 'I'm raising children for the psychiatrist's couch,' I said. I could have been signed off sick once more, played a long game, with generous NHS sick leave, but I couldn't see how this would help. Eventually, I'd have been expected back and nothing would have changed. I couldn't justify the effort that I put in to try and take care of my patients, whilst the organisation I worked for did so little to help me. It was my work, and not my children, that was the dementor. I handed in my resignation.

I worked my notice, shutting off from my feelings as best I could, but the tears were never far from the surface and the car was where they found their escape. In the car they overflowed.

26 May 2022

Unravelling at a service station, another series of tellings, condolences pour in

The tears come now, in these municipal loos. I cannot stop them. I gather all my courage and make my way back towards WH Smith, my basest instinct to find my mate. I keep close to the edges of the concourse, like a hunted animal trying to travel through scanty scrub unnoticed, keeping close to the concessions, which feel like they afford me some protection from the central atrium, which is too vast and exposed. I think if I walk out into this space I will collapse, like the weakest wildebeest, isolated from the herd and pounced upon by a ravenous predator. I hear my sobs getting louder and louder, feel my body convulsing. I look down to avoid making eye contact with anyone but I'm aware that people are there, walking past. I move over, with my back to a column, and begin to slide down it, as I feel the words 'someone help me' forming at the base of my throat, but they are caught there like an irritating fish bone that I can't swallow or cough up. Then a quiet, nervous voice asks, 'Are you ok?' A young lad is near me, asking again, 'Are you ok?' And I'm grateful and impressed that this twenty-something, not much more than a boy, is the first person to be brave enough to reach out to the deranged lady with buckling knees. I don't want my breakdown to be in his arms, but it will have to be. Then a woman appears, and although Covid still hangs in the collective consciousness, she reaches out and hugs me and holds me up and lets me cling to her. And the lad is still there, and they are both trying to ascertain what is wrong, and I'm saying, I'm waiting for my husband; he was here, by WH Smith, but he's gone, my husband, my husband, he's not here, he should be here, but he's gone, and then –

my dau …, my daugh … my daughter.

Is she here? they ask, looking around.

My dau … my dau … I choke. I cannot breathe. She killed herself this morning, I say, to these strangers, just like that. The next people to know. Then Peter appears and he takes me, so my rescuers can go back to their burgers or their noodles, and I collapse into his arms, losing all my physical strength. I'm deflated and empty. Nothing holds me up from within. The poets and the playwrights have it right, after all.

Peter takes over the driving and I doze a little. Then attend to a little life admin, compose an email to tell my clients, Mole Valley Pilates is closing down. Peter left work the previous Christmas – not retired but stepped down to take some time out and rethink, after years of worrying about Alice. A little sabbatical before heading off on another path. Not this path, though, Jesus Christ, not this.

As we get nearer to Leeds, my agitation returns. When we first set off, I couldn't get there fast enough. But now, as the clock ticks and the miles count down, I want time to stop. I don't ever want to arrive.

Kate's face when she opens the door: surprise, delight, confusion, concern and then I have blurted it out, right there on the doorstep and she's in our arms, crying and crying, and a new layer of pain begins.

Telling Harvey is a shambles. We try to FaceTime him several times – we want to see him across the continents – but get no reply. We try a regular mobile call, a WhatsApp; still no luck. We call Shin Ah and that too goes to voicemail. Peter and I completely lose our ability to use our phones, we can't function. Harvey calls us back and we don't know whether to press the red or the green icon to accept the call. The phone is treated like a hand grenade, tossed between us, like it might explode at any minute, and he's rung off before we answer. Finally, we get through. Harvey will know something is wrong, but he'll surely be thinking of one of his grandmas. Peter's mother is also in her nineties and has been unwell on and off since Christmas. Harvey's a bit belligerent, the way he can be when he's been disturbed in the middle of something. He's walking down a street; he's on his way somewhere.

What's wrong? he asks.

I see he's not alone, that he's with Shin Ah, and that's all the prompt I need as I blurt it out once more: Alice is dead. Me again doing the talking and Harvey covering his face with his hands, gulping for breath, Shin Ah with him, holding him, both of them crying and asking questions and the line breaking up. A disjointed, messy telling of bad news. It is, for now, the hardest thing I've ever had to witness: my child plucked out of his happy-go-lucky life and thrown into a turmoil of confusion on another continent, so very far away. I long to hold him. Instead, I hold Kate and Peter, and he holds Shin Ah. Thank God for this, at least. We agree to FaceTime again later when they're back at the hostel and have better internet. They will not climb the mountain; they will not trek into the jungle. They will return to base and make plans to come home.

We announce Alice's death on Facebook. We don't mince our words. She has died by suicide, everyone should know. I used to think it somewhat unseemly to post something so personal on such a public platform; now I am thankful for its efficiency. Immediately, our phones start to ping with a stream of notifications.

We have our first taste of a phenomenon that occupies us for months to come: the way people respond to our news. It's complex and varied and we're all drawn into discussing and analysing who said what, when and how. It's oddly compelling and a distraction, if nothing else. Getting cross with how other people behave stops us thinking in too much detail about what Alice has done, what we have or have not done, that she is dead. It's so wrong, so everyone and everything else is wrong, too. I examine the minutiae of messages, down to every emoji – a bright, round yellow face hugging a heart, job done. For words matter to me and people often do not realise their impact.

I imagine that when my mother told me my father had been in an accident, but was alive, I would have seen an unsettling look in her eyes, a look I didn't recognise, something that told me there was more going on. Her husband was dead. News as devastating as that would surely have been writ large across her face and I'd have seen it – the difference between what she said and what had actually happened. It's left me with a hypervigilance, looking for a hidden meaning in everything anyone says or does. And I do it now.

For many there are 'no words', which I find particularly lazy, because there are, people just can't summon up the effort to use them. There are big hugs aplenty – these sound so trivial; I didn't break my ankle or have my holiday delayed by a cancelled flight – and a fair smattering of OMGs, which superficially seem to care more than a simple, 'I'm so sorry', but make such an exclamation of themselves. It is too flamboyant, gossipy. But then that's what we are now really, isn't it? We have been the subject of gossip for a while, I imagine. Did you hear about the Litmans? You know, the ones with the transgender child that says he's a girl?

I've always been prone to worrying about what people think of me. As a mother, I certainly longed for 'well-behaved' children, so I could not be judged for any inadequacies of mothering, either openly, or worse, behind my back. Alice was the classic well-behaved child. But before her came Kate and Harvey.

1996–2009

Two little devils and an angel, an anonymous letter

The three children looked like three peas in a pod, but when it came to personality, they were land, sea and air. When Kate started nursery, I was regularly caught at the end of the day by Lynne, the owner. Lynne could never quite tell me exactly what Kate had done wrong. 'It's just her stubbornness,' she said. 'If Kate doesn't want to do something, she won't. I've never seen anything like it.' This was not news to me or to my closest friend from medical school, Emma, Kate's godmother. When Emma married, she chose Kate to be her bridesmaid, not anticipating that every single wedding photo would feature a scowling three-year-old, hands on hips, refusing to smile for the camera. But it was a relief to know Kate was like this with everyone and that Lynne didn't judge me for my child's strength of will.

Harvey was a little rascal. I can hear his deep, throaty chuckle even now, amused at his own mischief, always getting into trouble. Looking after him was exhausting. He was forever fiddling with things, breaking them, clambering and careering through his day. And he also had his stubborn streak, for this little boy who could never keep still, was 'sleeping lions' champion of the world. A hide-and-seek hider of extraordinary determination, who would not give up his coordinates to anyone, not even Grandma when she thought she had lost him for good. He's such a little devil, she said, whilst loving the very bones of him. He was such a contradiction, provoking strong feelings in people – a Marmite toddler. And one day at nursery, I found out just how much people could loathe my child, or maybe me, when I received a disturbing letter.

It was poking out of the little wall pocket that the nursery used for nursery–parent communication. I was curious. It wasn't a brightly coloured notelet – oh, the thrill of a party invite, getting Harvey off my hands for a few hours' respite – nor a branded missive from the office, about fees or the like, but a smart, crisp white envelope, addressed to: 'THE MOTHER OF HARVEY', like that, in capitals. I strapped Harvey into his car seat and opened the letter there and then. It was typed, by someone who professed to have 'thought long and hard before writing this'. I started to feel a bit wary, looking around the car park to see who was about. 'I write with the best intentions,' it said, 'and hope you will appreciate my bravery and honesty,' it continued. I began to shake. A character assassination of my four-year-old ensued. In particular, he was a problem at parties, where he shouldn't be left unsupervised. He was hostile and aggressive; he pushed other children, made them cry. I didn't see it because I didn't stay, it said. It wasn't only a judgement of Harvey, but of me and my mothering. It wasn't addressed to the father or parent; it was addressed to me, the mother. And worst of all, it was unsigned. The 'brave and honest' author of the typed note had confusingly left that bit out. I'd no way to respond. The powerlessness I felt that day made me quite sick. I was under attack, hypervigilant, checking all my interactions with other mums for signs, clues. I couldn't just throw the letter away and forget about it, as Peter suggested, and as Lynne also insisted was best. I read and reread it, reading between the lines for hidden meaning, trying to find, if not something kind about me, then the contrary, some evidence that both I and my child were truly such monsters that we deserved this. Eventually, I did throw the letter away, but it didn't stop me worrying. I found it even harder to trust other people and myself than ever before.

No one would have been inclined to write a letter like that about Alice. She did lash out at her siblings from time to time, when they pushed and pushed her for a reaction, something they admit to now

– that her outbursts were entirely justified. But she rarely got angry outside these sibling rivalries. She was a compliant child; she didn't push my buttons the way her siblings did. Kate and Harvey sometimes found her infuriating, in that she never felt the sharp end of my tongue. I babied her, and let her get away with stuff, they said. Maybe I did. There was definitely something about her that completely protected her from the angry mother her brother and sister sometimes had to endure.

27 May 2022

Friends reach out, I wish it had been me, I wish it had been you

Back in Leeds, after a fitful sleep, we pack up enough of Kate's things to tide her over for a few weeks and the three of us return home. Alice has been dead for a day.

Some of my closest friends start to do more than message. Emma drops off a box of emergency food rations. Ali and Elis, also medical-school friends, ring and arrange to come down from Shropshire to see us the very next weekend. Ali is one of the few people who picks up the phone to actually talk, and who continues to do so. Jane sends a beautiful photo she has of Alice as ring bearer at her wedding. Trevor, Peter's dearest friend and ex-work colleague, and his wife, Julie, drop by with a picnic lunch. Julie sits on the garden sofa next to me, but turns to face me, gently turns my face towards hers and looks deep into my eyes. She wipes a stray strand of hair away from my face and then another, tucking it behind my ear, then tucking it again. She has her other hand on my knee and she is scratching at me, as if scratching at the scruff of a dog's neck, and picking away bits of fluff, real or imagined, from my trousers. I start to mirror her. We are like a couple of monkeys participating in a grooming ritual. It is profoundly moving and I feel completely understood.

Peter and I go to see our respective mums. We have to do it separately; Kate doesn't want to come with us, nor be left alone. Peter goes to his mum, Gill, first, because she's still to be told the terrible news. She's old and frail, has faced death several times over the last decade, but always bounced back. It should have been me, she says. It should have been me.

I go and see my mum when Peter gets back. I'm anxious, I'm a child again and don't know my place. I don't know how she will react.

We've had the same thing happen to us, Mummy, I sob.

What's that? she asks.

An officer at the door, I say.

Oh no, she replies. This is not at all the same, nothing can compare to what you're going through.

I melt in her arms, fifty years of prickle soothed in a sentence, just like that. Though within minutes, she makes a fine stab at reinstating some of the intermittent, yet long-standing brittleness between us.

Gill's been on the phone, she says. She said it should have been her. Why would she say that? my mother asks. As if it's a wholly improbable thing, for an ailing ninety-three-year-old to dare to venture such a wish, to trade their life for that of their twenty-year-old grand-daughter. Why would she say that? she asks again. The question is apparently not rhetorical.

Because she feels it, I venture, because of her age.

My mother is eager to tell me why Gill is wrong. She takes me in her grasp, a hand on each of my upper arms, and stares at me in the rather intense way she has sometimes, now that she cannot really see it's me she's talking to. How is that helpful? she asks.

It's not, I agree.

Which gives my mother permission, I suppose, to continue. Well, I'm not saying it, she says. I'm glad it wasn't me. I have my life to live and I want to live it. I'm here for you. What use is there in saying a thing like that?

There is a brief silence after that. I'm dumbfounded. If there was an urge to scream – I wish it had been you – like I used to sometimes as a child, I don't register it. In this moment I am paralysed, defeated. Anyone can just say or do anything to me now; I am utterly defenceless. So, she ploughs on and fills the silence with her words. And without me to pull her up, instead of an argument starting, she navigates her own way back to safer territory and I feel secure once more. I lie with my head in her lap and she strokes my hair, calling me Cazzie, Caz, the childhood nickname I loathe. But now, Cazzie feels right; it is her deepest term of affection. Ultimately, my mother's house has always been a place of safety when it's really mattered.

1971–1979

Several moves, a certain competitiveness, another trauma

Thirteen days after my father died, the army booted my mother and me from our quarters and put us on a plane back to England, with nowhere to live. Fortunately, my father had a brother, with a large family home and older children who had moved out. We lived with his family, in Berkshire, for four months. I started school, made friends, then we moved to a rented cottage near by. I turned five and we moved again, this time north, to Blackpool. My maternal grandmother, Gaga, lived there. She'd been widowed before I was born and had recently married Stan, my mother's uncle, two brothers for husbands. Gaga and Stan encouraged my mother to buy Stan's house with what little savings she had. Now she was without a husband of her own, she should move back home and look after her mother, Stan said.

I started a new school, made more friends, but Mum hated it there, describing it as a bleak and soulless place. I think she would have hated it anywhere. It was less than a year since her husband had died in an accident, she was alone but for an elderly mother, and an uncle where her father had once been, a five-year-old in tow and her eleven-year-old in a boarding school 250 miles away. We lasted there just nine months before we moved again, to the housing-association semi that remains my mother's home today. It was an hour or so from my uncle's house, so visits to see my father's side of the family became a regular fixture to look forward to.

Once Mum and I had settled in, and there were no signs of another move, I must have grown a little in confidence and the arguments

39

began. My father was regularly hauled out at these moments, to disapprove of me: 'Imagine if your father could hear you?' 'What would your father say?' I had a strong sense that this was not fair, but I knew I was supposed to consider my mother's feelings before my own because that's what other adults in my life said. I didn't have the same claim on my father's love as she did, but as I grew older, I began to think that if my father was as nice as she said he was, he might have been kind to me, might have seen my side. A certain competitiveness built up between us.

So, it was always a relief to have the cousins over to dilute our intense, mother–daughter relationship. Including my brother, there were seven of us in all. I, like Alice, was the baby. We saw some or all of them often, at weekends and holidays, Christmas gatherings. Until one hot summer Sunday in September 1979, when my world, once again, lost its axis. I was twelve and sat on my uncle's lap in our living room whilst everyone else played French cricket in the garden.

A penny for your thoughts, he whispered, very gently in my ear.

I'm thinking about Daddy, I said. I was feeling very sad, but also nurtured by this trusted man, my dead daddy's brother, when, quite suddenly, the comfort I was feeling became something else entirely.

With his stubbly chin against my cheek, he stroked my knee, a bit higher, a bit higher still. Do you like it? he asked.

No, I whispered. Though to say no was rude, to say yes was worse, a lie.

He mumbled something else in my ear, with his hot, sour breath. Will you do that? he asked.

No, I said. I want to get down. I wriggled free, ran up the stairs, shut my door, but his heavy footsteps followed me. My bedroom door opened a crack, his head peered round, he said something, asked me to keep our secret.

Yes, I said, heart racing. I was wondering if he might kill me, for he must know that as soon as he was gone, I could say what I liked.

Later that evening, after they'd left, my mother ran me a bath and came in to chat, as we sometimes did. Wasn't that a lovely day, she said.

No, I replied.

What's happened? she asked, recognising immediately that something was amiss.

Though it had been a hot September day, I had changed out of my flimsy cotton dress into jeans and a polo-neck jumper. When my brother had gone out for an hour to play tennis, I'd begged him not to leave, and when he'd returned, I'd sat so close to him at tea as to be almost glued to him. My mother had noticed everything. She helped me tell her and she believed me. Do I ever have to see him again? I asked. No, of course not, she replied, with a wisdom far greater than many mothers of her generation.

And I was grateful, but it came at a cost. By saving me, another loss was inflicted.

And when my mother told her sister, yet another. My aunt was of the opinion that little girls made things up and shouldn't be believed.

———

Now, it is Alice, as a trans person, and those like her, who have become society's foolish, lying children, unreliable witnesses to their own thoughts and feelings, silenced from explaining what is happening to them, whatever their age.

28 May 2022

To Brighton, a jar of Nutella, a moment of light relief

We have been without Alice for three days. Peter, Kate and I travel down to Alice's home in Brighton. We cannot wait for Harvey and Shin Ah to return from Central America, where they are tied up in bureaucracy, waiting for an ESTA to allow them to catch a return flight via the US. The police want to know if Alice left a note; so do we. We're sorry Harvey's being left out but not sorry enough to delay. We're not really travelling for a note; we don't expect to find one. We make the journey because this was her home, the last physical place Alice was in before she got up from her desk, careful to close her door behind her but not lock it, walked past Keith's bedroom door and, finally, through the last door, the front door, closing it softly behind her, so as not to be caught in the act, then out on the street, deciding, right or left? Yet we do not know she even left from home. Perhaps she was with a Tinder lover the night before; perhaps there had been a squabble, a lovers' tiff. Maybe this, maybe that. We head to her room to find, if not a note, something, anything of herself that she has left behind, an answer.

Her smell, as we open the door, so specific to her, but already a little less heady than when it emanates directly off her, a residue of her smell, from her things. It's a warm day; the small room is crowded and stuffy with the three of us in it. I find her full-length, quilted coat and despite the heat I put it on, climb into her bed, under her covers, inhale deeply. The room is messy, but no more so than usual. Peter or I, or both together, have been weekly visitors to Alice over the preceding months. We're familiar with the detritus of her life. There's

42

a half-drunk bottle of vodka, a staple for many a student bedroom, although Alice is not a student. There are dirty plates smeared with ketchup, a McDonald's takeaway bag, empty cups and glasses, an overflowing bin. My eye catches a bumper jar of Nutella, scraped out, every last scrap, the glass almost clear. At home, Alice would have been profligate with the chocolate spread, opening a new jar whilst there were still several servings in the old one. But at home, there would have been another jar in reserve, whereas here, she would have had to go to Aldi – just a five-minute walk away – to top up, and that could have been a walk too far, on a bad day. Perhaps that's why she did it, I say, because she ran out of Nutella. Kate is appalled at my suggestion, the frivolity of it. I've said it in an offhand way, so she thinks I'm joking. Am I joking? Not really. This image of the empty jar haunts me for months. But Kate is more than appalled; she is quite disgusted with me, I think, that I could be so flippant. Sorry, I say. Obviously, running out of a spread for your toast isn't the reason. But inside I'm thinking it could be, couldn't it? The tipping point? Not the real reason, of course, but a very particular trigger? What had, metaphorically, and literally, taken her over the edge? She had been so well. If only I'd come down in the week and bought her some more.

Peter makes to start tidying up and clearing away, begins to talk about throwing away her furniture, her ugly office chair, so worn out from a life lived, of late, in front of her computer that the fake leather fabric has all but rubbed away. Kate and I ask him to stop. We need to absorb the room as it is. Preserve it as it was in life, at least until Harvey has visited. And to throw away her chair seems akin to discarding Alice herself. We cannot have that.

This makes Peter feel uncomfortable. Action is his way of coping, getting on, doing something practical, whereas Kate and I need time to sit and reflect. In this way, in Alice's room, Peter and I are together, yet worlds apart. These signs that there will be differences in the way we will grieve, that first appeared in our reaction to the policeman's news, keep making their presence felt.

Tomorrow, Peter will be going mountain biking because tomorrow is Monday, mountain-biking night, and he goes every week. Throughout our marriage, in the heat of the summer sun and the dank dark of a winter's evening he has taken to the hills. He sees no reason tomorrow should be any different. When asked if I mind, I say no, but Kate and I trade conspiratorial looks, roll our eyes – how can he carry on as normal? we say, without saying it. Poor Peter, it must be hard. We're a close-knit three, but in our grief, mother and daughter are stitched a little tighter.

You can go through drawers, I say, removing anything important, or special, that elusive note to take home, but leave everything else as it is, for Harvey.

We find a notebook, a poem:

That sums it up, I say.

2005–2008

A puppy, a piss-couch, a new career, Alice and *real* Alice

We'd always been a sweary, loud, chaotic family. And now that I'd stopped work, to help me restore my mental health, cope with the kids, eight, seven and just three, whilst managing the complexities of now having two mothers, we decided to add to the chaos and swearing and get a dog. Peter had a dog growing up. I had my Alice. It seemed only fair he got his extra family member, too.

The day I was due to collect Poppy, Kate had an inset day, so she came with me. As we turned down the access road to the motorway, my mobile rang. It was Kate's school. She didn't have an inset day at all. Oops, I said, turning to her with a wink. She was thrilled.

I was a slightly flaky parent in this respect. Once I sent Kate and Harvey to junior school in mufti on the wrong day. Again, Kate was thrilled, relished being different from the others. Harvey hid in the cloakroom and refused to come out. Alice was still at nursery when this happened, not exposed to this particular mufti-day faux pas. My guess is, if she had been, she would have felt Harvey's anxiety but been 'good' and stayed in class like Kate did. She would have endured, not enjoyed, being different.

When I was working, I often missed letters home, forgot cake sales and permission slips. My job could be very stressful. I treated a sister raped by a brother, assessed a brother who raped a sister, a teacher with a computer chock-full of child porn. I cared for homicidal and suicidal patients. The stakes were high. So, at work I dotted every i and crossed every t. At home, though, I was disorganised and slap-dash. I guess it mattered less if I made mistakes.

But on the other hand, I worried so much about the responsibility of parenting. I was only too aware of how mistakes could shape a child, but back then it was Kate and Harvey who I worried about, whilst Alice seemed like nothing would ever faze her.

When she was three, I was woken one morning by her tugging at my arm, Mummy, who's the man downstairs?

What man, sweetie?

The man in the kitchen, she said, quite calmly.

Peter was up in a flash, running full pelt downstairs. I dialled 999. Police, please.

Who the fuck are you? I heard Peter yelling. What the fuck are you doing in my house?

I didn't hear any replies. The situation didn't seem perilous. Wait here, sweetheart, I said to Alice. I'm just going to take Daddy his dressing gown.

In the kitchen stood Peter, stark naked, confronting this stranger who was trying to light his cigarette on the hob; he looked quite perplexed. Whether it was the nudity or the complexities of an induction hob, I do not know.

Put this on, I said to Peter. The police are on their way.

He says he knows us, said Peter. Says we were out drinking together last night, that we invited him back.

The man took some convincing that we hadn't all been up into the small hours getting shitfaced. We pieced together what had happened: he'd simply got tired walking home and let himself in for a kip. Moments before the police arrived, we let him leave. The police came in to take some details. As I sat on the sofa, I discovered where our intruder had slept the night and emptied the contents of his very full bladder. The policemen failed to stifle their laughter. Later, they had no trouble picking the man up from my description. He was known to them – not a criminal, really, just got in a few scrapes from time to time. Did we want to press charges? Not much point, to be honest, they said. No, we said, leave him be. We made a claim on our insurance for the sofa, but once the cushions were rinsed and scrubbed and left out in the fresh air for a few days, they seemed ok to us. We'd rather use the insurance money for a holiday, we agreed.

And so, the piss-couch was christened, and for years to come, friends were regaled with our amusing anecdote of the intruder, the naked confrontation and my wet backside. Most of them seem more appalled to be told the history of the sofa they were sitting on – the residue of the intruder that might remain within its padding – than by the intrusion itself. Alice, too, did not seem at all scarred by this incident. Later, her friend had a break-in at his house, car keys were taken, no car on the drive in the morning. That child couldn't sleep easily for months, regressed and spent time in his parents' bed, but Alice was fine after our experience. We congratulated ourselves. Turning it into a funny story had spared her the anxiety that now played havoc with her friend.

———

But perhaps this incident played out later in Alice's brain. She had learned that people could do quite bad things, but it wasn't always scary, yet when she realised she was transgender, though *she* hadn't done anything bad at all, half the country suddenly seemed to be against her.

———

Back in 2005, it was Kate and Harvey who were cause for concern. Kate was being bullied at school and struggling to get in at all some days. Harvey was always in some sort of scrap and had already been excluded from school once for running off with a friend. I was irritable and snappy. Sometimes, to my horror, like my mother before me, I would raise my hand. My professional knowledge didn't seem to help me be the mother I wanted to be.

Though now I was no longer a practising doctor, I could not allow myself to be merely a mother. Jane and I hatched a plan. She needed an excuse to leave her City job, which was challenging her sobriety at every turn. I needed to feel I was good at something. With no experience at all, Jane and I embarked on a naive plan to run a catering business. We lasted a year and made no money, though ultimately, this didn't really matter. It was the friendship, the camaraderie that our venture gave us, that helped us feel a little better about ourselves, and it was a stepping stone to something else, though neither of us knew what.

During this period, now Alice no longer required Lynne's expensive daycare, I moved her to a local playgroup. On her first day, she came home announcing she'd made a new friend, Zack. Zack told their mum they'd made two new friends that day, Alice and *real* Alice.

Alice and Zack became the best of friends but Zack's family moved away when Alice was four. They were close enough for day trips, and I loved their mother, so keeping in touch was not a chore, but once their teenage years hit, they became awkward in each other's company. Alice started to say she didn't want to go.

Then, sixteen years after they first met, around two years after Alice came out, Zack told their mother that they too were trans and would like to talk with Alice. But Alice couldn't manage it. They never did meet again. Alice and *real* Alice. Zack and *real* Zack.

In September 2006, with all the children now at school, I found myself in the peculiar position of being the stay-at-home mum I hadn't been when they were all pre-schoolers. Whilst other mothers were thinking about returning to the workplace, I was without a job and at something of a loose end. I embarked on an Open University Creative Writing diploma. I lost myself in the exercises and assignments. I would stay up half the night, the house quiet, free from mothering interruptions, and write. I might catch a few hours' sleep before taking the children to school and then would nap during the day. Napping is a skill I learned as a junior doctor that has never left me. I felt unusually vibrant and alive. I *wanted* to read, study and write; it engaged and motivated me in a way my medical training never had. My wonderful tutor praised and encouraged me. Even the chair of the examining board wrote to congratulate me on my mark, to pass on the external examiner's comments that my work was of publishable quality and to wish me luck pursuing a writing career.

But I didn't pursue a writing career. Instead, after turning to a Pilates class to fix the chronic bad back I'd endured since Harvey was a toddler, weighing in on the 99.6th centile, I chose to retrain as a Pilates teacher myself. It would pay the bills and work around the children. It was perfect, I said. But it wasn't. Writing was perfect, just not in a financial way.

29–31 May 2022

The challenge of just being, a round of applause, a grief-couch

Not that my career change did me any good, I think, as I wait impatiently for Harvey's return, with Alice dead at her own hand. If I'd stayed in psychiatry, maybe I'd have been able to get Alice's needs met more easily. Maybe as a doctor, people would have taken me, and her, more seriously. The seeds of self-recrimination and guilt take root and grow. I should never have tried to have a career, I should never have given up my career, I should have done this, I should have done that.

I start to write in a journal, my inner voice so critical and demanding it spills out on to the page. I lose my appetite, skip meals and poke food around my plate like a fussy child. I'm full before I've eaten a third of what's been dished up, Peter eats my leftovers with gusto. I'm living on air and adrenalin. I can't nod off, then can't stay asleep once sleep arrives. I pace the living room, rearrange the flowers that turn up in a constant stream, often accompanied by smiles and jollity from the delivery driver, how lucky I am. Peter sleeps the sleep of the innocent. I cry and cry, am so dehydrated. Peter's tears that flooded from him so readily that first day appear to have dried up. He's been out mountain biking, is planning his timetable for CrossFit the following week. I cancel my membership.

Because I'm not going to the gym and lifting heavy barbells or swinging from a rig, I search out my rings to put them back on. I have not worn my wedding ring for years, not just because it might get damaged at the gym, but as a little menopausal hint of defiance against the patriarchy and the institution of marriage. I put it back on

50

now, as a talisman to keep our union strong. I slip my eternity ring back on, too. Peter bought it for me as a Christmas present the first year after Kate was born. Such a gesture was quite out of character for him and I treasured it, but one time, whilst working in the garden, one of the five little diamonds fell out and was lost. It seems right to put it back on, now that Alice is also lost, the ugly empty setting symbolic of the ugly empty hole in my soul.

Harvey's absence feels exquisitely painful and I long to be reunited with him. Until he's in my arms, I fear he too might never come home. Though I'm not really eating I want his homecoming dinner to be special. He asks for steak and chips. This involves a trip to the shops and I'm newly afraid of leaving the house. The thought of walking towards the car, driving out into the world, even as a passenger, where people are carrying on as usual, and I am, too, doing something as mundane as a trip to the supermarket, is terrifying. I cannot do it. Eventually, Peter persuades me. He's carrying on with the things he enjoys. It will do me good, he says, come on. In the end I manage it because it's for Harvey.

We choose Waitrose, as it's the smallest store for miles, parking is easy, we can slip in and out unnoticed. But they only have three sirloins, so someone's found and goes to see if they've another two in the storeroom. Whilst we're waiting, Peter pops to another aisle to find wine, a nice red with our steaks, although I've no appetite for alcohol either.

Whilst Peter's out of sight, I notice an old acquaintance, someone who's known me since our children attended the same infant school. I turn my back, try to make myself very small. Has she seen me? My heart begins to race. Does she know? What will she say? What will I say? What if she says nothing? What if she's jolly and uninformed? What will I do then? Will I play along? Will I tell her? Will I cry? Won't I? Where's Peter? Oh, Jesus, why did I want to cook Harvey a steak dinner?

The encounter is avoided and the shopping trip survived. Back at home, I take to my bed, seeking the oblivion of sleep.

———————

But today, day six, we're finally going to collect Harvey and Shin Ah from Heathrow. Nothing will keep me away. I'm a poor timekeeper, habitually unprepared and late. Today will be different, I will not have them walk through the arrivals hall with no one to meet them. We debate the best place to stand, so they'll see us most easily. We choose our spot, and I sit on the polished airport floor and cry on and off whilst we wait.

Harvey and Shin Ah make a striking couple. He's tall, six foot two, and broad, with hair cut short like a military man, whereas she is petite with long black hair almost to her waist. Yet we mistake them dozens of times, in couples of all shapes, ages and sizes, so desperate are we to see them. We've been waiting forty minutes or so when there's a commotion. A man steps forward into the arrivals funnel and, in a bold American accent, makes an announce-ment: a United States veteran of World War Two who was at the D-Day landings, 6 June 1944, has travelled to the UK for the first time since that day seventy-eight years ago. Would we all please give him the honour of a round of applause when he comes through? He thanks us all warmly, in anticipation of a unanimous cooperative spirit.

Kate pleads with me, beseeches me: make it stop. This joyous event, to be celebrated with clapping and maybe cheers, it mustn't happen, not as Harvey and Shin Ah arrive.

I dig deep, find my best maternal reassurance: it won't, I say. Thousands of passengers have passed in front of us so far; what are the chances that these two arrivals will happen at exactly the same moment?

Then, as we finally spot them, Harvey first, searching the crowd for his family, and we burst forth as one, running to meet them, the whoops and applause begin. We stand amongst it, sharing our tragedy in person for the first time, the five of us in a tangle of grief, with Harvey and Shin Ah, of course, utterly perplexed at the incongruity of it all. What the fuck is going on?

Once home, I can't find my glasses and I only have one pair. I can get by without them, but I do need them to read. Every corner of the house is searched but they can't be found. I will call airport lost property in the morning, I say, though I never do.

I can still see to cook the steak dinner, but the preparation of a simple meal, one I've made many times before, becomes a task of *Krypton Factor* proportions, with some *Taskmaster* comedy thrown in. It's as if I've been asked to cook the steaks whilst blindfolded, without touching any of the utensils, in a race against my opponents. The steaks are overdone, the chips are underdone and I'm done in. Though it is wonderful to have Harvey home at last, our family is not complete. I retreat to my bed once more. Snatches of sleep where I can.

The next morning, I wake at dawn. This is my new rhythm. I take Pippin for a walk, before anyone else is up. A baby badger potters towards us from a distance, getting closer and closer. It brings a glimmer of something close to happiness. And then it is gone.

I return home and throw myself on to the sofa, like the heroine with the vapours from a Victorian novella. The piss-couch has only recently been dumped and the remaining sofa is short with high sides, and you cannot stretch out on it fully lengthways. It's not one for lounging about on, for wallowing in grief. And that is what I want to do. Wallow. Though looking wallow up in a dictionary, it says devote yourself entirely to something, usually in pleasure. There is no pleasure in my wallowing, but for great swathes of the day it is all I can manage, all I want to do, so I suppose it is a pleasure of sorts.

I can't grieve on this thing, I announce, gesticulating at myself, wedged in, like a corpse in a suitcase. I need a grief-couch. I open my laptop and order one online, fairly cheap and self-assembly. When it arrives, it's broken. Of course it is, I say.

Later, when the post is delivered and I cannot read the condolence cards, the floral tributes, I can ignore it no longer: I need some over-the-counter specs. After the Waitrose trip, I'm wary of going out again. I can't do it alone, so Kate comes with me. We go to Sainsbury's first, for a few bits and bobs, the daily staples that the newly founded WhatsApp group 'Feed the Litmans' misses out: milk, eggs, bread. I hold Kate's hand like I'm the child and she's the parent. Then on to Boots, to choose glasses. Kate needs stationery, some files, and she would like to go to WH Smith. I feel bold. You do that and meet me back here, I suggest. I find what I need, and in a kind of fugue, a lot of things I don't, then join a queue.

When I reach the front, the man serving points to the other end of the store – you need to purchase these items at the cosmetics counter, he says.

My knees begin to buckle, just as they did a week ago, at Northampton services. Please don't make me stand in another queue, I say, managing to get the words out, playing my trump card. My daughter killed herself on Thursday and I can't do it, I just can't. He obliges me, the poor man. Sorry, I say.

When Kate returns, she can see I'm agitated. I feel more like her elderly grandmother now, frail and confused, a little lost, as she guides me gently back to the car. Just like the trip to Waitrose, I'm exhausted, and head back to bed.

I have to go to the supermarket again, of course, random things need replacing. When Harvey accompanies me the next time, he isn't aware of how anxious I've become and he wanders off in search of something. When I notice he's gone, I shout loudly, Harvey, Harvey, where are you? Like the parent of a missing infant. What an odd sight we must make when he reappears and I cling to him. Please don't disappear like that again, I beg.

Tasks that were previously simple and commonplace have become Herculean challenges. I begin to wonder, is this what it was like for Alice every time she left the house: to attempt college, to shop at Aldi, to appease me and Peter with our repeated offers to take her out somewhere nice for lunch? Is her death bringing me closer to an understanding of her life?

2011–end 2016

A house move, a school move, a new friend, a rumbling problem

Alice's first episode of mild anxiety started around the age of nine or ten. A boy in her class was being mean to her, cosying up to her one day, then snubbing her the next. Alice didn't know what she'd done to deserve it. School became an unpredictable place, but she was able to talk to me about it, so I could help her. I talked to her teacher and the other mother, whom I knew. The situation resolved.

My Pilates business was doing well. When Alice was ten, we moved, so I could teach Pilates from home. None of the children were happy to leave the house they'd grown up in, even though the new one was less than half a mile away. They were not taken with the panoramic views from their bedroom windows, nor the potential for enough off-street parking for all my clients.

In 2013, Alice moved to secondary school, aged eleven. On her first day she made a new friend. As she told me about 'crazy Keith', she had that same animation she'd had telling me about Zack at nursery. And whilst Keith is not trans, he does later come out as bisexual. Another coincidence, or something else, something deeper and more meaningful than just chance?

In her first term, she came home and announced she was thinking of performing in the school talent contest.

Really? What are you going to do? I asked.

I'm going to play guitar, she said.

Alice was no musician; she enjoyed her lessons but rarely practised and I was floored that she was brave – or foolish – enough to think of performing in front of the whole school. I questioned her thinking: she couldn't string two chords together, was she sure? And because of me, or maybe not, she decided not to. In this way, Alice was such an enigma to me, so full of naive optimism at times, yet paralysed by her insecurities at others.

Upon moving into year 8, in September 2014, Alice, aged twelve, started to experience intermittent nausea. I took her to the GP, but they weren't concerned. The problem rumbled on for almost two years, until, at the end of year 9, in 2016, I finally took her back to the GP. Again, they couldn't explain it and suggested nothing that I can recall. Two months later, at the start of year 10, I tried a third time. Her nausea had developed into recurrent stomach pains, accompanied by episodes of retching, which sometimes led to vomiting, particularly first thing in the morning. When this happened, she'd then sleep for most of the day. This time they referred her to a paediatrician. But yet again, there were no notable findings. She probably just has a little acid reflux, the doctor assured me, nothing to worry about. Alice was prescribed antacids and discharged. But I felt fobbed off. I was sure something was being missed. I didn't know what was wrong, but I didn't think it was acid reflux.

Nausea and vomiting continued to disrupt her schooling until one morning, the attendance officer called. Why was Alice off school again?

I was defensive. What was I supposed to do, send a vomiting child in against policy?

No, she agreed, but Alice is always sick on a Thursday or Friday – we need to talk.

I somehow persuaded Alice to attend a meeting that morning. As soon as we entered the school building, Alice felt sick. She commented on her nausea again as we walked back to the car. I don't feel too bad now, she said. I can see her fourteen-year-old face as she turned to me, looking quite pleased with herself, like when she'd finally worked out the answer to a difficult sum. It's like the building is making me ill, she said.

I stopped in my tracks. She was anxious. How could I not have seen it? Alice was compliant, she cooperated and endured as best she could, but after three or four days at school, her anxiety became too much, spilling over into physical symptoms, until she vomited. This kept her off school and a pattern had developed. It was so obvious, but as a trained psychiatrist, I'd missed it – in my own child.

The very act of naming her anxiety alleviated some of her distress. The nausea and vomiting eased up, and the school refusal, too, for a time. But beyond Alice's own inference that the school was making her sick, no one gave much thought as to whether anything else was at play. We never knew definitively what Alice was anxious about, but now I can guess.

3–4 June 2022

A garden party, a broken glass, a plant on the windowsill, a job to do

Now, I am overwhelmed by anxiety, as Alice once was. I take to wearing a baseball cap and dark glasses whenever I leave the house. I don't want to be seen. I continue to rise early, not out of choice, but because I'm unable to sleep for more than three or four hours at a time. It soothes me to be alone in the countryside. Some mornings, I find it rather hard to return home. But when other walkers appear, I head back, for once the world around me awakens, I prefer to hide away.

We are due at my mother's for tea, all of us. My brother and his wife will be there and their three children. No one wants to go, to see so many of them, it's overwhelming. The date is in the diary because it's the Queen's platinum jubilee celebration. My mother is a staunch royalist. She's the same age as the Queen and her spitting image; it's a family joke that they've never been seen in the same room together. I'll go to the tea party, I tell my brother, as long as Mum is aware it isn't about Liz. For us, this is no time to celebrate. Let the country be glad that the Queen, who is clearly in poor health, has lived for this momentous occasion; let them enjoy their four-day bank holiday, 'Platty Joobs', in the sun. But for us, the bunting hanging from gate-post to telegraph pole, adorning homes and public buildings, is an insult to our grief. Privately, we voice a very real fear that the Queen might die any day and we don't want our personal grief overshadowed by the collective mourning of a nation, for a woman that none of us really knows. Our publicly unspoken mantra: please wait, please wait. And of course, she does, and we are grateful.

As we are about to head out of the door, the phone rings. It's the coroner's assistant. In England and Wales, the coroner must hold an inquest where the death is a suspected suicide. He is careful with his language as he talks to us. There must be situations where parents are keen to avoid a verdict of suicide, I think. Maybe it still holds a certain shame for some. We tell him, as a family, we will not shy away from a suicide verdict, this is not an accident or misadventure. Alice had good reason to feel suicidal and people should know what brought her, and her family, to this place. Alice's inquest is booked for 31 August, he says.

I feel quite agitated after this call. I have some diazepam that a friend has given me, just in case, and I take one for the first time, to get me through. It does reduce my anxiety, but I become quite disinhibited. The last time I spoke to my brother he'd said something about Alice being in a beautiful garden now and I bring it up, tell him never to say such bollocks again or I'll be inclined to punch him. I comment on Michael's tan, ask too loudly if he uses Bondi Sands or some other brand. I could do with something to make me glow at the funeral, I quip.

Shh, Auntie Caroline, he says.

I'm chatting away, like the first time I had wine at a family lunch in my early teens, wittering on and on about nothing. Then, just like that family lunch – where, wondering how hard I'd have to bite the wine glass to make it break, I bit down and broke it, fragments of glass in my mouth – I am jolted back into the moment. Alice is dead. A few days ago, she was alive and now she is not. I can't be here. With my mother, who is glad *she* is still alive, so she can fulfil her maternal role, help me be without my daughter. With my brother, sitting here, with his three children, whilst I sit here with only two of mine. Will only ever sit with two. Birthdays, Christmas and weddings, all these days reaching ahead that should be, will be, things to celebrate, will also remind me that Alice has died, for she will not be there when she should be. I understand for the first time why occasions such as these are hard for the bereaved. On an ordinary day, Alice could be anywhere, but on Christmas Day, at a sibling's wedding, where would she be, but home?

Sometimes, in these early days, her absence is not felt strongly at all. I know she's dead, I weep, have nightmares, stop eating. At others, she's still in Brighton, might text at any moment to ask me to pop down with something she forgot at Easter. But tea in my mother's garden has brought the reality of her death hard up in front of my face. Time expands and contracts. The capacity to reflect on dozens of memories within moments. I remember Alice on the beach in Cornwall: ice creams, rock-pooling, swathes of golden sand, a raft of washed-up starfish, mackerel fresh from the sea. I see her dancing to Tchaikovsky in the kitchen, standing to attention in her royal guards' outfit, a school-book-day triumph, recorded for posterity in a photograph. I remember her fearlessness somersaulting on the trampoline. Her deep, throaty laugh. The subtle inflections of her voice, a mid-Atlantic drawl from too many hours gaming with strangers across the ocean. I will never hear her speak or laugh again. See her broad smile, or her odd little skip when she's happy.

Peter takes us all home and I climb the stairs. I feel like never getting up again. But I must because we're heading to Brighton, with Harvey this time, to visit Alice's room, so he might have the same experience we did a few days ago. But it's not the same. As we open Alice's door, her scent is already less potent and the room rather disappoints me, as if I expect it to be different somehow, that she might have tidied up for us since our last visit. Harvey takes some time with Alice's things on his own and we loiter outside in the small hallway. I'm anxious to get back into her room, to find anything of significance that we might have missed the first time. And we do find things, things that plant seeds of doubt into our understanding of her mental state.

There's a handwritten appointment for Blue Dragon tattoo parlour, the date sometime in the future, towards the end of June, a deposit paid. Kate phones and speaks to them. Alice was halfway through a tattoo, along her ribcage and flank, says the man. The tattoo the policeman mentioned when he made his house call, we realise. The session ended early, he goes on, because Alice was finding it too uncomfortable. How did she seem, asks Kate? She was fine, he replies. Chatty, in good spirits, keen to schedule the slot to finish it off.

Kate finds a receipt from Lidl, from three days before her death. A simple thing. What did she buy? I ask. Vegan burgers, pasta, loose onions, brioche buns and a basil plant, she replies. That would need watering, I say.

Earlier in the week I'd emailed to cancel Alice's speech therapy. Her voice coach had told me Alice had been doing well and seemed very motivated. In their last session, Alice was excited with her progress feminising her voice and had booked two more appointments. This, her tattoo appointment, a basil plant on the kitchen windowsill all say to us Alice was getting better, had plans. What changed her mind?

After the bank holiday weekend, Sandra calls from the undertakers. Someone from the mortuary has been in touch, she says. What do I want them to do with Alice's clothes? Would I like them returned?

Yes, I want them back, I say without hesitation. Whilst the sofa is soon to be discarded, I cannot do the same with her clothes.

Sandra calls back later. I sense a pause, something delicate to be said. It's the mortuary again, she says, as if the mortuary itself has a voice. Alice's jacket and shoes are – another pause – unscathed. Would you like them, her jacket and shoes, back?

Yes, we would, I say. We want everything.

Her other clothes, she says – yet another pause – are not in such a good state. Would you like them disposed of?

No. No! They are Alice's, we want them back.

They can be washed for you first; would you like them washed?

Again, no! I don't seem to be able to make her stop with this line of enquiry. She is not listening, or she can't quite believe what I'm saying, maybe because she wouldn't do the same. But we aren't all the same. No, I say again. No. We will have them as they are, we will wash them, I will wash them. I will not have what's left of her disappearing in ever-diminishing circles, spiralling down the plughole of a municipal stainless-steel sink. (Though of course, I think later, they would have used a machine.) I will not outsource this act. This is not laundry. She is not laundry. Send me the blood-soaked clothes, send me everything.

Alice's clothes arrive back from Brighton before she does. I go to collect them. They are folded neatly in transparent plastic bags. As with most days now, only so much can be achieved before a mental wall appears that stops me doing anything more. The bags are stored away in the rarely used study at the front of the house. Occasionally, Kate and I talk about washing the clothes, but the bathroom in this house, which we've owned for less than a year, needs renovating, is grubby, small and awkward. It's not a place fit for the task. We delay and I put it out of my mind.

Early 2017

Little by little, day by day, week by week, month by month

In February 2017, Alice turned fifteen but didn't want to spend the day with friends. We had a meal at home, a cake. It was a worry. She was of that age where most children begin the natural steps to separate from their parents, begin to hide parts of themselves, a withdrawal that often hurts parents, but is part of growing into an independent adult. But here she was, celebrating her birthday with just her mum and dad. Not that you could call it much of a celebration. Alice was quiet and withdrawn.

She was still quite slight at this point, had not entered a noticeable puberty. My puberty was late, as was her sister's. Peter's puberty was slow and gradual over many years. Harvey continued to grow well into his twenties. At school, those around her were physically changing, but she was not, not yet. But behavioural changes were clearly starting to kick in. Though these were quite foreign to me. She didn't rage at me, for a start. We didn't fight. She didn't throw things, slam doors, yell that she hated me or tell me to fuck off, that she wished she or I were dead. This was the puberty I understood. For me and her brother and sister, the confusions of adolescence were merely an exaggeration of an already tumultuous engagement with the world. But Alice would have found the whole experience utterly alien, having been so at peace with herself for so long. And her unvoiced gender dysphoria must have amplified her distress immeasurably. She seemed uniquely inaccessible and uncooperative.

Her nausea returned, accompanied by vague symptoms. She was intermittently tired, not well, fluey, achy, all very non-specific. She was sleeping badly, becoming nocturnal, and some mornings she wouldn't get up for school. Peter left for work at six, so I was always on my own. I tried everything to get her to go. What's wrong, sweetheart? You can tell your mum.

Nothing.

Please, sweetheart, I can see something's up, I want to help.

Go away.

It went on and on like this. What started as kindness and concern turned to cajoling and cursing, from me, at any rate. Will you just get the fuck out of bed? I'd pull the covers off a few times; she'd pull them right back over her again. And although I was no longer working as a doctor, I had Pilates clients relying on me, classes to teach, not a desk job with work that I could delay and catch up on later. So, when I had work scheduled, I left her in bed and got on with my day.

I guess the looming onset of puberty was playing heavily on Alice's mind, but there was no way I could know if she wouldn't talk to me. Alice lost her art of communicating so effortlessly. I lost my art of reading her. But there's no one moment where I can look back and say, yes, this is where it began. It was insidious, happening slowly, little by little, day by day, week by week, month by month. Her undemanding nature, which had been so charming, making parenting her such a breeze, was no longer an asset. It became a hindrance; she didn't ask for anything. Her needs, which I had always been able to meet, almost outside of regular communication, were now quite unknowable. Things were changing in a way that I couldn't put my finger on. Something was up and I didn't like it. Alice was not herself and she needed help.

7–8 June 2022

A mole, a looky-likey, a different Pippin

Now it is Peter and I that need help. He wants me to be more like him. I want him to be more like me, to share his inner world, to talk. He can no more do that than I can get on a bike, do some exercise. We row about something. Fuck off to the gym, I yell. He's already half out the door.

I turn to Kate. I soon come to rely on her to help navigate my relationship with Peter, my husband, her father. It's a strange state of affairs. And her sister has died. I put a lot of pressure on her; I do not mean to, but it's her support that enables me to carry on. She is a buffer in the space that separates Peter and me, as we hover at opposite ends of this spectrum of grief.

So, when Kate comes into my room with a cup of tea and in a casual manner says she thinks she should get her mole checked, it's as if I'm about to lose everything – the doorbell is about to ring and I'm to be asked once more, is there somewhere we could sit?

A few years previously, Kate had been seen by a dermatologist for a suspicious mole in a prominent position on her décolletage. Kate was afraid of an unsightly scar if it was removed, so the doctor arranged a compromise: she would remove a similar mole on Kate's forearm, and if that was clear of malignancy, the other one would be monitored annually in clinic. The forearm mole turned out to be benign. The follow-up slipped through the cracks of the pandemic.

———————

Two years later, no one's looked at the original mole. Now here is Kate, in my bedroom, just a fortnight after her sister has died, telling me it has grown, is itchy and has an irregular border. Show me, I demand. Now!

I'm horrified. The mole is huge, far bigger than the end of a pencil, a giant paint splat with a dark border. Perhaps it has already spread. I'm losing my second daughter. I can't breathe. I'm out of bed opening the window, pacing the room, flapping my arms like the wings of a bird that can't yet fly. I can't live like this, I say. I need to see a doctor, and so do you. We'll go in the morning. We'll be first in the queue. And we are, though there is no queue, no one falling in line behind us. I need to make an appointment, I say. Two appointments.

We don't make appointments face to face, the receptionist replies.

But I'm here right now, I say.

You need to call us to make your appointments, she insists. Please step outside.

I won't, I say. I'm telling her about Alice, causing quite a scene, a garbled story about a dead daughter and another one at death's door. I'm crying and beginning to hyperventilate, I talk in snatches, catching my breath. This way, we get our appointments (suicide's silver lining), both of us seen together, me holding Kate's hand, waiting for bad news.

But when Kate shows the doctor her mole, I almost burst out laughing. It's half the size it was yesterday, much smoother and paler, the rim around it barely there. I'm not a reliable witness at all. The doctor refers Kate to the dermatologist just in case, so I don't feel such a fraud and I get my medication: sleeping tablets and some diazepam of my own, to subdue panic when it hits. I leave feeling better than I did an hour ago. I can stand.

Which is just as well because we are due at the marina to meet the police, who are investigating Alice's death. There's a free multi-storey near Asda, the officer I've been liaising with tells me on several occasions. I suppose this detail might materially matter to some people. To me, it seems a little tasteless, as if we care how much we pay to park, to do this thing we're about to do.

We're following satnav. It doesn't take us to Brighton seafront and then left as I'd expected. We turn left earlier, along the A27, towards Falmer, then right on Falmer Road, the B2123, through Woodingdean, in the direction of the coast. I've never travelled this road before. It sweeps unexpectedly upwards, not down towards a beach. We turn a corner, a vast expanse of green in front of us, leading the eye forward, to the horizon, where it comes to an abrupt halt, turning suddenly into sky. It's not a view I'm used to. Not an askew glimpse from a Cornish coastal road running parallel to the sea, not the urban descent into Brighton or Hove, nor the rolling Surrey Hills – a hill behind a hill, behind a hill – but the land stopping abruptly in mid-air, head on, like a half-built bridge, a sweeping breadth of cliff. I swallow around a large lump in my throat.

We're being taken to the undercliff walk to see where Alice jumped, where she died. It's a drab and blowy day, the threat of drizzle in the flat sky. Two officers meet us in the car park in their unmarked car. One, a woman, remains somewhat remote throughout; the other is a man. He must be the officer I've been talking to over the phone, since the first day. He looks like a young Boris Becker, I whisper to Peter. He laughs; the tennis player was jailed not long ago. We drive behind them to get nearer to the spot, before continuing the last stretch on foot.

Peter starts sobbing, everything he's managed to keep at bay so far pouring out. Kate and Harvey walk either side of him, a hand each. I accompany Boris. He speaks in a voice that sounds like it's been practised in the mirror. Like a vicar who doesn't really believe in God. As he was the responding officer at the time, I ask lots of questions. In particular, Harvey wants it to have been light when Alice jumped. He finds this image less frightening than the thought of her shrouded in darkness. I set out to establish the facts. What time did the call come in?

Just after five.

How long did it take you to respond?

Not long.

So, it was definitely around five o'clock when she died?

Around then, or a little earlier.

Could it have been much earlier?

No, I don't think so.

How can you be sure?

I don't think he answers. On a morning in late May, it would be light at 5 a.m. I look it up: sunrise on 26 May 2022 was at 04:57.

———

It is not until almost two years later, when I review the police paperwork, that I read the ambulance was called at 04.38 and took just five minutes to arrive, at which time the paramedic noted rigor mortis had begun to set in. So, Alice died sometime between 2 and 3 a.m. It had been dark. Harvey is reassured when we tell him that Alice was not actually afraid of the dark, rather she embraced it – the dark was where she felt safest, unscrutinised, hidden from view. But I don't know why this correct version of events, so simple to understand and convey, wasn't told to us at the time.

———

I continue with my questions. Have you answered calls to this spot before?

No, not personally.

But there must be other cases?

Yes, it happens.

Does anyone survive?

I don't know.

Is it much further?

No, not far now. After a few minutes he stops. It was here, he says. The ground is chalkier here.

Was she on the chalk bit or the path? I ask.

The chalk.

Did they close the path?

Yes.

How long for?

An hour or so.

Is that all? I think. An hour isn't nearly enough time to erect a white tent, procure a sarcastic forensic pathologist in boiler suit and white wellies. But there had been no signs of a struggle, no suspicion of foul play. I've already been told this over the phone. Did you look, I'd asked, for anything under her fingernails? Yes, we looked, he'd said.

The others huddle together and wait for me to run out of questions. When I do, the police officers step away, leaving us together. We don't really know what to do. It feels a bit like stepping into the arrivals hall of an unfamiliar airport, everyone looking around for something, a sign or a symbol that they can understand, that will tell them which way to go. We look down, we look along, we look out to sea. It's hard to look up.

We've brought some flowers with us and a card. We start to make a little shrine, gathering beach stones that have been thrown up to the path in stormier weather. I spot a particularly appealing one, the size of a small fist and smoothly rounded. It's dark grey but within it there is a white ring around a paler grey area, a thumbprint-sized indent.

I pick it up and rub my thumb against it. Look at this, Kate, I say. I'm going to take this home as a memento.

Can I hold it? she asks.

Of course.

You could put it in Alice's hand, she says. Make a contact relic.

What's that? I ask.

It's from medieval Catholicism, she says. A physical object acquires properties of the deceased, due to the physical proximity to the body.

That's a lovely idea, I say.

When we are done, we stand back and observe our handiwork. From the bottom of the cliff looking up, it doesn't seem that high to me. I wonder out loud if Alice might have survived the fall, made a full recovery if she'd been found sooner.

Kate takes me by the hand and turns me to look along the path towards Rottingdean. Look at those people walking in the distance, she says. And look at the size of them next to the cliffs.

I step back and look up; I cannot see the top. Come here, everyone, I say. Come and see how brave Alice was.

Brave. A word I will think about a lot over the coming years. Both in the context of what Alice did and how I respond. For I am told over and over again that I am brave, and I loathe it, hate this word that's used so carelessly about me, when people have no idea how I feel inside and will not be told. When I say I feel weak, defeated and barely here, no, no, they say – you are so brave, so very brave. Shut up, I want to scream, you do not know. Shut up. But it is the word I use about Alice on this day. Was she brave? I said it then, but would I now? Surely she was, if nothing else, very, very scared. But to do something anyway, despite that fear, isn't that one definition of bravery? She was determined, that's for sure. Perhaps that's a better word, for us both.

I plonk myself down on a high concrete kerb at the edge of the path and invite the others to join me. We're all out of words, but the tears flow. A dog walker approaches with her rag-bag crew of canines. Most of them ignore us, but one approaches and sits stolidly at our feet. He looks like Pippin – not our Pippin, but his namesake, Auntie Mabel's Pippin, from *Come Outside*. A favourite CBeebies show. We pat his head and scratch at the scruff of his neck. He presses his body into us.

The dog walker smiles. He's a lovely dog, she says.

He's just what we need, I say. Can we keep him?

I wish I could say yes, she replies, kindly. She begins to walk off, with her other dogs in tow, but our new little friend won't budge. She calls and calls him, but he seems determined to stay. The dog walker is quite far away and hovering, maybe considering coming back.

It's ok, I say, to the dog. You can go, we're all right now. He looks up at us, stands, shakes himself off, then potters after the others. I feel quite calm, as if he has taken some of my burden away with him.

Spring 2005–August 2016

Kindred spirits and friends forever

Our Pippin is not that kind of dog, and neither was Poppy before him. I cannot say Poppy ever sensed any need in me for comfort or reassurance. She was a timid dog and therefore always by our sides, for her own reassurance, not ours. But for Alice she was a loyal and dependable friend, a constant who remained the same, whilst things around her changed. School moves, house moves, a new granny who came and went, friends who confused her by saying one thing but doing something else instead.

But I will not call Poppy Alice's best friend, for that title is reserved for Lucy. Alice and Lucy met at infant school aged four. It was an instant connection, just like she had with Zack, when they were only three, and with Keith, aged eleven. And Lucy too was in the LGBTQ+ gang. At their first meetings, did they all see something in each other, before any of them saw it in themselves?

Lucy and Alice in particular seemed destined to be friends forever. They shared a creative imagination, made spaceships out of cardboard boxes and flew to galaxies far from our own, drew treasure maps and navigated to make-believe lands with dragons, trolls and mythical beasts. Their friendship endured when Lucy's family moved overseas when they were both six. Then, when Lucy returned, around three years later, they took up where they left off, with regular sleepovers, spending entire weekends in each other's company. Now they were a little older, they built fires, toasted marshmallows, spent winter evenings wrapped up warm in the garden, stargazing and chatting endlessly about what lay beyond.

We went on long dog walks over Leith Hill, built secret camps and dens. Lucy was more adventurous than Alice and loved to climb, steep banks and fallen trees. Alice followed cautiously, whilst Lucy led, giving her courage. But Lucy's family moved again at the end of junior school. They kept in touch over the years, first at weekends and during school holidays, when I or Lucy's mum did the ten-hour round trip to keep their friendship strong, and later via social media when a particularly unpleasant trip to see Lucy meant we never took that journey again. Poppy, who was old by now and on borrowed time, did a wee in Lucy's father's study and he was furious. I heard the yelling before I knew what had happened, then there was a flurry of commotion, Lucy's youngest sibling rushing to find me, another arguing with his father in Alice's defence. I found Alice, reduced to tears and shaking. I had rarely felt so protective of her, had never needed to. I want to go home, wept Alice. We swept up our things and left never to return: Lucy's home was no longer a safe space for either of us.

Safety in our home and in each other's company was something Alice and I shared and took for granted. Alice would hold my hand in the street until well into her teens, so that if I saw someone she knew approaching, it was me who let go, so as not to cause her any embarrassment. I called her sweetie, or sweetheart all her life, so that sometimes Peter would say, do you think you should call her that at rugby? But Alice didn't mind, or never said she did. She just smiled.

Alice didn't partake in many activities outside of the home. She attended Stagecoach, but not for long, and then gymnastics, but when she started rugby, she gave up the gym because she didn't want to be busy both days of the weekend. I encouraged trips to London and tried to drum up enthusiasm for visits to the beach, but being at home, with friends or family, was what she liked best. We'd bake together, listen to music and dance, curl up on the sofa to watch *Deadly 60* and *Harry Potter*. Simple day-to-day pleasures were what made her content, rather than a childhood of structured and planned activities.

Early June 2022

The nuts and bolts of a suicide, the need for an investigation

Now I am planning Alice's funeral. I insist on asking certain people when they are free, not just family but friends, too. Eventually, reluctantly, we settle on a date: 20 June. Lucy will not be able to come. I worry about whether we should tell my birth mother that her granddaughter is dead. I decide not to. She has never known Alice as Alice; it will just make everything more difficult.

Peter's mum is frail. She cannot be our responsibility on the day, I say. Get one of your sisters on it. I worry that she, too, like Liz might die at any minute. She will have to go on ice if she does, I think. Later, after she dies, I confess this thought to Peter. Thank goodness I held my tongue, I say.

Oh, you said it several times, he replies.

Should we invite Mr B? I ask. He was Alice's headmaster at junior school. Alice was friends with his son, was invited to parties and sleepovers at his house. Mr B would occasionally say, with a twinkle in his eye, that the offer was still open to swap our children at any time. Now, ten years after Alice saw Mr B for the last time, we email him, to at least let him know she has died. He comes to her funeral, on a school day. This speaks to me of the place she held in his heart.

Alice's post-mortem has already taken place, but she cannot come home until the pathologist has completed her report. We are not offered the opportunity to go and see her in Brighton and it does not occur to any of us to ask, during any of the many calls we receive or must make to chase up the police and staff at the coroner's office who are rather haphazard with their communications. When the coroner gets the interim findings, we're told Alice died from multiple injuries. Just that. It's entirely unenlightening. I find myself thinking graphically about what happened to her. Perhaps it is my medical training. Perhaps it is my experience with my father.

Whilst my grief for him over the years has been complicated and fanciful, my relationship with my father's death began to improve from one specific starting point. One day, not until my early forties, I imagined his body in the jeep, very clearly, smashed against the windscreen, blood everywhere. I saw him as physically dead and gone for the very first time – not this mythical father figure who might have saved me if alive, who I regularly wished would reappear, like a knight in shining armour, to rescue me from an evil stepmother of sorts, but simply dead, and no bloody use to me at all.

With Alice, I don't have to wait decades for similar images to flood my thoughts. Was there a blow to the head on her way down, so that she was already unconscious or even dead before she met the ground? Had her neck snapped at her cervical spine, no connection between her brain and the rest of her body as it suffered the impact of a fall from a height? Had she severed her aorta, so her life blood, instead of taking its journey from her left ventricle to sustain life in the rest of her body, seeped out into her thorax or abdomen and failed to return to the right atrium for another cycle, denying her organs the oxygen they needed to survive? Was she alive when she landed and could have been saved? She had taken the necessary precautions to factor in this eventuality, having jumped in the small hours of the morning, when she was less likely to be found. Did she lie there a long time, in pain? To know she had died instantly, like my father, would indeed be some sort of comfort. Was it one single injury that finished her off or the sum of several blows? Was she drunk, high, both or neither? We are told the toxicology results will take some time, but once they are back, would that be it as far as the coroner was concerned? That Alice died because she jumped from a height, sustaining multiple injuries. We don't think so; there are other questions my family want answered.

I google 'Boy lured to his death online'. The first hit has the story I'm after, about a fourteen-year-old boy from Surrey, our home county, who was murdered in 2014 after being groomed online. The article references that, like many of his peers, the boy spent lots of time gaming, playing with other online 'friends' (the article's speech marks, not mine). Alice did this, I think. Was she lured to the clifftop by a murderous transphobe? But I've already discussed this with the police, we know there were no signs of a struggle. Nonetheless, they still appear to be looking at things from the perspective of a criminal investigation, trying to construct a picture of her last forty-eight hours. Who saw her? Who spoke to her? Where did she go? They have Alice's mobile, which they found at the scene, but we don't know the password and without one it can take months, sometimes years to access, plugged into some software designed for the job of codebreaking. We tell the police we think they are better off trying to access her computer. She lived her life there, we say. If there are answers, this is where they will be. They come to take it away for examination. What are they expecting to find? Since they do not say, I am left to imagine. If there was no actual attacker at the scene, maybe there was a dark and malevolent presence in Alice's online world. A charismatic, persuasive troll. Had Alice fallen under a spell? She spent a lot of time on Reddit, always quoting something she'd read on a subreddit thread. Could there be evidence of virtual conversations, where little by little, whatever confidence Alice had found in her new gender identity, her new name, was being eroded, being manipulated? Was she persuaded to take her own life? The police appear to be taking this line of enquiry seriously, and anything they find will be made available to the coroner in their report, but without access to the content of either her phone or her laptop they are at something of a dead end.

March–April 2017

A series of different questions, rare tears, a dismissive doctor

One morning, when once again Alice would not get up for school, I sent out a message to all my clients. Class was cancelled. I sat down on Alice's bed to put my best medical and maternal-detective skills to the test. We need to sort this out, I said. Alice turned her back to me. Please, I said, I've cancelled my classes to be here with you. Alice just lay there impassive. She was so stubborn; a quality her siblings had as toddlers, she had now, in her teens. I started asking direct questions.

Are you gay?

No.

If you are, you know it's ok.

I'm not gay.

Are you being bullied at school?

No.

Are you sure, darling?

Yes. Go away.

Is a teacher being mean to you? Has something happened on the internet? Has someone asked you to do something you didn't want to do? Have you done something you didn't want to do?

No, no, no and no. Leave me alone.

I was so worried. I knew something was wrong, but I couldn't get her to open up. Not by direct questioning, not by open-ended questions. Not by leaving her alone, not by bombarding her with my concerns. Have you committed some sort of a crime? No.

Is it your sexuality? I asked once more.

80

No!

I took a deep breath. Are you sexually attracted to young children?

This finally elicited more than a one-word response. She raised her eyebrows, No, you weirdo! Why would you say that?

Because I'm clutching at straws, Alice, I said. I was thinking, if I can make her understand I still love her, even if it is this, then surely she'd feel safe enough to share whatever was on her mind. It never crossed my mind to ask if she was trans. Perhaps subconsciously I thought being trans was worse than being a paedophile, and to ask that was beyond the pale. Maybe if I'd asked that, Alice would still be alive. Finally, I asked: have you been looking up ways to kill yourself on the internet?

She didn't say no, she didn't say yes. She slowly crumpled into rare tears and pulled the sheets up over her head. I'm sorry, I'm sorry, I'm sorry, she said. And I must have reacted the right way, for we hugged, she clung to me, buried her head in my chest, repeated herself over and over again: I'm sorry.

I even allowed myself to enjoy the hug, the closeness, for it had been absent for so long, and to feel pleased with myself that I had an answer. But I felt sick inside that it had come to this. For the relief, almost thrill of getting to this point came at such a cost. My carefree, happy-go-lucky Alice had disappeared and from that day forward, my happiness would be measured in how close or not I feared she was to death.

Now I had to work to get her seen by a doctor. It took weeks of plotting and persuasion to get her to agree to go. As I entered the consulting room to see Dr W with a sense of trepidation, I felt relief that we were finally there, and hope that help was at hand, but I was afraid Alice would be misunderstood. I'd had my fill of the myriad friends and acquaintances who'd compared Alice's behaviour to that of their own children. All children spend too long on their computers, they said, are withdrawn and sulky, don't care for their

schoolwork, could do better. So many had an idea or a recommenda-
tion – have you tried tai chi or swimming? Could she get a paper
round? She won't get out of bed for school, I said, sometimes wanted
to scream, when they suggested these things again and again.

Dr W was no different. What can I do for you? he asked.

As would become a pattern for most of our meetings with doctors
and nurses, a lot of the talking was left to me.

Alice has been looking up ways to kill herself, I said.

He must have asked did she have specific plans to do something?
She must have said no. I don't remember him seeming particularly
bothered, or me feeling that we were listened to or understood. I
described how Alice had ongoing problems with anxiety, which had
improved but were worsening again. She was struggling to get to
school, was socially withdrawn and spent a lot of time in her room
on her computer. Attempts to engage her in any activity other than
gaming were met with extreme resistance, and too much pressure
often resulted in Alice taking to her bed and covering her head with
the sheets. As a family, we always ate our evening meal together, but
lately, Alice had been refusing to join us. We'd enabled her to some
degree, I conceded – we took meals up to her, and we'd try not to in
future. But the real problem was her mood. She seemed so flat, so
disengaged, wasn't living, wasn't experiencing the life we envisaged
for her: studying and sports, friendships and parties, splashing about
in the Mole. She lived in her room.

But like it was with all parents who have children who do
cooperate and can be cajoled, bribed or threatened to do whatever
their parent wants them to, Dr W's answer was that she needed to be
more active.

How? We have tried.

She should play more football, he suggested.

She doesn't like football, I replied.

She should get some fresh air.

What is this, the 1950s? I thought.

Her first words were garden and outside. She was raised ruddy and wholesome. Only last summer she played imaginary fishing games in the stream that ran through Lucy's garden. But things had changed. How could I make him understand? I'd never met such resistance in a child, and her siblings had stubbornness in abundance.

We were sent away with a prescription for football, fresh air and some stronger parenting. It was a grim experience for both of us. Although Alice said little during the consultation, once we left, she begged me not to make her see that horrible doctor again. I promised. I was furious with Dr W, taking what I feel was a very particular line with me: that mothers would do better to listen to the doctor.

––––––––––

I subsequently came to understand that this type of interaction is one that the trans community endures on a daily basis: a damaging and disturbing parenting of their experience by cis adults, who assert with such moral authority that they know more about the trans experience than trans people themselves. Cis people are the self-proclaimed experts, whilst trans people are not to be trusted, are wholly unreliable in knowing themselves, they imply. A collaborative approach is the very least trans people deserve, but their voices are rarely heard, and even when they are, they are not believed. After this appointment, Alice retreated back into herself.

A week in mid-June 2022

Private moments with Alice, a support-group rant

Sandra from the undertakers calls. Alice will arrive with them in the morning, she says. Tomorrow is Harvey's birthday. I have already been fretting as to how I can make my twenty-four-year-old feel special, eighteen days after his sister has killed herself, when he should be celebrating in Central America. We agree we will postpone seeing Alice for one more day.

Peter leaves for Brighton again, to empty Alice's room. There's no rush, I say, it can wait, but he wants to do it. Maybe it is a way for him to absent himself from worrying about Harvey's birthday, one child getting older reminding him that another never will. I do not mind; I am grateful he is prepared to undertake this task that I do not want to do. When he returns, Pippin sniffs at the boxes of Alice's things. Here is her smell, but where is she? He darts about the house, looking for her.

———

Sometimes Alice would hide away and I would dart about the house myself, searching high and low for her. Often, she would be curled up in the large eaves' cupboard in her bedroom, an outgrown childhood den of cushions and comics that now seemed to offer sanctuary, and where she would read by torchlight. Other times, depending on the weather, she might be somewhere in the garden, tucked away out of sight with a book. I would call and call for her, quite shrill in my panic at times that she had run away, but she would never reveal herself, even if she was right under my nose.

Now I long for her hiding skills, if not to disappear entirely, at least to escape for a while from the despair, the guilt, the endless tasks that must be undertaken. For the rest of the world carries on regardless, and so, to a certain extent, must we. Now I'm no longer in business, there are contracts to cancel, refunds to process, so much admin that only I can attend to. It all seems so unnecessarily demanding and trivial when other demands on me are so immense.

We are going to see Alice.

I never saw my father's body, never even went to his funeral. I know without any question that I want to see my daughter. I've seen lots of dead bodies, from medical training before I specialised in psychiatry, but never in a coffin, never a family member, never my child. Peter's seen a couple – his grandma and a colleague who died in his sleep, at a hotel, after a work bash. For the children, Alice is their first.

These most private moments with Alice are the hardest to recall. The surviving fragments aren't necessarily the bits I wish to remember. There's a box of tissues, for tears, but when I look around for a bin there isn't one. Alice would have found that funny, says Harvey. Leave them on the table, he adds, she'd find that funny, too. She certainly has a smile on her face, a smirk, we all see it. She looks like she's trying not to laugh, might sit up at any minute. Surprise! Just kidding!

We've chosen a white cardboard coffin. We think she'd approve. The undertakers charged less for it than Amazon. Is it awful that I checked? Kate's picked out her clothes: a cream long-sleeved roll-neck top and a black skirt, but she's covered by a cloth from the neck down, so the skirt's hidden and just the roll-neck and the sleeves of her top show, where her arms are neatly folded across her chest. Kate and I have been spending rather a lot recently, on matching Tiffany necklaces with a pretty lower case '*a*' and silver lockets, for her ashes. I'm now glad we didn't spend more on some fancy trousers Kate wanted Alice to wear. This is what I'm thinking, as I gaze down at her, that I've saved some money.

I touch her cheek and kiss her cold forehead. When I'm alone with her I find myself pulling down her roll-neck towards her throat, past her clavicles. I see the wound left by the pathologist, where she opened Alice up. I run my finger over the puckered skin. I've an urge to pull back the covers to trace the zipped-up skin further, to see her half-completed tattoo. I don't, and I don't ask, though I think about it, and later wish I had.

I only remember a few phrases of the long conversations I have with her. Silly, silly girl, I say, my silly, sweet, darling child. We'd have worked it out, sweetie, it could have been ok. I repeat myself. I say much more. Some of it is quite ridiculous. Promise me you'll never do it again, I ask, more than once. Calling back over my shoulder as I leave, I'll come back to see you tomorrow.

The next day, I'm immersed in more admin for the funeral, which is five days away. Peter and Kate are out sorting the order of service and Harvey's spending more and more time with Shin Ah's family – he finds being in the house as a family of four too much to bear.

I'm home alone and in charge of putting together the visual tribute. I'm having trouble choosing the photos that will play as everyone enters the chapel. So many of Alice before she transitioned and so few after. I ask Keith to set up a Remembering Alice Facebook page, which quickly proffers up lots of pictures I've never seen. My favourite is a picture of her in a deckchair at a barbecue, legs crossed, chatting with friends. She looks so relaxed. In that moment, she was utterly safe; all her friends accepted her as a woman, so she was one.

Amidst this intense task, I must return to Alice because I made a promise, and I cannot break it. But looking at all the photos has left me so distressed, I feel unsafe to drive. I find the wherewithal to phone a friend, ask her to get me there, between sobs. I have the stone from Rottingdean with me. I place it in Alice's hand. It's a little fiddly to get her thumb upon the right spot. Look after it for me, I say.

We have an appointment with the celebrant to discuss Alice's funeral, what music to play and who will want to speak. Jane has written us a beautiful letter, with memories of Alice as a toddler. How I took Alice to see her in the Priory when she was detoxing and that it was such a treat to hold a baby in such a stark and clinical place. And how I asked her to babysit Alice overnight the following summer, when Alice was only eighteen months old and Jane had not long been sober, so that Peter and I could have a night away. So pleased I trusted her.

I would like her to read it out, I say. It's important to me, given what we've been through together.

I return a third time to Alice, to take the stone away. I hold it in my hand, my thumb against the memory of hers, the contact point in the relic. And perhaps this will somehow help me hear an answer, as I ask Alice questions about herself that I long to know. Were you ever in love? Were they kind to you? Did you experience the intimacy of sex? Was it good? I hope it was good. I won't let you be forgotten; I'll always speak up for you. I'll be a better person. I'll be who I want to be because you no longer can. I go on and on, until my words dry up and I turn my back and leave.

When I get home, Peter is surfing the internet for help with our bereavement, for counsellors or support groups. I'm not interested, I say. I feel beyond help. He persists, so I humour him. Maybe it would do me good, I say, without believing it.

How about this one? he says, SoBS, Survivors of Bereavement by Suicide. Jesus Christ, I say, imagining the pumping fists in the brainstorming session when they came up with that. SoBS, for fuck's sake. He finds another: Suicide & Co.

Really? I ask. Suicide & Co?

Yes, he says, what?

I can hear their theme tune now, I quip, something jolly and child-like, something out of *Sesame Street*, or a musical. I sing it out to illustrate my point.

Peter is undeterred by my flippancy. There are others: Cruse, that's one we've heard of, Sibling Link, for the children, though they will soon be too old to benefit from it. As if you stop becoming a sibling after the age of twenty-five, I tut.

What about this one, The Compassionate Friends? he continues. They only support people whose child has died, that might work?

They sound like they all wear crucifixes and might stretch to half a shandy down the pub, I say. Though why I should be critical of them on this basis is unclear, for whilst I consider myself an atheist, the local church has been drawing my gaze a lot recently, and though I've historically been quite a big drinker, I do not touch a drop of alcohol between Alice's death and her funeral, have no urge at all.

In all these snarky responses, what I'm really saying is, I'm not ready. Attending a group is admitting to others that Alice is dead, so I find any reason not to go.

April–end 2017

Another doctor, a referral to CAMHS

After her encounter with Dr W Alice refused to see another doctor and a month of ongoing low mood passed before she agreed to try again. I took her to see Dr A, a female doctor who'd treated me with care and dignity through my own episodes of crisis, my postnatal depression and the emotional fallout of reconnecting with my birth mother. This doctor will be kind, I promised, and she was.

Dr A referred Alice to Child and Adolescent Mental Health Services (CAMHS), where she was offered an anxiety-management group. It was difficult to get her there, she didn't find it helpful and didn't do her homework, but she managed five of the allotted six weeks. Her computer usage and gaming history were discussed and steps were taken to reduce it. I asked Peter to do something specific – to work some IT magic to limit Alice's computer time. But we fundamentally disagreed on how much of a problem we thought it was. I felt a massive unease. But I never took the matter into my own hands. I didn't want to offend Peter. I didn't want it to be my job. And Kate and Harvey had been the same at Alice's age and had self-policed their computer usage in the end, coming out unscathed.

At the end of the course, the psychologist's report said Alice did well, but it merely taped a sticking plaster over a gaping wound. The reason for her referral – her suicidal thoughts and related research – seemed completely forgotten.

Might a more positive intervention have been made? If the assessor had been wearing her ID on an LGBTQ+ lanyard, or wearing a pronoun badge, maybe Alice would have approached her privately, mentioned her growing, but hidden, gender dysphoria. Maybe. I'll never know because she wasn't. What I do know is a six-week course of group cognitive behavioural therapy for a working diagnosis of generalised anxiety isn't going to help a fifteen-year-old with unvoiced, yet highly specific issues around their gender. And if the environment doesn't show acceptance and understanding, or at the very least an awareness of difference, and a willingness to explore it, how are these important conversations ever going to happen?

———

Alice trudged on, sometimes going to school and sometimes not. She was academic, so the school didn't seem that bothered. She passed all her tests. It became our normal. This withdrawn child we shared a home with but couldn't seem to help.

June 2022

Recriminations, triggers, a proper plot

Now we are learning to navigate our new normal: a world without Alice at all.

The police keep talking about the forty-eight-hours before she died, keep repeating that she doesn't appear to have been seen or to have spoken to anyone. This evidence of her aloneness and isolation exacerbates my incessant feelings of guilt and self-reproach. I am distraught that I did not reach out to Alice in the days before her death, when I was aware she'd gone quiet on the family WhatsApp. Peter is quick to reassure me. She was always going quiet on the chat he says, over and over. It does nothing to ease my pain.

It is Kate who is able to talk me down each time a new wave of recriminations engulfs me. Imagine if you'd rushed down to see her and you'd had a row and then she'd done it, she says. Imagine if you'd had a lovely time and everything had seemed fine, but she'd jumped anyway.

I know, I know, I say, agreeing with her intellectually, before repeating as I will so often: but I'm her mum, I should have been there for her.

It's an impossible demand you place on yourself, to hold so much power and control, so much responsibility, she persists.

Yes, I concede, ok, thank you. I smile weakly and blow my nose.

You cannot take the blame for this; you weren't even there, she says.

Exactly, I think, and I'm back to square one, with my ifs and buts.

I try watching TV to distract myself, but I'm triggered by almost everything. Not just the obvious – jumping scenes (of which there are many), other suicides (also abundant), the occasional trans joke – but also the less obvious: happy young children, happy older ones, happy parents, angry parents.

I try writing my journal. I replace my desk chair with Alice's old, tatty one, another contact relic to help me connect with her whilst I write, but I barely sit in it at all. I mostly curl up on the new grief-couch, which has finally arrived in one piece, and continue to wallow. The grief-couch is my safe space from where I deflect the frequent calls to action: a walk will do you good, get some fresh air, stretch your legs. The GP said this to Alice, now my husband is saying it to me. I've no motivation, no impetus. Leave me alone, I say. Go on your own.

Our old sofa sits in the hallway area, at the bottom of the stairs, waiting to be hauled on to a roof rack and taken away. We navigate our way around it. One morning I come down and find Peter curled up, fast asleep on this old, familiar sofa, not the new, luxurious, clean grief-couch a few steps away. He is folded in, uncomfortably tight, at one with the stains and memories infused into this sofa, one that Alice sat on her whole life. It is hard to let it go. Eventually, Peter does take it to the dump and we all feel some regret as another little bit of Alice leaves the building.

We all agree Alice would choose cremation, but I suddenly want her buried. My father is buried overseas and I've never had a place to go, to be with him, to mourn. When I was around eight or nine, a friend's father died and was buried in the local churchyard. I used to go and stand by *his* graveside. It was better than nothing – someone's dad, if not my own. Now I feel strongly I need this for Alice, a proper plot and a traditional headstone. When the others say she wouldn't like it, I use my occasional new retort: if she wanted a say, she shouldn't have bloody killed herself. But in the end, I agree to cremation quite easily. It is what everyone wants.

March–September 2018

A child restored, a letter by the kettle, watch and wait

Alice was formally discharged from CAMHS in the spring of 2018, many months after her last anxiety-management session. We were asked if we thought she still needed their help, but it was an odd question, since she hadn't been seen by anyone from the team for over six months. So, we said no. She'd just turned sixteen.

Rather than mental-health workers, I came to rely on a few of my closest friends for support. Jane had moved away but still worked near by, so we'd meet a few times a year in a café for lunch and a catch-up. The last few meet-ups had been dominated by my worries for Alice's mental health.

Do you think she's gay? she asked.

She denies it, I said. And it wouldn't make any sense – she's known Kate was gay since primary school, Kate's girlfriend came to Cornwall with us last summer. Why would she be so secretive about something that's so normal in our family?

She better not be transgender, Jane said, laughing.

I remember my reaction, saying nothing, looking down at my plate, poking my food around but not eating, swallowing uncomfort-ably, tingling teeth in my jaw and a strange vibration in my body, as if I could feel my individual atoms on the move. Eventually, I must have said something, something like yeah, I hope not, or no, that would be difficult, or outright denial: no, I'm sure she's not, there's no signs, oh God, no, not that!

I'd never thought about it, that my child might be trans. Jane planted a seed, but it was not one full of hope and promise of growth and new life, but a seed that was toxic and harmful, a seed that must not be watered. I didn't go home and ask Alice if she was trans because I didn't want her to be. Another opportunity missed. It was not just Dr W or the psychologists at CAMHS who saw the world through a heteronormative lens.

Despite her school attendance sitting at 62 per cent, Alice sat all her GCSEs bar one when she was sick again. She got good results – 8s and 9s in the subjects she loved (physics, in particular, chemistry, maths and biology, too). In those she didn't, French and English, it was 4s and 5s. I found it pretty impressive she'd managed to pass a foreign language without going to class.

When Alice was around eight or nine, she and I were chatting about what was out there beyond the stars, how had life begun?

I want to be like that cool science guy, she said.

I was at a loss as to what cool science guy she meant and she got quite frustrated because neither of us could remember the names of any cool science guys.

And then I said excitedly, 'Ooh, I know, Brian Cox. Is that it?'

But it wasn't Brian Cox. And I kept on struggling to think of any cool science guys, when suddenly she shouted, Einstein! I want to be like Einstein.

Wow, I said. That's one cool science guy. Aim high.

And she went on to tell me all about some of Einstein's work, but I began to only half listen, the way mothers tend to, when they have other things to do, like getting dinner ready. If I had my time again, I would listen; I would let dinner wait.

In the summer holidays, after GCSEs, Lucy came down unaccompanied on the train for the first time. We travelled up to London to meet her at King's Cross. Took a peek at Platform 9¾. It was magical to see them together again. Alice was back to her usual self, full of life. She was a child restored. On her last night, they sneaked out to stargaze in the middle of the night, so for one brief moment I thought I might have to phone Lucy's mum to tell her I can't find them, they have run away.

Once the summer holidays were over and Lucy had gone, some of Alice's courage seemed to leave with her and she withdrew again. But to my surprise, she asked if she could go back to see the doctor. Could it be that nice one she saw before?

Appointments with Dr A were like gold dust, but I made it my mission to get her one. Alice liked Dr A enough to speak privately to a doctor for the first time. She came out of the appointment in a buoyant mood.

The following week, a letter arrived for Alice when she was out. I knew it was from the GP, but it didn't cross my mind to open Alice's mail. She was sixteen and a half – I respected her privacy, though I desperately wanted to know what it said. When Alice returned home, she took the letter upstairs. I waited for the right moment to talk to her.

The next morning, Peter came into the bedroom in an agitated state. A letter had been left open on the work surface next to the kettle. He rattled out a blow-by-blow account: I was just getting ready for work, I didn't mean to pry, I was only tidying, putting away, making tea, the letter was already open, I scanned it to see who it was for, it said gender dysphoria, I haven't read any further, I didn't open it, it was just there next to the kettle, it was for Alice and it said gender dysphoria. I don't know what to do, he said. As if I did.

It was a complete shock. We'd talked about the possibility of Alice being gay, but the possibility she might be trans, even after Jane planted her seed, was never considered. There hadn't been any signs. What would they even be?

As a baby, Alice had been bigger than her sister, smaller than her brother, exactly in between the two. She was smaller than the average boy. She played with her sister's toys and her brother's toys. She played at cooking and Power Rangers. She had a particular fondness for a neon pink handbag of Kate's that she carried around with her everywhere. Whilst Harvey had occasionally dressed up in Kate's clothes and fairy outfits, Alice never did. Maybe she would have done if she'd had a sister closer in age. She loved to dance but wouldn't go to dance class because it was full of girls. I took her to an all-boys one instead; she didn't seem comfortable there either. I took her to the ballet when she was nine or ten, a special children's production. The whole theatre was full of mothers and daughters, the little ones kitted out in their ballet clothes or princess costumes. We saw one other child in jeans and a t-shirt. Alice didn't seem to notice, or care. Her best friend was a girl. Most of her friends were boys.

She'd started playing rugby aged seven, because her older brother did. I used to love watching her. As one of the smallest players on the pitch, she could often look a little out of place, but despite her size, she was good. She quickly earned the nickname Scrappy, to go with the nicknames for Harvey (Shaggy) and Peter (Scooby). Why Scrappy? Because once she dived into the ruck, nine times out of ten this little whirlwind of fierce determination would come out holding the ball for her team. It was to our constant amusement that between these displays of courage and physical strength, she would skip across the pitch. I was sad when she gave it up, aged twelve or thirteen. No reason, she said, she just didn't like it anymore.

We decided to speak to Alice about the letter. Surely, even if only on a subconscious level, she wanted us to read it. Why else would she have left something this personal so publicly on display? This was her way of letting us know. But when we sat her down to talk, she clammed up immediately, wouldn't be drawn. I talked to Kate about it, maybe she could help. She would reach out to Alice, she said.

Much to my surprise, in early September 2018, a few weeks after Lucy's visit, and eight months before she fully came out to me and Peter, Alice overcame her fear of public transport, of travelling alone, and made the solo journey to Cambridge, to spend the weekend with Kate, to seek support and advice about her gender identity. She thinks she is a girl, she says. Kate is sworn to secrecy, a promise she keeps. After Alice's death she will question that promise. Should she have broken Alice's trust? Would that have saved her? How often we both ask ourselves similar questions. What did we do wrong? How did we let her down?

I didn't demand to see the letter. I walked the tightrope between love, concern, control, respect and trust. Perhaps I respected Alice's privacy too much. The letter, which I read much later, revealed that whilst Alice had spoken about her gender identity, Dr A didn't refer her to Tavistock Gender Identity Development Service (GIDS). Instead, she sent Alice away with some leaflets and an invitation to make another appointment if she wanted one. A child – who the previous year she'd personally referred to CAMHS for crippling anxiety, who she knew had looked up ways to kill herself, who had disclosed worries about her gender identity and who hadn't told her parents – was sent away without follow-up.

Kate knew this, and urged Alice to book another appointment, to get herself referred to GIDS. But Alice came home and did and said nothing.

I know Dr A well, she's a good doctor, but it's my belief her uncon-scious prejudice at the time sent my child away with nothing of any practical help. Dr A adopted a watch-and-wait approach. Worse than that, she wasn't even watching whilst she waited – for Alice to change her mind, whilst her hormones were about to surge.

Without any more disclosure from Alice, life continued, superfi-cially at least, much as before. I approached her intermittently about her gender identity. Would she like to talk to someone about it? There were organisations, groups. No, she said. We didn't look for support for ourselves. We were in a semi-denial. If Alice wouldn't talk about it, then why should we? We continued at work, and Alice struggled to get to school. In year 12, her time at home began to overtake her time in class and both her performance and her confidence declined.

20 June 2022

Preparing for the funeral, getting my needs met, having a lovely time

The day of the funeral arrives. The heat's dropped a little, it's going to be a perfect June day. Kate and I, between us, have bought and returned more than a dozen black dresses to try. If internet shopping existed for no other purpose, I feel it should exist for this. I've narrowed it down to two, quite different in their style. One is an expensive, classic shift dress, to be worn with power heels and a string of pearls; the other, a much cheaper affair, a figure-hugging thin-ribbed cotton knit that encases me from my throat to my wrists, down to the floor, bar a small, off-centre slit. I'll wear it with boots, or wedges – quite a different vibe. My head's telling me to go with the former. It's so classy, so sophisticated. But my heart's saying no. I cannot put my finger on it, then it hits me. In the first, I look quite the grieving widow, but I'm not a widow. I'm mourning my daughter, a child. I'll wear something young.

We get ready in the same way we'd get ready for a wedding or christening, a black-tie do, making sure there's enough hot water for everyone to shower, plus steam-free mirrors for make-up. Do people need something to eat before we go? It's about ten minutes before we are due to be picked up when I realise I don't have my glasses on. Where are they? They're lost again. I search all the usual spots: hall table and bedside locker, coat pockets, a slew of bags. The search is widened: the bathroom, my desk, the loo. I'm getting desperate: the fridge, the kitchen bin, the airing cupboard, back to the hall. That fizzing feeling rises once more, bubbles in a soda bottle with nowhere to go, pressure building.

I can't go to the funeral without them, I say, to no one in particular. Peter is trying to settle me, but I cannot be reassured. I won't be able to read my speech, I say, as I pace back and forth. Then it strikes me with the utmost clarity: you'll have to go without me.

Peter takes hold of me and sits me down. I think you maybe need a diazepam, he says.

Ok, I say.

Harvey, Kate, he yells, please stop whatever you're doing and help look for Mum's glasses.

All the rooms are searched again. No one finds them. The diazepam isn't working. I'm overflowing; soon there will be nothing left in my bottle at all. I've lost my glasses, just like I've lost my daughter. I've been careless, put them down somewhere and forgotten about them, whilst I was busy with other less important things, fripperies – jewellery and make-up and hair – when what I really need is to be able to see.

I'm transported back to the day before Alice died. I was at iFLY with Peter, cashing in a voucher that Harvey had bought us for Christmas. Whilst Alice lived her last day, I bounced around in an air tunnel in Basingstoke. I'd put her out of mind, to have a day out and I'd enjoyed myself; it wasn't the sort of thing I did these days, it was a perfect gift from a loving son. But, like jewellery and make-up and hair, it was a frippery, it took attention away from life's realities. Whilst I was carefree and literally buoyed by air, my daughter planned her plunge in the opposite direction. I'm selfish, thoughtless and cruel. I may as well have taken her to the cliff and pushed her over myself. I'm entirely and singularly culpable.

Peter shakes me out of my reverie. I'm back in the house on the day of the funeral and I'm inconsolable. My glasses are lost forever. Alice is lost forever. I'm in such a state of agitation. I will take more diazepam, get into my night clothes and go to bed. Then Kate shouts, found them!

The car arrives and we're ushered in by the driver. It's only when I'm installed in the back row of seats, where I'm at some distance from the driver and unable to speak to him, that I notice there's no second car. Where's Alice, I ask? My heart begins to race once more.

We've instructed the undertaker that we want to drive behind Alice from our house to the crematorium. I've been very clear; I don't want the first time I see the coffin, lid down, to be just moments before we step out under the gaze of all the other mourners.

Peter is saying, We have to go, we're on a schedule, what's done is done.

But I wanted her here, I wanted to follow her, I gave clear instructions, didn't I? To Sandra, Peter?

Yes, yes, but we can't do anything about it now, he says.

I'm feeling utterly ignored and everyone's saying, it's ok, it'll be all right, but it isn't all right. It's already all wrong and now this is making it intolerable. I asked and it hasn't happened, and I can feel it coming back, the feeling I've had all my life: I've no voice, no authority, I don't matter, I'm not good enough. I want to run, but the diazepam must be having some effect, slowing down my racing brain, and I realise I am good enough, because no one else is trying to get what we asked for, and I rise from my mute, helpless, hopeless place and find my voice. If I can't find it now, when can I? I will get what I need on our final day together. I'm thinking out loud. If she's already left the undertakers, could we meet her at the train station?

Do you really want that, Mum? asks Harvey, gently. We don't want her hanging about waiting for us there, surely?

No, you're right. Somewhere else, then, on the one-way system, outside Sainsburys? It's a funeral scene from *Fawlty Towers*. But somehow it is sorted. I'm in the back with Harvey and he's taking me seriously, relaying my needs, via Peter, to the driver. Without me hearing, calls are made, conversations happen and we're driving towards the undertakers to meet Alice in a local residential road.

A suitable compromise has been reached, everything is ok again. I take another diazepam as we sweep up the drive to the crematorium and the funeral begins.

And it turns out to be just as I had imagined it on that first day without Alice, twenty-five days previously. Except it is also better than I imagined. Kate has been determined to speak at the funeral from the outset, but Peter, Harvey and I weren't sure we could. Our wonderful celebrant is an acquaintance from happier times – care-free, child-free nights down the Leg of Mutton and Cauliflower. He has broken his self-imposed rule (no friends, no family) and agreed to perform minister duties at Alice's funeral. And with his quiet forti-tude and compassion he encourages us all to think about how we too might be involved. Peter and I are both able to speak in the end and Harvey asks his godfather, Ginge, to read a poem written by Alice on his behalf. The family have found it a great source of comfort and Caroline, in particular, has been quoting from it regularly. Ginge gives me a wink as he reads. Fuck, fuck, fuck, fucking, fuck.

Back at the rugby club, we're met with a sea of old faces from the past, the rugby mums and dads, flipping burgers and sausages, manning the coffee urn. We are surrounded with goodwill. Preparing for the funeral service itself was an ordeal, but the wake has all been taken care of by friends and I have not had to do a thing. Picnic blankets are strewn across the grassy slope; there are deckchairs for the oldies. Peter's mother has made it. I've never heard quite so many fucks at a funeral, she says. People drift out of the club-house with their beers, their gin and tonics. I could do with one of those, proclaims my mum to a group of Alice's friends. All I got was coffee in a nasty paper cup, she adds, working the room, as usual, even now.

I haven't drunk alcohol since Alice. I will break this new-found abstinence later today, but for now, I am a little giddy on diazepam. I waft around amongst our friends and acquaintances with a broad smile on my face. I am having a lovely time, I say, to anyone who asks how I am.

Last orders are called at the bar and the light fades. A few final stragglers head off and finally it is just the inner circle who walk across the playing fields towards the gate that opens opposite our road for the short walk home.

There are lots of little details about Alice's life that I won't ever know, but I learn some wonderful things from her school friends after she's died. They tell me stories at the wake, out on walks, at our house, when we meet for tea one afternoon, which turns into pizza and beers, and they stay until almost midnight. I learn the answers to some of my questions at the undertakers. Alice was loved, she did experience intimacy. Some try to hush Bea, who is telling me, but I am so grateful for her truth, for her startling ability to know how to talk to her dead friend's mum. She speaks so openly, without fear, with such love and tenderness and understanding. I cherish these stories.

November 2018–May 2019

A bit of backstory, my early transphobia

Alice had lost her art of talking to me almost completely. Her silence did not protect her; it created a hole for me to fill. Around this time, articles about trans people became increasingly prevalent in the press, and they were mostly hostile. I read them and I worried. Had my child been brainwashed? If young people could be groomed to be suicide bombers or have underage sex with multiple men, then couldn't they also be groomed to be trans? It was a cult, an epidemic. Alice was a victim. If Alice was trans, she would have told me years ago, just like Kate had told me she was gay when she was thirteen. I argued with Peter. It's only since she's become so withdrawn and entered an online life that she's turned this way, I said.

The computer's her lifeline, he said. You hear her laughing and chatting with her friends online.

Yes, I do, I agreed.

I continued to follow trans stories in the news. In 2018, a trans man had given birth to his child. In February 2019, there were stories in the press; he wanted to be named as father on his child's birth certificate. If this were to happen, the child would be the first in the UK, if not the world, to legally have no mother. In the way of Victor Meldrew, I didn't believe it. If you had ovaries and a uterus and had given birth, you were the child's mother. I was happy for this trans man to adopt the role of father to raise his child, but he couldn't erase his biology, that he had given birth, and that was a thing only women did. I talked about this at the dinner table when Kate was home because she was a passionate LGBTQ+ activist. Kate tried to explain why his legal challenge was reasonable. Harvey and Peter just said it didn't matter. Alice kept quiet. But she was there, listening. No wonder she didn't want to talk to me about her burgeoning trans identity, though she didn't talk to Peter either.

I chose to read her silence on the matter as evidence that she probably wasn't trans at all. And crucially, although there had been little change in Alice, and she wasn't much better, she was no worse. There was no immediate cause for concern. Most of the time we lived as if her gender had never been brought up. Perhaps it was, indeed, a phase.

I met with Jane for coffee. Told her that Alice was questioning her gender, that I wasn't coping very well, that I wished it wasn't so. She was sympathetic. She wouldn't want it either, she said. Since the last time we'd met, Jane had been spending more time on the internet, specifically Mumsnet, learning about 'the trans problem' in the feminism section.

She shared her knowledge with me eagerly. She'd learned there were two 'types' of trans women: suppressed homosexuals, who became women to accommodate their internalised homophobia, and those who were autogynephiles – men who became sexually aroused by the idea of themselves as women. The latter is a term for a sexual fetish proposed by a single psychologist in 1989 that gained early traction, but has since been by and large discredited, and has never been recognised in any version of the World Health Organization International Classification of Mental and Behavioural Disorders (ICD*) that was my diagnostic bible as a psychiatry trainee. But what Jane read on Mumsnet she believed. I challenged her.

Alice isn't gay, I said, so she can't fit the first category. Do you think your goddaughter is in the second category? That she is a fetishist?

* ICD is the WHO International Statistical Classification of Diseases and Related Health problems, a subdivision of which is the ICD Classification of Mental and Behavioural Disorders. The latter includes clinical descriptions and diagnostic guidelines for all psychiatric disorders.

No, she said.

I didn't believe her.

We were both fifty-two at this time. I was entering menopause. My sudden lack of oestrogen and progesterone exacerbated a deep-seated resentment of the life challenges I'd endured: adoption, childhood bereavement, sexual assault that had left me feeling unimportant and powerless. I raged against Peter, his career over the years. He'd escaped to the City five days a week, away from the emotional load of parenting, whilst I'd juggled medical training, childcare and house-keeping. My retrospective resentments loomed large. I had not triumphed, the way women were now meant to, both at home and at work. I didn't consider my Pilates business a success, although it certainly was. I raged that I may as well have climbed the medical career ladder if all my years of compromise and sacrifice had come to this. A suicidal child who was talking about transitioning. I was only a few steps away from aligning with Jane and her more radical anti-trans views. Back at home, I repeated what Jane said. Don't listen to her, said Peter. But I did wonder: what if she was right?

June 2022

Another trip to Leeds, a story heard for the first time

Two days after Alice's funeral, Kate has a scholarship interview for her law-conversion course that she plans to start in September. We are in awe that she's able to focus at such a time. They tell her within days that she's been successful. We are all delighted. Kate decides not to continue her master's. She will start afresh in the autumn with her law training. But she wants to return to Leeds for a mini pupillage she has booked, and she may as well move out that week, she says. She has no ties to Leeds and wants to be home with us. Peter offers to come but Kate wants a girls' trip. So, it's agreed, I'll drive her – the same journey Peter and I took the day Alice died. I'll keep her company in the evenings and help her pack. It's a long schlep up the M1, and Kate doesn't drive, so I break the journey. I'm careful not to pull in at Northampton.

I keep myself busy whilst Kate's at work. On the first day, Rebecca, a housemate of mine from medical school, comes over. We head to a nearby café. It's the first time I've been out in a recreational capacity. I walk so slowly, I'm like a learner driver having their first lesson, never getting out of second gear. In the café, I feel observed, as if my grief must be issuing from me like a bad smell. But Rebecca takes her time with me; she has an understanding. Her brother Huw died unexpectedly from medical complications of epilepsy when she was just nineteen and he twenty-one. She used to wear a locket around her neck that contained his ashes. At the time, I thought it macabre, now I understand. Whilst a student, I never asked Rebecca about Huw, although we shared a house for three years. She was a mature student when she started her medical training in Cardiff, and Huw's death had happened during her first undergraduate degree in Bangor. I ask about him now.

I was home for Christmas, during my first year, when it happened, she says. Huw had never visited me at university, so when I went back in January, I could kind of forget about it, as if he were still alive back home. I have that feeling for many months – that Alice could still be living in Brighton, that she'll be back for the weekend, that I'll see her at Christmas. Rebecca, thirty-seven years earlier, maintained the pretence by not going home herself for almost a full year.

And what about your parents? I ask. They must have been around the same age I am now.

Yes, she says.

How did they deal with it?

My dad never talked about it, not until his final months, when he was diagnosed with cancer. He began to reminisce about Huw then.

And your mum?

Well, she grieves for Dad now, she replies. Grief for her son held in her hand, like a baton, for thirty-five years until it could be passed on, I think.

After Rebecca leaves, I'm at a loose end. I message Lucy who's at university in Sheffield. By chance, she's going home tomorrow to celebrate her birthday – she'll be passing Leeds on her way and will drop in. I cry and cry in advance of her arrival. I don't want to scare her, but I cannot stop myself. I think Lucy, of everyone in Alice's life, knew her the best. I thought nothing would ever separate them. But their relationship did falter. As Alice's anxiety took grip and her depression deepened, she stopped replying to messages that Lucy sent. I kept encouraging Alice to keep in touch, was afraid that she was losing her strongest ally.

But on this visit, I find out it was still Lucy to whom Alice turned when it really mattered and that she holds no grudges for Alice's difficulties communicating over the last few years.

Lucy tells me how Alice came out to her as trans during that summer visit after GCSEs, the visit when Alice seemed so well, so completely herself. It was Lucy who was Alice's very first confidante.

I came down on the train on my own to visit in the summer holidays, she says.

I remember, I reply. Your first big journey alone.

Yes, you both came to King's Cross to pick me up.

Were you sharing a room?

I think so, she says. You and Peter had gone to bed. Kate and Harvey weren't there. I don't know where they were.

They were at university, I say.

Alice was in an unusual mood. She picked up one of my bra tops, like a vest top, sports-bra thing, and disappeared into Kate's room. When she came back, she was wearing a pair of Kate's denim shorts, which were really tight, like hotpants.

She always loved wearing tight shorts after she transitioned, I interrupt. That and oversized sweatshirts.

I know, Lucy says, I saw some pictures. And on her top, she had my bra stuffed with socks.

I haven't ever heard this, I say.

She was very excited, Lucy goes on. She was saying, 'I'm a girl, I'm a girl', and skipping up and down the landing.

And Peter and I were asleep in our room?

Yeah, says Lucy. And Alice was being so loud and shouting, 'Look at me, look at me, I'm a girl!' And I was shushing her, urging her to calm down. I was worried one of you might wake up. She just said, 'Let them, I don't care.'

Wow, I say. The tears are streaming down my cheeks.

I have a photo of it on my phone, would you like to see it?

Yes, please, I tell her. She looks so happy, I say.

She was, says Lucy.

If only we'd woken up, I say.

Peter and Harvey arrive that evening, in a hire van. Kate's life is dismantled, boxed up and loaded on. The next morning, they head off. Kate and I follow, after a final sweep of the flat. As we drive through Leeds, heading south, a fresh unravelling begins. A city seen from a new perspective; tall buildings rise like cliffs from their tarmac beach. Images from 9/11 flash before me. I narrow my focus to the car in front, which pulls me along under bridge after bridge after bridge, each one a reminder, an insult, a threat. Bang! A body bounces off the bonnet. I blink, grip the steering wheel a little harder. Breathe, Caroline, breathe. Kate cannot help with the literal task of driving, but by being with me, talking, sharing that she's thinking similar thoughts, of Alice on the cliff, she navigates me out of the city and on to the open road.

Kate asks if she can put some music on. In the car, on a road trip, I usually have music blaring, but since Alice I've not wanted to listen to anything. Everyone else has downloaded her playlist from Spotify, the soundtrack that accompanied her at the end. I cannot, not yet. We agree on *Rumours*, Fleetwood Mac. It's a good choice. We're quiet for a while and we cover a chunk of our journey held together this way, by the comfort of the familiar.

After a service-station break, we start talking again. We're back on the clifftop with Alice, attempting to climb inside her brain and fathom this all out, and Kate revisits a subject that's been troubling her. Do you think she was drunk, Mummy? Or that she'd taken something?

I don't know, darling. We'll have to wait for the toxicology results.

I don't want her to have been, she says. I wonder how long they'll take? I really need to know. I really want them to be clear, she continues.

Me too, I say.

This is our mutual wish: for Alice's actions to have been considered, that she made a choice whilst of her own mind, unadulterated by psychoactive substances that made her temporarily insane. If you can agree that suicide, in and of itself, isn't always the result of insanity, by definition. We want her to have had agency. We want to believe that her choice was rational, given the insurmountable barriers being placed in her path, the value, or lack of it, that society seems to place on trans existence. This idea that Alice got what she wanted, comforts us at first, but our grief deludes us. Death is an escape, that is all. What she wanted and deserved was to live her life free of judgement and fear, as she knew she needed to.

This line of discussion untaps something deep inside. I begin to shake, like the seismic activity of a volcano that sends warnings of an imminent eruption. But I'm on the M40, hurtling along at 70 miles per hour. I mustn't explode. Here they come, the tears, my lava flow, pouring out of me, snot streaming from my nose, as I wipe it away with my sleeve. I peer through the haze, a sign, for another services, not far to hold out. When I pull to a halt, I throw open my door, stagger out, lean against the car and howl.

We finally arrive home. Peter and Harvey have made better time than us and dinner is waiting in the oven to nourish us. My appetite has returned and I sit down, grateful to eat with my family.

It is five weeks since Alice died. In that time I've: told my brother, driven to Leeds, told strangers, told my daughter, told my son, told Keith, told my clients, told everyone. Driven home, driven to Brighton, driven back again, to Brighton, and back, to Heathrow, for Harvey, to Brighton and back again. Been a mother, a wife, a dog-walking insomniac florist, entertained guests – welcome and unwelcome – visited family, visited friends, visited Alice, visited Alice, visited Alice. Called the coroner, the undertaker, the police. Waited for the visits and the calls that never came. Shopped for food that others ate, lost a stone, lost my glasses, found them, lost them, found them. Shopped more, a sofa, that important black dress, and glasses, so I can see. Closed my business, answered emails, processed refunds. To Brighton, and back again. Planned a funeral, a speech, a wake. Imagined doing it all again. Driven to Leeds, driven back.

We're home. Kate's never lived here, so it doesn't feel like home to her. And her new housemates, her parents, on whom she's previously relied for consistent love and support, within a marriage that was warm and stable, are on the edge of a precipice themselves. It's the last day of June.

End May–2 June 2019

Taking a break, a life in the balance, driving home alone

We continued to worry about Alice, but because she remained so reluctant to talk to us, we gradually put any gender-identity issues on the back burner and started to think about doing more things for ourselves.

Towards the end of May, Peter had a walking weekend booked with old school friends. At the last minute, I was invited to the Netherlands to support a friend who was competing in an international triathlon event. Her travelling companions had pulled out and she didn't want to go alone. The dates clashed. Alice was seventeen, old enough to manage a few nights without us, as she had in January, when Peter and I had taken a short break for our own sanity. But we knew she was in a bit of a dip, had at times felt suicidal again, wasn't perhaps as robust as she'd been back then. Peter and I discussed whether I should go. I really wanted to, to support my friend, but also, to get away. To escape the daily battles about school attendance, computer use and leaving her room. The one-way street of interaction with Alice who gave nothing back, not even a fight, was soul-destroying.

I talked to Alice about going away.

I'll be fine, she said.

Do you feel suicidal? I asked.

No, she said.

Would you like me to ask Kate or Harvey to come home?

Nah, I'll be fine.

Are you sure?

Yes.

I need you to look me in the eye and say that again, I said.

She turned her head and met my gaze: Mum, I'll be fine, go and have a nice time. She smiled a generous smile. It was so lovely; she was my Alice again.

I'd be away Wednesday to Sunday, but Peter was only going from Friday. She'd be on her own for two nights, that was all. She'd managed before. We encouraged her to have friends round. I left Alice Emma's number to call if there was an emergency.

Peter and I communicated with each other whilst we were away, but we didn't expect Alice to answer texts or calls. It seems ludicrous to me now that we would have accepted this, but we were so inured to her silence.

I arrived home before Peter. My first impression was that Alice had held the gathering we'd encouraged. Lights were on in the kitchen, there were cupboards left open, clothes discarded on the floor, plates and glasses scattered about. I called up the stairs, I'm home, as I started to clear up. Alice didn't reply, which wasn't unusual, so in no particular hurry, I carried on, muttering to myself about the mess, before carrying my case upstairs and popping my head round her bedroom door. She was tucked up in bed, fast asleep. She looked so peaceful. I sneaked in and knelt down next to her.

I'm home, I said.

She roused ever so slightly. Hello, she said, with a small smile.

I tousled her hair. Are you going to get up for roast? I asked, then went downstairs and started to peel the potatoes.

Peter arrived back just in time for dinner. Good timing, I said. Can you call Alice down?

I popped to the loo. The next thing I knew Peter was shouting, come here, Caroline, quick, come here. Caroline!

I remember my irritation. Just let me pee, I've cleaned up, I've cooked dinner, whatever it is, can't it wait?

Caroline, I need you.

All right, all right, I'm coming, give me a minute.

In the kitchen Alice was bent over the sink, Peter stroking her hair.

What? I asked. What's the matter?

Peter was shaking, he looked quite grey. Alice has taken an overdose, he said. He choked on the words, as if his mouth was full of stones. She's taken lots of tablets.

I was immediately in doctor mode: what have you taken, Alice?

I don't know.

You need to know, what did you take?

Stuff, just stuff.

Where from, from the kitchen drawer?

Yes.

Just the stuff we already had?

Yes.

How much?

I don't know.

You need to know. It's important. Peter, look in the drawer.

I don't know, I feel sick, leave me alone.

No, Alice, I won't. Answer me. What did you take? I scanned the kitchen, nothing. Where did you take them, Alice?

In the living room. Can I go back to bed?

Through the door I noticed, for the first time, packets strewn across the coffee table: paracetamol, ibuprofen, co-codamol and antihistamines, their blister packets emptied out, every foil compartment popped. Enough to kill her, for sure, if she'd taken them all and kept them down. Depending on when she'd taken them, the paracetamol could already be irreversibly poisoning her liver, so the only chance of survival would be an urgent transplant within days, a few weeks at most. I felt cold and sick. I was falling through infinite space, spinning in a vacuum, like an astronaut cut loose from her mothership. I've killed her, I thought, my selfish need to get away, unload, put her out of mind. This was on me. I noticed an almost empty bottle of gin. Please God, let her have been sick.

I returned to the kitchen, firing out instructions. You're not going back to bed. We need to get you to hospital. Peter, she's taken paracetamol, she'll need the antidote. My mind was racing, it was twenty-five years since I'd treated a paracetamol overdose. Did they need the treatment within twelve or twenty-four hours? I couldn't remember. Call Emma, I said, she'll know what to do. Ask her if we should go straight to St George's. They have a poisons unit, and if Alice needs a transplant she'll be transferred there, anyway. Alice heard it all.

Alice, darling, you must listen to me. Look at me, listen to me, we need to get you to hospital. When did you take these tablets?

I don't know.

You have to know.

Last night, maybe, she said.

Do you mean Friday night or Saturday night?

I don't know.

Daddy left on Friday, did you take the tablets on the first or second night?

The second, I think.

Good, good, that's good. And what time last night?

I don't know, can I have a glass of water?

Here, drink this. Was it dark? When you took the tablets. Was it dark?

Yes.

Were you sick, sweetie? Please say you were sick, I prayed.

Yes, she said.

Oh my God, oh my God, thank God, thank God, I thought. How soon, darling, how soon after you took the tablets?

I don't know.

Was it still dark?

Yes.

That's good, I said. Good, well done, good. In early June, the nights were short, maybe she'd been sick quite quickly. Maybe, just maybe, she was going to be ok. I couldn't let myself think that she wouldn't be.

Emma recommends St George's, said Peter.

Ok, I said, get her in the car. We need to leave. It was well over twelve hours since she'd overdosed, the clock was ticking.

I used to work at St George's, in the liaison psychiatry department, where I gave my opinion on medical patients with suspected psychiatric problems. So, I drove because I knew the way. But I took the A3 instead of the familiar A24 because I thought it would be quicker out of rush hour. I sped up the dual carriageway, then slammed on the brakes for the speed cameras. But when I got to red traffic lights, and saw my way was clear, I broke free of authority and drove. Then I took a wrong turn and didn't know where I was. Peter, who can't navigate a shopping mall, was in the back with Alice, trying to direct me using his phone. My veneer of calm peeled away; my child was going to die, if not because I left her, suicidal and vulnerable, so I could have a mini break, then because I took the wrong route to Tooting. Then I saw it, the cemetery, on my right, where it should be from this end, and I knew we were moments away. In the rear-view mirror, I saw Alice staring at the row upon row of headstones and gulping.

———

She explained that moment to me later. She'd wanted to die, but thought she'd survived. Now she was realising she might die, after all. She was not scared, but she hadn't wanted the end to be so drawn-out. It was embarrassing to have been discovered.

———

I dropped Alice and Peter at accident and emergency and went to park. When I returned, they were nowhere to be seen; a clerk was on the phone, taking notes. Constrained by manners, I bounced from foot to foot, as if on hot coals, to attract her attention without speaking. But my bobbing up and down, my rising panic were unremarkable – stressed mothers so commonplace, we are invisible. I found my voice. My child's been brought in, but she's not in the waiting room. She held up a palmed hand: wait, it said. My child and her father, where are they? She continued with her call. I couldn't catch my breath.

A lady sat waiting leaned forward. They went through there, she gestured.

Thank you. I barged through the doors, found them quickly, in a cubicle. Have you been seen?

A nurse has been in, said Peter.

Has anyone taken bloods?

No.

Are they coming back?

I don't know, he said.

I left to find someone. I'm Alice's mum, I said, to the first nurse I encountered. She needs bloods: liver function, clotting, paracetamol levels.

It's all in hand, she replied.

But there's no time, she needs the antidote now, she might need a transplant, we must be quick, I used to be a doctor. I went on and on, said everything I could to persuade her to move a little faster, except the words too unbearable to speak: that I thought Alice was almost certainly going to die. The nurse wouldn't be swayed and went about her business. There was nothing I could do. I returned to Alice and Peter, tried to climb on the bed. To lie next to her, skin to skin, like we did when she was a newborn. I wanted to feel her heat, her warm, living body. I pressed as close as I could, as if by embracing her, enveloping her, I created a womb of safety. She could breathe my breath, bleed my blood, I would sustain her.

It seemed like an age, but in reality, she was seen quickly, calmly and efficiently. Bloods were taken, the antidote, the acetylcysteine infusion, started and we could do nothing but wait to find out the damage she'd done to herself. The following hours were the longest of my life. I didn't google the treatment window for the infusion that ran through her veins, I didn't want to know. I allowed myself a few more hours of hope before I would have to face the consequences of my actions. I would never forgive myself. Never. My baby, who needed me, yet I'd abandoned her. What had I done?

But when the results came back, they couldn't have been better. Everything in the normal range. It was a relief beyond words. A puzzle. Alice was admitted to the ward and chose Peter to stay with her overnight. I tried to arrange my face to hide my feelings; it was hard to speak. I might as well go, then, I said, try and get some sleep.

Yes, you do that, Peter agreed. We'll be fine.

Night-night, then, I said.

Night.

I leaned over the bed and kissed Alice on her forehead. Love you.

Love you, too.

I wanted to stay with her; I was her mum. But Alice chose her dad. I knew why. Alice knew that I didn't want her to transition, didn't want her to make changes to her body that she might later regret, didn't want her to change at all. But she was so unhappy, she'd tried to end her life; she'd already changed beyond all recognition.

I returned home alone, and as I climbed into bed, thanked a god I didn't believe in for the return of my child alive, and physically, if not mentally, well.

July 2022

Shaking it out

Something odd is happening to my physicality. I can no longer judge where I am in space and I knock into things constantly. I spill my tea when I reach to place it on a nearby table and miss, I cannot manage zips and buttons, or the putting of my arm into a sleeve.

And I start to experience violent whole-body spasms that startle not just me but anyone in the vicinity. If you experience hypnic jerks (the involuntary spasms that can happen when you drift off to sleep), you will have some awareness of my experience. But it doesn't only happen at night, though these have become far more marked; it happens at any time of the day, and for quite sustained periods. The minute I stop, take a moment and allow myself to completely rest, they arrive in volleys like bullets. It's as if my body is physically trying to shake off an irritant fly that keeps landing on me and disturbing my peace. But it is not entirely unpleasant. It feels like it is doing me some good, serving some purpose. Perhaps it works a little like the aura after a seizure – nowhere near as disabling, of course, but a kind of absence, creating a few moments in the day when I am a little switched off and able to rest and restore myself for the next challenge.

June 2019

A lie and a false confession, a promise of help, a battle begins

The paediatrician was ready to discharge Alice after one night, but she remained in hospital for two more for psychiatric review. In my year on rotation with CAMHS as a junior psychiatrist, I often assessed children who'd self-harmed. I was always happy to discharge the patients I saw for community follow-up, never worried enough to seek a second opinion. But the CAMHS nurse who assessed Alice asked the on-call consultant psychiatrist to come in. Dr P was the right side of middle-aged, old enough to have experience, young enough to talk to a teenager. She was dressed in a simple skirt and shirt, nothing fancy. A no-nonsense sort of a woman, with a slow, deliberate manner. I felt Alice would be given all the time she needed. Dr P talked directly to Alice from the outset, making her her priority. They left for a side room together, where Alice talked openly to this complete stranger. Some people have the knack.

Alice cited the death of our dog Poppy, in April, as a provoking factor. She'd been diagnosed with heart failure three years previously and given less than a year to live. She'd exceeded all expectations, but in her final months had found it hard to walk, had become incontinent. We'd all agreed she would be put down. Undoubtedly, we'd underestimated how much her loss meant to Alice. Poppy was the member of the family Alice confided in the most. She'd lost her lifeline.

Alice also talked of anxiety about school, having fallen behind. She admitted to drinking on her own at home, for the last few weeks, to zone out. And, this wasn't her first suicide attempt, she revealed. A while back she'd removed a kitchen knife from the cutlery drawer, whilst Peter and I slept, and walked to the woods next to the local park, planning to cut her wrists. She'd sat there in the darkness for over an hour, she told Dr P, before returning home unharmed, leaving the knife behind.

Ah, that's where the knife went, I sighed when the doctor told us. I'd noticed its absence. It was my favourite from a set of three, expensive and very sharp. This must have been at Easter because all the children were home and I'd asked repeatedly, has anyone seen my knife? The middle one from this set, I said wielding the other two around, so they knew exactly which knife I meant. What could've happened to it? Maybe I threw it out with the compost? I mused out loud. Doesn't anyone know where it is?

Alice shrugged. Not me, she said.

———————

As a youngster, Alice tended to admit to crimes she hadn't committed. Like the Christmas all the chocolate decorations on the tree were eaten without permission. I called the children downstairs, made them stand in age order, like some sort of police line-up in front of the fireplace, pointed to the tree, the evidence, the empty wrappers still hanging from its branches.

Was it you, Kate?

No, Mummy.

Was it you, Harvey?

No.

Was it you, Alice?

Yes, she whispered.

Kate, at the other end, looked so surprised – perhaps Alice had eaten just one, what a stroke of luck!

These are the stories we repeat to ourselves now that bring Alice back to life. Little anecdotes of a life that make us smile, then cry, then smile again in an endless cycle of grief.

———————

Alice talked to the psychiatrist more fully about her sexuality. She was bisexual, she said. She'd had a boyfriend. She liked to wear nail varnish and women's clothes around the house when we were out, had been questioning her gender for a year or more. Dr P suggested Alice needed admission, since she'd planned to overdose as soon as she'd realised that she might be left on her own and she wasn't expressing regret. Both serious signs of intent. But Alice didn't want to be admitted. We agreed we could support her at home, with the full backing of our local CAMHS team. An urgent referral was made. She was discharged with a diagnosis of social anxiety and her ongoing risk of suicide was rated high. She'd soon be assessed for talking therapy and a trial of antidepressants or anxiolytics. At least that was Dr P's expectation and ours.

Alice's survival was a gift, the chance to know her as she truly needed to be known. But it wasn't an instant acceptance, not by me at any rate. There was a journey to be undertaken.

Alice came home and slept on our floor for the first couple of nights, but soon asked to return to her own room. She asked so casually, but it felt like she was asking to leave the country.

Let's wait and see what CAMHS think, we said.

Can we get another dog? she asked.

Would a dog give you something to live for?

Yes, she said.

There was no checking with CAMHS about this. Six days later, we'd a one-eyed Romanian rescue dog to share our home. Alice named him Pippin and her mattress was moved downstairs, so she might sleep overnight with her new dog whilst he settled in. She appeared a lot better, and it wasn't just the dog; Peter agreed. The overdose had acted as some sort of release valve, like the time in year 10 when her nausea improved once she'd named her anxiety about school. She was more like she used to be. Smiling more readily, spending time with us, chatty and open. She began to talk about her gender identity, but she didn't have much to say.

When did you first start thinking this way? I asked.

A while ago.

How long's a while?

I dunno, a year or two, more.

What makes you think you're a woman?

I dunno, I just do.

Lots of men like to dress up in women's clothes and that's ok, I said. The obvious implication hanging in the air, unspoken but plain enough. Have you been looking things up online? I asked.

Can we talk about this later? she replied, wandering off to find the dog.

Alice had her first appointment at CAMHS. She was encouraged to use a traffic-light system – a red, amber or green card Blu-Tacked to her door to show us how suicidal she felt. I asked for her to be seen by a doctor. The nurse made a note.

She was seen by the nurse again the following week.

Alice needs to see a doctor, I said.

I will take your request to the team meeting, she replied.

We worry every day whether Alice will be alive in her bed in the morning, I said.

Are all the medicines and knives locked away?

Yes, we said. But this felt like flimsy defence against what she could do if she wanted to.

Instead of a doctor, Alice was referred to Heads Together, a charity-led counselling service with an outpost in our hometown.

She would have to wait a month or two for an assessment. Ok, we said.

Ten days after her overdose, Alice returned to school. As far as we were aware at the time, no one there knew about her gender identity, but we found out later she had confided in one friend, Zev. Peter and I took it in turns to drive her in. When it was my turn, I watched her disappear into the woods, between the school and the car park where I dropped her off, and felt anxious, sick. Sometimes I got out of the car and followed her, did a recce of the woods, looking for a body swinging from the branch of a tree. I asked the school to always let me know that she'd arrived.

We had to let Kate and Harvey know what had happened. Kate was in the middle of finals, so we decided not to tell her until they were over. We couldn't tell Harvey if we weren't telling Kate. The secrecy was challenging. We allowed Kate one day of celebrations before we rang to break the news. The timing was bad – the following day was Harvey's birthday, but he simply had to know, now that Kate did. She's doing ok, we said. Try not to worry.

A few weeks later, Alice was finding it hard to go in again. She'd got dressed, had some toast. Peter, who'd been working from home to support me since Alice's suicide attempt, called up the stairs: time to leave. When Alice didn't appear, he climbed the stairs, found her curled up on her bedroom floor. What's the matter, lovely?

She managed a choked reply, I can't go.

What can I do to help? Peter asked.

Make me a girl, she said.

Alice didn't make it into school for the rest of the academic year.

2–9 July 2022

A breakdown, an uncomfortable encounter with an old colleague

I am curled up in the classic foetal position, gripping Alice's stone in my fist, and Peter is trying to soothe me. The details are scant; I ask Peter for help with remembering but he remembers less than me. It's two days after my return from Leeds. Everything that has needed to be done has been done. With no more demands to be met, quite abruptly I become acutely unwell. I'm telling Peter I want to be dead, that life has no point. I'm asking him to fetch me razor blades so I might cut my wrists.

Don't be silly, darling, he's saying.

Please, I'm begging him. Just get them for me, just let me do it.

Peter reaches out to several of my friends. Sorry to drop this on you but I'm scared, he writes on his phone. Caroline is talking a lot about killing herself. I don't know what to do. Emma texts straight back, she's on her way. Emma is the right person for a crisis; her years of treating babies and children hovering between life and death, managing the expectations of their desperate parents, have made her the embodiment of unflappable, calm made flesh. She enters the bedroom. I'm going to make a call, she says, without hesitation.

She relates my story to her psychiatrist friend and we're steered towards Safe Haven, a mental-health crisis service with hubs across the county. None of us has heard of it. The nearest is just twenty minutes away. Emma sits down on the bed to look up the opening times on her phone. There's a sudden creak and a jolt. The mattress

126

drops a few inches underneath me. I think I've broken your bed, she says. I think you have, I reply. She's laughing and I hoist myself up and manage a smile.

Remember when I broke Russell's bed, shagging Andy that summer I was resitting my anatomy exam, I say, once Peter's out of the room.

Lordy, she laughs, I didn't know that. We chat a little as we wait for Peter. Where's he gone? she asks.

He's probably gone to get some gaffer tape; he uses that to fix everything, I say. Perhaps he could try it on me, I add.

I think you need something, she agrees.

It is so good to have her here. One of my oldest and dearest friends. Telling me firmly, you know you can't, it will devastate everyone, then breaking the bed and making jokes about getting her stomach stapled.

When Peter returns, Emma tells us the opening times: 6 a.m. to 10 p.m., she says. She needs to leave, take her daughter somewhere or other. Will you be ok?

Yes, we'll be fine.

Peter coaxes me into the car. I sit in the passenger seat, enveloped in Alice's quilted coat, despite the heat, face pressed against the glass, staring into nowhere. We drive in silence except for my sobs. Peter is overwhelmed by my haemorrhaging emotion. The silence presses in on me like a judgement. I'm screaming at him, stop the car. We're less than a mile from the house, approaching a bus stop, pull in here, STOP ... THE ... CAR. I stumble out and lie on the bench in the grubby shelter, curling up once more, reaching for the stone in my pocket. Peter approaches. Get away from me, I hiss.

He's on his mobile. Caroline won't get back in the car, he says. I don't know what to do. Will you go with Emma? he asks me.

Yes, I nod.

Will you come back to the house with me and wait for her there?
Another nod.

Soon we're off again. Emma driving and Peter next to her. Me sprawled across the back seat, rocking.

When we get to the centre, it's shut. Opening hours 6 p.m.– 10 p.m. it states on the door. For fuck's sake, Emma, I say, but I'm smiling.

It must have been the bed breaking that distracted me, she says.

She takes us home. I'll come back at 5.30 p.m., she says. We'll try again.

This time the door is answered by a jolly lady who seems surprised to have a visitor. I'm afraid we're not open, she says.

Well, you clearly are, I reply.

Oh, yes, she responds, airily, but only for phone calls. We're under-staffed, I'm the only one here.

Then what am I supposed to do? I ask.

She offers me the choice of a couple of other centres. She's so cheerful; she's like a waitress at an American diner, my choice being between chocolate or strawberry ice cream.

I turn my back on her, walk to the car and prostrate myself once again on the back seat. If I'd been on my own, alone without a family who loved me … we're so near the river … I can imagine I would have carried on walking, towards the water.

The next centre isn't far away. It's not well signposted; I'm not sure we're at the right place. But my knock on the door is answered and we're ushered into a huge room, with a large central table where a man sits, talking to a woman with her back to us. We're asked to wait on seating along one wall. I hear everything that's being said between the couple at the table; it immediately becomes clear that this is a consultation, that the woman is in crisis. This is wrong, I'm whisper-ing to the others. We shouldn't be here. For a moment they're thinking I'm asking to go home. No, I say, this – I point towards the table – *this* is wrong. No one does anything. It's me, the patient, who makes the others get up. We find a side room with a few chairs in it.

We're going in here, so you can have your consultation in private, I say pointedly and shut the door behind us.

With this start, my expectations are low, but I'm seen in under twenty minutes, no nine-hour wait like in accident and emergency, and the man who sees me, with his good eye contact, steady voice and sensible questions, inspires confidence. I forgive him his confidentiality faux pas. You're having an acute grief reaction, he says. It's frightening but totally understandable. You need looking after. I'll refer you to the psychiatry acute home-care team. They'll see you at home tomorrow.

The next day, we're not convinced anyone will come. There'd been confusion the previous evening about which team I should be referred to, our postcode being on a boundary between here and there. The man and I disagreed. But a nurse does come, spends two hours with me. Talks about admission. I'm shocked. I know the threshold to be admitted to hospital, the pressure on beds, I'm not that unwell, surely? What have I said to necessitate this course of action? I've told him I'm thinking about burning the house down in the middle of the night, that's what. I know killing myself will be awful for my family, so taking them with me would spare them that pain, I reason.

Unless you tell them, I'll have no choice but to suggest you go in, he says, and I'll have to tell them myself.

I can't, I say. It's only a thought. I won't do it.

But you need to tell them, he repeats.

I can't, I say. I'm so ashamed.

It won't be too bad, he says, if you do come in. You'll probably get a bed in the Priory, he adds to encourage me.

It's tempting, in the same way I sometimes used to feel, if I could only commit a crime, I could have a welcome break in Holloway to alleviate me of my daily responsibilities. I manage to speak to Peter and secure my place at home for the night. The doctor will come tomorrow, the nurse says.

When he does, I wish the man at the crisis centre had been right about my catchment area and I'd been wrong. Because the man who walks through the door is someone I used to work with back in 1995, on my first job as a junior psychiatrist. We were equals back then, both on the same training scheme, on the bottom rung of the ladder. He was a little squirrel of a man, always darting about here and there, looking busy, then scurrying off up the nearest corridor when you needed him. The nurses used to ask me to do jobs he should have been doing; they, like me, were avoidant of conversations with him, tired of trying to decipher his mutterings from under his 1970s moustache. Yet he carried an air of confidence that did not match his level of competence, a habit of holding eye contact a little too long, once you had tracked him down.

And here he is, unchanged, except for a smattering of grey and no crumbs in his facial hair today. He is the psychiatrist in charge, standing in my living room, in his smart suit, whilst I sit under the duvet, unwashed and in my night clothes at midday.

I know you, I say.

No, I don't think so, he replies.

Yes, I say.

No, he repeats.

Definitely, I say. I recognise you, we used to work together.

No, he repeats, a look of confusion on his face.

At Brookwood, I say, we were trainees together.

That was thirty years ago, he says.

Yes, I say, thinking he's still the same – just because it was thirty years ago doesn't mean it didn't happen.

He stares at me a little more intently, a flicker of recognition appearing in his eyes.

Ah, I think I remember, he concedes, yes, maybe.

Privately, I mock his powers of recall and observation. I'm in the midst of a mental breakdown, but still, I recognise him. Yet he's the consultant and I'm the patient, and my sense of superiority soon melts away as I pull the duvet up over my head.

Kate has come downstairs, the tone of my voice during this exchange having alerted her that she's needed. Please go and get Dad, I beg.

Peter comes and sits beside me. I'm hiding under the duvet; I have to lift it up to talk. It's him, I whisper.

Who? he asks.

You know, *him*, I repeat, trying not to use the nickname I once used, which would identify him immediately. Him, I repeat unhelpfully, the doctor from Brookwood, Dr Dolittle. Finally, Peter understands. I can't talk to him, I say.

Somehow, we cobble together a consultation, me under the covers, Peter a sort of translator, and I'm prescribed medication to help calm my suicidal thoughts, olanzapine 5mg. I used to prescribe it to patients with schizophrenia, but in much higher doses. I don't object. I'm not delusional. My protestations that killing myself would be the best outcome for everybody are not fixed and unshakeable, but I'm not well.

Once Dr Dolittle has left, I turn to Peter and plead, just as Alice did about Dr W: never make me see that man again. The home-care team rally round, find a way to manage me without another encounter. Being seen by this man I don't respect, who's reached the pinnacle of a career to which I once aspired, whilst I've fallen by the wayside, only serves to add to my relentless feelings of guilt, shame and worthlessness.

As with Alice, all medicines, prescribed and over-the-counter, knives, too, are locked away, in the same lock box we used for her. I refuse to have it anywhere I can see it. I hold out my hand and Peter places the olanzapine into my palm, as if I'm a sinner accepting sacramental bread. It has a profound effect on my body. Quite quickly I feel the 'chemical straitjacket' effect. I am pinned to the bed, as if gravity has trebled. Don't make me take that again, I slur to the nurse who comes to visit the following day. A reduced dose is agreed. The next day is similar. This will wear off, says a third nurse the day after that. And they're right. Gradually, I begin to emerge from under my duvet. I empty the dishwasher, Peter runs me a bath, I take a turn around the garden, like a convalescent from a period drama. I'm encouraged to leave the house, only manage a ten-minute walk with Peter to the post box and back, my arm hooked through his. He's become my carer. Thankfully, he doesn't have to cook; I am grateful for the rota that still feeds us. But today's meal isn't a meal, it's ingredients. A thinly veiled message that we ought to be doing better than this, I feel.

That first week, I am visited on a daily basis in my own home. The contrast with the treatment Alice received during her times of crisis is not lost on me.

June–August 2019

Fighting to be heard, a family holiday, a new name and some history

We took Alice to more CAMHS appointments. The nurses changed. We retold her story. Each time I spoke to or saw anyone, I asked for Alice to be seen by a doctor. Five times I asked and five times was denied. Throughout this long summer, we battled with a gamut of gatekeepers. And Alice was a witness to our frustrations, was aware of how little she seemed to matter to the array of staff she encountered. A consultant psychiatrist in the hospital had offered her an admission, but now she was apparently not much of a worry at all and yet so little had changed.

But in the midst of all this she could still do some quite normal things.

I'd bought my brother Billy Joel tickets for his birthday but now had no appetite to go with him. Instead, just three weeks after her overdose, Alice went with Keith. She was so animated when she returned, not because of the music, but due to her and Keith's mutual horror that the mother and baby Billy Joel brought on stage were not his daughter and granddaughter, but his wife and child.

A week later, Alice came with us to Kate's graduation. She wore her favourite floral shirt and beamed for the camera. The next week, she went to her first and only Pride march in London, and the next she managed our family holiday to Spain, to a villa in the Cordoban countryside. For the previous half dozen years or so we had abandoned our Cornish beach holidays for guaranteed Spanish sun. The luxury of a private pool to keep cool in and each other's company were what we loved. On this, our last family holiday, Alice wouldn't leave the villa, so we spent most of our time reading, eating, playing cards. This was the last time I saw Alice topless, in trunks by the pool, the last time she swam. Once we returned home, she covered herself up at every opportunity. If she was in bed when I went into her room for anything, she pulled the sheets up tight to her chin.

Zev became a regular visitor to the house. He arrived the first afternoon laden with shopping bags. Later that evening, they came downstairs. Alice was in full make-up, wearing a floral knee-length dress, a kind of cross between turn-of-the-century Monsoon and 1980s Laura Ashley. It was the first time I'd seen her in women's clothes. Zev had brought the outfit over, but he was still dressed as a boy.

Wow, look at you! I said.

Alice was giggly. Perhaps they'd been drinking. I'm hungry, she announced and set about finding ingredients for a meal.

I ran off to tell Peter, our child's in the kitchen in a frock. And not even a nice one.

Peter saw my distress and veered me away from any intervention. He protected Alice.

Each time Zev came over, he brought a new bag of tricks with him. And each time, I was taken aback that he didn't dress up, too. He was like the child that persuaded you to play knock down ginger or steal apples from your neighbour's garden, but was careful not to do it themselves, I thought. No consequences for them when you were caught. Who was this young man who'd entered Alice's life so quickly and become so influential, even manipulative? This was the word that echoed in my head. I perceived the whole situation as incredibly threatening and alien. I had no idea how to handle what was happening to Alice. I continued to hope that an answer lay within the health service.

We took her back to another CAMHS appointment. She was asked, as she had been before, how her sexuality and gender were impacting on her mental health. Alice repeated that she was bisexual, was comfortable with this, had been involved with a male friend at school, but also liked girls. They wrote something in the notes.

During this period, Alice asked to change her name.

Would that help? we asked.

Yes, she said.

So we agreed. She could change her name without parental consent anyway. And arguing with her would feel abusive, putting our desires over hers. Not that it wasn't hard for us, to let her old name go. But Alice was thoughtful in the matter of choosing a new one. She included us in the decision-making process.

I loved your old name so much, I said.

Well, you better learn to love the new one, she quipped.

It was not easy to use a new name when the old one had been used for seventeen years. Peter and I slipped up constantly, but we kept at it. Yet in the clinic that was charged with taking care of her, where there was no lengthy history of using another name, no brain rewiring to be undertaken, the nurses constantly deadnamed and misgendered her.

We were repeatedly asked about what we knew of Alice's inner world. The answer was very little. But we were asked, so we answered. When did we first become aware that Alice was transgender? How did it present itself? What were the signs? We repeated the same answers we'd searched for ourselves over the previous weeks and months. We had no idea Alice was trans, we said, until the letter, and even then, we were not sure. Then there was the overdose, of course. The nurse nodded as if she understood.

We were being asked for proof. How simple it would have been if we could have just had an X-ray (look, there's the break) or a blood test (here's the deficiency or the excess) or a classic set of symptoms pathognomonic of what it is to be trans. But there is no test. And all these hint at disease or defect, something bad to be got rid of. Perhaps there is nothing much wrong with her at all, I wanted to shout, this could just be her normal.

How are your counselling sessions going? asked the nurse.

Good, said Alice.

Alice certainly seemed happiest when her gender identity was embraced and other people showed her respect, as her Heads Together counsellor, Anne, did. Inside, a bit of me loathed Anne. It's easy for her, I thought, when Alice sang her praises; she's not actually looking after you.

Peter and I never spoke to Anne, only saw her, when we were dropping off and picking up each week. She had the appearance of a kindly young granny. When Alice came out of the sessions, she looked like she'd just been enjoying hot tea and a selection of chocolate biscuits.

I was so contrary. I was cross with both Anne, who was helping, and CAMHS who were not. I wasn't getting what I wanted. Can Alice see a doctor? I asked again.

No.

In the end, I took Alice back to Dr A, her GP, where, dressed in a tartan dungaree dress and full make-up, she was called in over the tannoy by her deadname. I was furious, wanted to weep, but Alice just said, It's ok. It was Dr A who started Alice on antidepressants at this appointment, whilst she was 'under the care' of CAMHS. On our way out, I complained to the reception staff about the deadnaming; it didn't stop it happening again.

When our sixth CAMHS appointment came around Alice refused to go. Peter and I went without her. We encountered yet another new nurse.

Where's Alice?

We couldn't get her to come.

Why have you come?

Because she's not well, she's suicidal, she needs to be seen by a psychiatrist.

She's not suicidal, he said, reading the notes.

We think she is, I replied.

How do you know? he asked.

We're using the traffic-light-system, I said. It's often red.

Has she told you she's suicidal?

No, I said. She's very guarded.

So, this is an assumption, he says.

The card's often red, I repeated.

He wrote it down, that I was only assuming, as if he knew more than me about my child's mental health. Peter and I both repeated our request for her to be seen by a doctor, our voices rising. We cannot get through to him, get past this condescending nurse. Well, it would be nice if she were here, for me to assess, he said.

I'm sorry, I said, I couldn't get her out of bed. She's unwell. Why was I apologising when I wasn't surprised she wouldn't come? She'd had all these appointments, repeated her story to various strangers, yet nothing had happened. Why should she think today would be any different? She needs to see a doctor, I repeated. Why hasn't she seen one yet?

She's been assessed as not needing one, he said.

That's not what Dr P at St George's recommended, I persisted. The consultant who referred her.

That doctor didn't know what they could offer, he said. It was not their job to say what we will or won't do. She's made bad lifestyle choices, he continued, speaking confidently, disparagingly about my child, this man who had never met her. In his mind, there was no doubt that he was right, he was not assuming. His arrogance disgusted me. Yes, he tutted, bad lifestyle choices.

What do you mean by that? asked Peter, jaw clenched.

She drinks, takes drugs. He read this from the notes.

This behaviour isn't typical of her, we said. We know our child, she's dabbled, that's not unusual.

The mother is defensive, he added to Alice's notes. I know this because we see the records, after Alice has died.

We want her to see a doctor, repeated Peter.

No, no, no, he said, shaking his head with his I'm-the-professional-here air.

The GP has had to start her on medication, I pointed out. She needs to see a psychiatrist, my voice rising and shaking.

The mother is a very difficult parent, he added to my litany of faults in the notes. (Later, I ask our solicitor if he wrote that about Peter, too, since he was there and asking the same questions. No, she says.)

The nurse told us Alice was eligible for long-term psychotherapy through CAMHS, but the wait was over a year, by which time she'd be eighteen, so there was no point referring her.

Could she be referred for adult psychotherapy in anticipation? I asked.

No. Our psychotherapist takes private work, if you would like his details.

Yes, we would, we said, whilst muttering something about what would we be supposed to do if we couldn't afford it?

He wrote that I was cross, demanding it for free. Recording my observations of the failures of a system that is supposed to care for everyone as another unpleasant character trait of this difficult mother.

In the end, though I don't remember it, I said we would take legal action. Or I presume I did, for the nurse wrote that in the notes, too – that I had threatened him with a lawyer – and this alone appears to be what finally made him refer Alice to see a doctor.

Two whole months after her significant life-threatening overdose due to mental-health struggles as part of her gender incongruence, Alice was at last seen by the consultant child and adolescent psychiatrist. The doctor was lovely. At that first appointment, she referred

Alice to GIDS, who quickly referred her on to our local adult Gender Identity Clinic (GIC) because Alice would soon turn eighteen.

How long will she have to wait? I asked.

Dr S did not know. A couple of years or so, she guessed.

It was disappointing. It had taken almost ten months of gatekeeping, first by the GP and then by mental health services, to get to this point. It was a significant delay. But Alice didn't seem to mind, the referral alone lifting her spirits, for now.

After that initial appointment, Alice was seen once every six weeks by the consultant psychiatrist at CAMHS. Peter and I felt vindicated, but it didn't feel like much of a win.

9 July 2022

A march and a different type of overdose

London Trans Pride is scheduled to take place just a week after my visit to Safe Haven. Kate wants to go, wants us all to go. I feel too unwell. It will be too noisy, too crowded, too far from home, with too many tall buildings, too many trans people – walking, dancing, chanting trans people – parading their very aliveness. Kate is quietly persistent. It won't be the big corporate carnival of Gay Pride, she explains. Whilst it will be a celebration of trans joy and existence, there will be a strong emphasis on political protest. We should make placards; we should march for Alice.

Everyone else is keen. But I'm barely leaving the house, still having daily home visits from the psychiatric acute home-care team. How will I manage? And on top of this, I'm still considered a suicide risk. If I don't go, someone must stay behind with me, and no one wants that task. I discuss my attendance, my non-attendance with each successive nurse that visits, a different one each time, no rapport building. The days pass by, with me no closer to a decision.

On the eve of the march, Zev texts. Some of us are going to Trans Pride, are you? It would be good to meet up.

I text back: I'm not well enough, but the others are going. I pass on contact details. The decision's made.

At 9.30 a.m. on the morning of the march yet another nurse, Daisy, messages to arrange my daily appointment. We agree she'll visit at midday. Kate and Peter are busy making placards to hold high overhead.

I text Daisy back in a flap. I've got massive FOMO. It was my choice not to go, I text, but now I feel like a child who's been told they can't attend the party because they've been bad. I'm telling everyone I'll be fine if I take diazepam, but Peter's not sure. He wants to be assertive and say, you aren't well enough, you need to stay home. Or the opposite: yes, take diazepam, come with us, you'll be fine. But he doesn't know which.

And he has good reason not to. Less than a fortnight ago I was asking him to fetch me razor blades, to slit my wrists, to send me to Alice. Harvey's volunteered to stay with me, but I sense some reluctance. Whenever I bring it up, he speaks abruptly, occupies himself with Candy Crush on his phone. What? he asks, when I insist he puts it down and talks. Kate becomes worried – if I change my mind and come, then Harvey will bring his grumpiness with him. Everyone's in a bother and the train to Waterloo leaves in less than two hours.

I decide to walk the dog with Peter. I'll gauge my anxiety levels by getting in the car for a few minutes and walking around a small field, I jest. I smile sheepishly. I feel the question of my capability's been answered. How can I possibly manage a ninety-minute three-vehicle journey and a two-hour march in a crowded city if I can barely manage this? The walk leaves me feeling sick, but is it the walk, or is it the FOMO still nagging quietly but insistently in my ear?

I check my phone, Daisy's replied. Contrary to my expectations, she's not tried to put me off going. She's been positive and encouraging. Break the day into manageable chunks, she says.

I will, I proclaim, I'm a grown up. First, I'll aim to get to the station; if I manage that, I'll get on the train. If I need to get off, Harvey will come home with me. So, the day is broken down – at any point, I can step away and escape. Permission from a mental-health professional is enough to reassure Peter. I'm going to go. I even find time to make a small placard. Marching for my daughter. The relief is physical. We're on our way.

Peter gives me my first diazepam just before we leave the house. I'll keep an eye on the time and top you up when it's due if you don't ask first. Ok?

Ok, I say.

The march starts from Wellington Arch, a monument to the victories of war. An apt starting place, I think, the transgender issue so often framed in the language of war, this side against that, lines drawn in the sand, though victories are few and regained ground can quickly be lost again to opposing factions. Alice in no man's land, Alice as cannon fodder crosses my mind. Before the off, Peter gives me another tablet, easier now than once we're on the move, he says.

I bump into someone I used to know when Alice was little. She's here with her daughter who's several years older than Alice. Her transition is complete, because it began when she was seventeen, in 2015, three years before Alice first came out to her GP, when NHS gender services still functioned and the wait to be seen was less than a year. She is thriving. It is both heartwarming and a massive slap in the face to know this.

We meet Zev and other friends from school, Keith, Bea, Iona and others. It's good to see them. This is only my second march ever, I say. I tell them that the previous year I attended Reclaim Pride, whilst Alice was still alive, raging and indignant at the delays in her treatment. We know, they say; Alice was so proud of you.

We don't seem to have gone far when Peter taps me on the shoulder and offers me another tablet, with a bottle of water, warm from the sun. It's a blazing hot day, and we all appreciate the shade cast across the street as we turn a corner, one step closer to Soho Square.

The universe sends me another unexpected familiar face. A journalist who covered Reclaim Pride is politely asking to take our picture, with our signs. They don't recognise me at first. They're about to leave when I touch them on the shoulder. Hi, I say, it's me, we met at the march last year. You took my photo. I'm speaking like I've just

bumped into an old college friend and am suggesting a drink. They
have a puzzled look on their face. Perhaps they are trying to reconcile
the recollection of the weeping mother at the last march, child still
alive, with the dry-eyed one in front of them now, brandishing a sign
for all to see, her child dead.

What happened? they ask.

She killed herself, I say.

They gasp, lift their hand to cover their mouth. Can we hug? They
open their arms expansively.

Of course.

And when they turn to go, I think they're crying, by the shape of
their shoulders and the wiping of their face with the back of their
hand. But I have not shed a tear. I don't feel anything at all.

I start to self-examine my state of mind. There's lots of joy, brightly
dressed people waving sunflowers. But I don't feel joy. My daughter
has died. My family appear sombre: Peter and Harvey often embrace
each other and cry as they walk; Kate wears her determined look.
I should feel sad or even angry, I think, but I don't.

Time for another pill, says Peter.

No, I don't think so, I say. I had one quite recently.

Yes, but two hours is up, he replies.

I have my answer. At home, I haven't even been taking diazepam
every day, and it's a four-hourly regime at most. On top of that I
usually cut them in half. But today I've been taking them whole.
Peter's been accidentally overdosing me. And maybe his mistake is no
bad thing, as it's allowed me to drift through this day, a twig carried
along by the stream, and at the end I am still afloat.

At Soho Square we gather, seated on the grass, to hear speeches.
It's a squash (an estimated 20,000 people have attended, compared to
1,500 three years before). As one speaker mentions trans lives lost, my
family stands, as one, holding our placards aloft. Someone captures
that moment in a photo, Peter and Harvey, my tall, handsome,

athletic boys, Harvey resting his head on his father's shoulder, Peter comforting him, an arm pulling him in tight. You can almost see his jaw trembling in the shot, whilst Kate and I stare straight ahead, impassive, holding our placards high. Read this, read this. This photo appears on London Trans+ Pride's Facebook page and Instagram, is tweeted and retweeted. Kate is commissioned to write a piece for *PinkNews*. But of all the mainstream media outlets, only one covers the march. Twenty thousand people protesting, met with virtual silence, whilst a single tweet from JK Rowling can circulate for months and reach millions.

The next day, a psychiatric nurse visits again. The regular visits and phone calls continue for three weeks. Where was this for Alice?

September 2019

Staring in Tesco, grandmothers to tell, a trans friend, persistent doubts

The school summer holidays were drawing to a close. Zev's regular visits had boosted Alice's confidence and gradually I'd become more used to how she looked. She wore dresses and blouses, applied too much blusher, foundation ending abruptly at her jawline. She was no different in this respect from many teenage girls, starting out with make-up pinched from their mothers or from Boots. But her skills improved, with practice and help.

I began to trust Zev; he had Alice's interests at heart. When he was here, helping her be Alice, she was her best self – playful, excitable, full of beans. Kate helped Alice to bleach her hair and her confidence shone as brightly as her new blonde pixie cut.

Early in September, there was much excitement when some of Alice's friends arranged a trip to Primark to kit her out with some suitable clothes for school. The girls all shared the same changing room. She came home laden with outfits. She'd developed a penchant for short dungaree dresses (she had great legs). I think that might be a little too short for school, I said. I laughed because I'd never had to say that to Kate.

It'll be all right, she replied, laughing too.

When Alice and I went out socially, beyond the confines of our home, with her dressed as a woman for the first time, I felt a certain dread. I didn't know what I would do if someone stared or name-called her, as she wouldn't want me to draw any attention. But I felt so protective of her, and couldn't promise I wouldn't. We walked

Pippin over the downs and headed for an ice cream. A woman pushing a buggy, rubbernecked us as we passed and I couldn't help myself. I said something – nothing punchy or smart: staring's rude, most probably.

The woman brought a hand protectively to her chest. Me?

Yes, you, staring, it's rude.

She turned to her companion; they both looked at me as if I was mad or maybe dangerous and hurried away.

What was that about? asked Alice. Why are you being so weird?

She was staring, I said.

Alice shrugged.

She was, I repeated.

Can I have a Cornetto? asked Alice.

Over the ensuing years, Alice always behaved as if she was completely unaware when people stared at her, whereas I was not. If I ignored it, I felt bad, if I interjected, I felt bad, if I talked to Alice about it, I felt bad, if I didn't, I felt bad. Finally, I settled on a tactic of simply staring back until eye contact was broken by the starer, who invariably looked vaguely embarrassed. If Alice noticed, she didn't comment. We both operated quite easily within our system of acknowledgement and denial.

Now that Alice was dressing as a woman, I developed a habit, when out and about, of scrutinising women in the street for any hint of transness. It was particularly bad at the supermarket, where people moved more slowly, stopping regularly to check sell-by dates, cross things off their list – and whilst they did so, I observed them. There were tall women and broad women, stocky women and snake-hipped women, women with thinning hair and facial hair, all sorts of women. I saw potential trans women everywhere. My habit became more troublesome when I developed a very strong urge to ask. It got me out of the supermarket run for a while.

Why did I do this? Because I had grown up in a household where appearances mattered? Where we could not have a milk bottle on the table in case a neighbour happened to walk past and see. Milk in a jug was a sign that we were still officer class, despite the relative poverty we had been thrown into. A household where people were judged by virtue of being well-kempt, natty dressers or badly coordinated scruffs, before they ever said a word.

I wanted Alice to pass. She was not a flamboyant person, someone who walked down the street head held high, look at me, look at me. She was reserved, shy. I didn't want her to be judged and suffer any more than she had already. And perhaps, like my mother before me, I didn't want other people to see our truth. Alice's gender dysphoria was marked, she longed to pass. Each day she remained untreated made this need more difficult to realise. I worried about it endlessly.

———

Now I couldn't care less how someone looks. I live for the day when trans people are accepted just the way they are, when they don't need to pass at all.

———

With Alice's name changed and a tendency to wear make-up and women's clothes most days, we needed to tell her grandmothers. They were both in their nineties when they learned they now had another granddaughter, rather than the grandson they thought they had. Peter went to tell his mum; I went to tell mine. I wasn't sure what to expect. I was bristling for a fight which never came. Poor Alice, she said, without a moment's hesitation. Imagine how difficult it must be for her, she said, switching name and pronouns immediately. Poor child. No wonder she's been so unhappy. The fight drained out of me and I began to cry. What's the matter, darling? asked my mum.

I'm so worried about her, I sobbed. I don't know how to help her. I'm scared.

Mum reached up to me, on her tiptoes and I folded down towards her. She wrapped her arms around me and said what she always says to soothe me: there, there. It will be all right. I sobbed and sobbed. Hush, Cazzie, hush, she said.

What will happen to her? I wailed.

There have always been people like her, said Mum, since God was a boy. You'll work it out between you.

———

And my mother was right about one thing. For although many people would have you believe that being trans is an entirely new phenomenon, it has been around for millennia. And it was definitely around in the 1980s, for I knew a trans woman when I was a teenager. There were rumours about her, amongst my friends at the local pub. Someone who used to work at a local menswear store had been off work for a few months, now they were back, but with a new name, dressed in women's clothes and wearing make-up. Jokes would have been made about her, I'm sure, behind her back.

I ask Peter, who I hung out with, but didn't date at the time. He agrees, there were definitely occasions he heard a warning: you don't want to get off with her. But they did call her, 'her'. No one said she was still a man. In everyone's minds, back in the mid- to late 1980s, during a time of rampant homophobia, Jess had her sex change and was now a woman. She lived, worked and played amongst us and no one questioned it, certainly none of the girls. We never discussed what Jess hid under her skirt, or in her trousers, what surgery she had or had not undertaken, what would happen to us if we ended up in the women's loos together. It didn't occur to us to care. Jess wasn't around for long; maybe there was more hostility than I realised, out of sight, or maybe she just wanted to start afresh, somewhere her history was unknown. So, when I popped into the chemist to collect a prescription for one of the children, a good ten years after I last saw her, it was such a surprise to see her behind the counter. She recognised me straight away. Hello, Caroline. How nice to see you, she said.

I was delighted she remembered me. We chatted, not in-depth, only as much as we could with a queue forming behind me. And this is all we did for the next few years – chat at the counter when I popped in for plasters and Calpol, emergency tampons. Then, one day, she was gone and I felt an unexpected sadness. She'd disappeared again and I didn't know why. We were never friends, not in the sense that most people might describe friendship – we didn't walk our dogs together or go out for beers or pizza; I didn't know her phone number or where she lived – but now she was gone, I missed seeing her.

———

Yet even with positive personal experience of knowing a trans person, I was still afraid of my own daughter's transition. I wanted it all to be some dreadful mistake. I didn't understand it and I didn't want it. Did I even believe in it? Yes, but for other people's children, not mine. Let them mutilate themselves and live half-lives in the shadows. And I didn't want another daughter; I was happy with the child I had.

I told Alice: I love you, I'm here for you, you can speak to me about anything. But despite all my protestations of love and support, in hushed tones (not hushed enough), in another room (a door left ajar), late at night (Alice practically nocturnal), I argued with Peter.

I talked about body dysmorphic disorder (BDD), as it was called back in my psychiatry days, when people presented to surgeons, asking to have a limb cut off. The horror stories I'd been told, of surgeons acting barbarically and operating on their patients with disastrous results. Obviously, doctors don't perform this surgery now, I said, they refer to psychiatry. It's not normal to want a limb amputated, so why is it ok to operate on genitals or breasts? I asked.

And I remembered my training; BDD was a sexual perversion. At least that's what I was taught back in the mid-1980s. I was panicked, I wouldn't hide from the possibility that my child might have a sexual fetish. My uncle was a paedophile, and I'd treated sexual predators at work. They were all someone's child, why should I be exempt? It was a nightmare. And in the middle of it all was Alice, my angel, the least monstrous person I'd ever known. None of it makes any sense, I cried to Peter.

In 2005, a researcher conducted a telephone interview with fifty-four subjects who had body integrity identity disorder (BIID) as it became called: the uncontrollable desire to amputate one or more healthy limbs or to be paraplegic.* Results were not what I expected. Medication and psychotherapy were ineffective, yet the six subjects who had received elective amputation expressed satisfaction – with their body image now matched to their internal representation of themselves they felt completely well. It is bordering on impossible to find surgeons who will do elective surgery of this nature, the first rule of medicine being 'do no harm'. But what looks like harm to some is of value and benefit to others. Who are we to deny a treatment that benefits someone, simply because it makes us feel uncomfortable and we wouldn't choose it ourselves? This is paternalistic morality medicine at its most fundamental.

* First MB (2005) Desire for amputation of a limb: paraphilia, psychosis, or a new type of identity disorder. *Psychological Medicine*, 35: 919–28.

Regrettably, I didn't know of this research at the start of Alice's gender journey. I was stuck with the stories I'd been told as a junior psychiatrist. It was nigh on delusional to think one could change from a man to a woman, I said. You've told me before that psychiatrists used to treat homosexuality as a disorder, Peter countered.

I know that, but this is different, I said, without being able to say why.

But my mother, in her nineties, not known for progressive views on anything, excelled herself. A few days after we told her about Alice, a letter arrived. It was a card from my mum for Alice, and in it a cheque for twenty pounds, with the message: For my beautiful grand-daughter Alice, a little something to go towards your new wardrobe.

What does that mean? asked Alice.

It's to buy new clothes, I explained.

Weird, she replied, but she was smiling. And I smiled with her. It was a heartwarming gesture and it meant the world to both of us.

We had a coming-out Mad Hatter's tea party, just the five of us, no other guests, to officially welcome Alice into the family. Alice, dressed in her new Primark outfit, was in a sunny mood, buoyant and optimistic.

She was so engaged in life in those weeks, preparing to go back to school fully, as Alice, for the first time. She would be studying physics, maths, drama and psychology. She was excited, not apprehensive. She arranged to go in with her friend Iona on her first day, for moral support. For a child who'd had so much anxiety for so long, it was quite something to observe her transformation. I dropped her off at Iona's, so they could go in together. The teachers knew Alice was coming back as Alice (we'd popped in to see the head of sixth form the day before and he had been fully supportive). But apart from an inner circle of six close friends, Alice hadn't told anyone else. She was in a group of around eight lads with whom she played Dungeons and Dragons on Saturday evenings. None of them knew. I didn't know that they didn't know. I'd have been beside myself with worry if I had. And just like that, she started her first day in year 13 as Alice, in a skirt and sweatshirt, hair bleached blonde, eyeliner copiously applied, as if it were the most natural thing in the world.

I went to pick her up at the end of the day in the usual spot. There was a big public car park near her school and children poured across the recreation ground to meet their parents there. I arrived early for a change and took Pippin, as my excuse to mill around on the playing fields, so I could come to Alice's aid if there was any trouble. When I saw her, she smiled and gave me a low wave, hand at her hip, just like she always used to. She looked fine, all the other kids were just walking along, not paying her any attention at all. A little hope crept in.

Mid-July 2022

An accident, a change of medication

A few days after Trans Pride, Peter falls off his mountain bike. He needs an X-ray, a lift to accident and emergency at the very least. I haven't driven for ten days, and apart from the anomaly of Trans Pride have barely been out. C'mon, I'll take you, I say. I'll have to drop you off. I won't be able to stay – in that place, I add, my voice wavering.

I understand, he replies.

Peter comes back by taxi, his arm in a back slab and a sling. He has fractured a bone in his hand. He looks so crestfallen. What will he do without the gym and cycling to ease his mental pain? Peter's pursuit of exercise is a distraction, no doubt a coping mechanism, but to me it doesn't seem entirely normal. Whilst everyone might think he's coping better than I am, to me, he is merely avoiding his feelings. And although it is a way of coping, it is not a way of engaging with what has happened to Alice, to us. But people prefer it on the whole, Peter's way. My raw emotions frighten more people than understand them, including Peter. He needs his escape from me. Since Alice died, Peter's days have had structure and routine: dog walking, CrossFit and visits to his mum, who is really quite poorly, regular as clockwork. I, on the other hand, am erratic and unreliable. I feel, with Peter's accident, things will have to change, but the next day, he brings weights in from the garage and does bicep curls with his good arm, tries out the home exercise bike that's been forgotten under a pile of coats for months, business as usual. I roll my eyes at Kate. She takes me to one side. Daddy isn't coping, really, she says. It might look like he is, but he's always on his phone reading articles about

153

couples splitting up after the death of a child. It's a kind of digital self-harm, she says.

Dad and I will be ok, I say, we're not statistics. But I'm not sure she believes me. We are putting on a reasonable act, but the foundations on which our relationship is built – intimacy, loyalty and trust – are shaking. We'll be ok, I say to Peter, but he too doesn't seem sure, and has every right to doubt me, because I don't really believe it myself.

Now I am back behind the wheel of a car, it's agreed I will stop taking my olanzapine, which I'm still finding very sedative. Plus, I've recently been started on an antidepressant, which, if it works, should soon help dampen my suicidal thoughts and alleviate the need for the chemical-cosh approach. I've been reluctant to take one, arguing that I am grieving and not depressed, that my thoughts and feelings are reasonably understood in the context of what I'm experiencing, that I should ride the wave. I am also concerned about side effects. When I took SSRIs in my thirties, they'd had an effect on my libido and my ability to feel sexual pleasure. Peter and I have only tried to have sex once since Alice died, in the very first week. We wanted intimacy but I found it impossible to participate in something normally associated with such pleasure, whilst my child lay on a slab in the mortuary. I cried and cried.

I explain all this to the prescribing nurse. I understand, he says, but you're not well. You really should give it a go, and you won't get this particular one from your GP, he says, to tempt me. I am persuaded, like someone buying something they don't need because they have a discount coupon and it's about to expire.

September 2019

Struggling to understand, a slow road to acceptance

I was not so easily persuaded about Alice. Even though her social transition had started, my support was half-hearted. I flip-flopped from acceptance to doubt, from one opinion to another. I didn't know where to turn. I didn't approach trans-friendly organisations such as Mermaids, who'd been receiving bad press at the time, and whom I mistrusted. Just like when it came to finding bereavement support groups, I made excuses for not contacting all sorts of organisations: they were too far away, met on the wrong day, provided for the wrong age group, because I didn't want to be part of all this. But I was. Alice was my daughter, so I had to find a way to help her, whatever that might be.

I bought a couple of books at random from Amazon. One, though I didn't see it at the time, was vehemently anti-trans. I was pulled in by its catchy title, referencing a frothy 1980s romcom, with a pleasant pink and blue cover, hinting at the colours of the transgender flag. I lapped it up. The author was not a stupid man; on the contrary, he was smart, with his clever promotional title and cover. The book was easy to read, full of persuasive and plausible evidence to preach his personal view, which led me away from my child not towards her. Later, I realised it was written by a politically right-wing US author and devout Christian. His other book: *What is Marriage? Man and Woman: A Defense*. So many red flags, but back then I missed them all. The book was as balanced as a guide to vegetarianism published by the meat marketing board. Yet I was not reading like a scientist. I was reading as a mother under attack from something I didn't understand, desperate to defend myself. My intense anger at the patriarchy made me wonder why anyone would want to be a woman. But Alice, my daughter, did. She was, she said. She was a woman.

Jane didn't think so. She came for supper one evening when Peter was out. We'd kept up our relationship this past year, but the gulf between us had grown. Whilst I was doing very little research, Jane was fully immersed in gender critical theory by now. She believed sex and gender were down to chromosomes and chromosomes alone, and that whilst there were intersex conditions and chromosomal abnormalities, these were so rare as to be easily dismissed, and that most trans women were, quite simply, men playing at dressing up.

I told her about the Primark trip, Alice's delight at her new clothes.

Did she try them on in the shop? she asked.

Yes, I said.

What about the fourteen-year-old girls in the changing room? she asked. What about the twelve-year-olds?

What about Alice? I countered. I just want to keep her alive.

I felt so deflated. Whilst it was possible to feel hopeful for Alice when we were able to protect her at home and, to some extent, at school, where she was in the company of close friends, Jane served to remind me that there were plenty of people who believed my child was a perversion and a threat. Even her godmother.

Whilst Jane had been able to write Alice a lovely letter after her suicide attempt, where she talked about her own mental-health demons, her Priory admission and how she had, at times, thought she would never get better, she couldn't maintain her support, keep her godmother's promise – because to Jane, Alice, like any other trans woman, was seen as a potential threat. Her research had entrenched her earlier views and she could not be swayed. When we parted, I had a sickening feeling that I was losing her.

In less than a fortnight, Peter persuaded me to chuck the anti-trans book in the bin, but this was not the sign that all was well with me.

I was no longer worried about contagion and coercion, but I still lived in fear of regret rates. Something I had no evidence for but which were increasingly part of the conversation around trans people. And, like Jane, I held that if I read it in the papers, it must be true.

My other reasons for doubt lay closer to home. Alice's puberty was late and slow, but it was marching on. Yet she appeared so passive. She was not pushing for us to get her started on puberty blockers or cross-sex hormones, did not seem nearly as concerned about the waitlist as I was.

You can't really want it if you don't fight for it, I reasoned.

I do want it, she replied.

Then talk to me, I beseeched.

Leave me alone, she said.

If she wouldn't engage, wasn't demanding and pushy, it couldn't be real, I said. And despite the fact that she'd never been a pushy child, this was all the evidence I needed.

Later, after her suicide, my deep depression that came from not being able to have the one thing I need most in all the world – to have my child back – would help me to understand her apathy.

One evening, when Peter was out, I asked Alice down to help me make dinner and have a chat. I was trying to talk to her once more about hormones and treatment options, trying to help her do something that, quite frankly, I wished she didn't want to do. She was being monosyllabic, didn't appear to be listening. The home phone rang and I answered, because it was usually my mum, and there was always that niggle that she might be in need. Can I call you back? I said. But it was too late. Alice was retreating up the stairs, eating an apple. Why the fuck would you want to be a woman anyway? I yelled after her. She didn't react, just disappeared into her room.

That night, I turned to Peter. I think I need some help with this, I said.

16 July 2022

A primitive ritual of immense importance

Now I need support with almost everything, though I am doing a little more, because I have to, until Peter's hand is mended. Occasionally, I take advantage of people's repeated offers to help – anything at all, they say. Can you unblock our loo? I ask Trevor on one of his many visits to walk and talk with Peter. Anything but that, he laughs. I pounce on one set of neighbours, say yes, you can tidy up the garden for us if you like. The weather is so lovely but the garden is such an eyesore, it is making my grief even worse somehow; there is an indecency in its burgeoning growth. They spend an entire morning getting to grips with the overgrown weed patch we call a garden. They work a miracle and I am so grateful for the welcome sanctuary it becomes, to which I can retreat when my battery is entirely flat.

An existence emerges that lasts for months, beyond the first year. I sleep on and off at any time of the day or night, whenever I can. I take to describing myself as a slug, sliding from one surface to the next, leaving a slime trail of squalor behind me, for I stop showering and fail to change my clothes. And it is so hot, the days melt into one another. One week becomes two, two become three. Some sweltering days, I pad about in just my knickers and a loose t-shirt, regardless of visitors. Other times, even though the sun is high in the sky, I feel a chill and don Alice's coat, whilst everyone else retreats inside to find some shade. I imagine buying a bivvy bag. I feel safer in the garden. I will stay outside through the winter; I will live my life this way from now on. It feels right.

One day, in the midst of all this heat, Kate comes to me in a panic. She has noticed a white mould on Alice's combats. The clothes that were collected from the undertakers, that have been put to one side and neglected.

We need to do something, she says. There's an urgency in Kate, a sense that we've messed this up, that Alice's clothes are ruined, everything is ruined. She's so distressed. Tomorrow's going to be another hot, sunny day, could we wash them in the garden?

Yes, we'll do that. We'll use buckets and we'll pour the dirty water on the parched plants, they'll be grateful.

On the day, Peter wants nothing to do with it. He takes Pippin for a walk. Harvey wants to be present but doesn't want to be involved, he will watch. Kate and I lay out a blanket on the grass. It's bright orange, the only one we have. We fill two large plastic tubs, one turquoise, one lime, with water. They are not muted and sombre; again, they are what we have. We open the first bag and a pungent sour ammonia smell emanates from it. We have to turn our heads to take a breath, but as we open the bag further and expose the contents to more air the smell dissipates a little, or we grow accustomed to it. We start with her socks; they are small and simple and fairly clean; we have one each to wash. The water runs immediately clear. Next, I lift her lace-trimmed cream t-shirt out of the bag, a favourite top. It's been cut to remove it from Alice's body. Kate and I take it in turns to swirl it in the water and rub at the cloth. We talk to each other as we work, we're in tune: it's disappointing, we agree, that the water has merely turned a dirty dishwater beige and we become half-hearted in our efforts. It's not as we'd expected. We move the shirt from the dirty bucket to the clean one and begin to rinse. The old water is poured at the base of the giant fig tree in the centre of the lawn.

Harvey is hovering by the patio door. I find a role for him: can you take the empty bucket and refill it with fresh water? I ask. I want the water to run clear before proceeding to the next garment, her navy hoodie. There's a lot of blood on the hood. She must have had it pulled up at the time and it's sandwiched closed, like pitta bread. We carefully peel the edges apart and when we wash it the water changes to a murky rusty red–brown. It's opaque, not the clear claret red I'd imagined, but like paintbrush water in a jar at primary school. I pummel and pummel, scrub and twist, I punch down into the water, to punish it somehow, and I'm splashed with it. It feels primitive, and I'm removed from the twenty-first century and connected through action to others who have enacted similar rituals for generations, whether out of custom or necessity or out of instinct, as I have.

As we proceed, Kate becomes less inclined to participate and content to watch as I continue. Alice's trousers are next. The ammonia smell is strong. I have to steel myself as the trousers carry a weight heavier than that of the cotton cloth from which they are made. They are damp, blood is congealed in clots, and as I pull the fabric apart, my hands are stained with Alice's blood, still wet, which I can smear between my finger and thumb, as if somewhere, just out of sight, she must be sitting on an outside step, nursing a cut knee, waiting for a plaster and a quick kiss it better. I use a pebble from the garden and make a fingerprint upon this grubby stone (which later I forget to bring in, so it sits where I left it for several days, enduring hours of monsoon-style rain, yet somehow, when I do retrieve it, the print is not washed away).

The washing continues. We use ten, twenty, maybe thirty buckets of water in all, and each garment, as the water finally runs clear, is draped, like bunting, on a branch of the many trees that overcrowd the garden.

———

People have asked me since, why did we do it? We did it because we wanted to, because it felt right for us. We did not turn our backs on her, did not hide or flinch from the harsh reality of what happened to her, what she did to herself. If she could walk to the edge of a cliff and step towards almost certain death, did we not owe it to her to take these much smaller steps, to acknowledge her act, to confront it? Or maybe it just helped us feel closer to her, for it was something of her physical presence that still remained.

———————

Weeks pass and Alice's clothes hang where we left them. For Kate and me, they have so assimilated themselves into the landscape of the garden, we no longer really register they are there. Visitors have come and gone, no one's mentioned them. Nor has Peter. It is Harvey saying that he'll have to move out to Shin Ah's parents' permanently if we don't take them down that tells us we should be mindful of differences in how we're grieving. I fold them and put them away in a new bag. One day I'll look at them again.

September 2019

Thank God for Allsorts

In mid-September 2019, two months after Alice began to socially transition, Peter and I finally attended a support group I found for parents of trans children, run by Brighton Allsorts Youth Project. I'd already spoken to Ben, the person who would be facilitating the meeting, over the phone and he had vetted us to assess our integrity; journalists had tried to infiltrate the group more than once, he said.

We arrived early to complete some paperwork. Ben ushered us in. He was a neat-looking chap, with a short beard and a quirky *Peaky Blinders* cap. All smiles. He took our hands in turn, a good, firm grip. Come in, come in, take a seat. Whilst we filled out forms, he busied himself, moving chairs, finding a box of stickers, some marker pens, for names, he explained. He chattered on – I'm so glad you could make it. How was your journey? Is it still raining out? He smiled again, such a lovely face; kind, if a face on its own can be such a thing. He made eye contact as he talked, but not too much, asked questions and listened to the answers – not just nervous banter, but conversation that soothed me. He had a boyish air, in his jeans and trainers, but soft creases at the corner of each eye suggested he was older than he appeared at first glance.

Other people drifted in and sat down, mostly women, only a couple of men. They looked like your friend, your neighbour, your brother, your sister, your mum. They looked like everyone and anyone, entirely unremarkable. No one displayed stigmata, look at me, my child is trans. But this was what we had in common, why we were there. It was the first time I'd met another parent of a child with gender incongruence.

The group took parents at any stage of their child's journey, from people like us, at the very beginning, coming to terms with their child's needs, looking for answers, through to the seasoned veterans – a sign of hope: the suicidal thoughts, the school refusal, the social isolation had been endured and they, and their children were through the other side. For the first time in months, I dared to imagine a future for Alice.

The meetings were helpful for practical reasons – how to change a name by deed poll, how to deal with school, the passport office, the bank – but most importantly for the emotional support they provided. I was struggling to use Alice's new name, accidentally misgendering and deadnaming her most days. I never meant to. If I spotted it, I corrected myself; if it was pointed out, I apologised. Alice was very forgiving. The other parents in the group were reassuring. Don't beat yourself up, it will come; the brain will rewire eventually, said Ben, his lopsided grin making me feel a bit better about myself. And he was right, though talking about the children in groups – Kate, can you call your brothers down for dinner, or, what do you boys want to eat? – took longer to overcome.

Here, I could talk about Alice's problems at school, her ups and downs, and people understood. My positive experience with my mum encouraged people to expect more from their elderly relatives. We were a community of concerned parents all experiencing a simi-lar thing, learning from and supporting each other. Here, I felt understood. It was a safe space, where it felt all right to speak my fears out loud: I don't like this, I don't understand it, why us? Ben made it clear: it was ok to voice these views, as long as the main purpose of attendance was to support and learn; the overriding aim of the group was to help not just us, but our children.

But there was one theme within the group that made me bristle when it was expressed, as it often was. Many parents framed the transition of their child in the context of loss. Ben nodded in agreement each time a new parent said, I feel as if I've been bereaved. I've heard this many times, he reassured.

I don't feel that way, I said. I felt like standing up and walking out, shouting over my shoulder as I left: listen to yourselves, you're not bereaved, who's died? Show me the body.

In a similar way, the term deadname was not one I personally liked or used. Again, it spoke to me of the ultimate loss, death, as if Alice had not existed before her transition and her past must be erased. Whilst it is a truth that in the early days it was hard to think back to the Alice we knew, when we'd called her a different name, it really did not take too long before we could talk about when Alice was born, when Alice started school and so on, until the logical conclusion sat quite comfortably with us: Alice was always Alice.

The purpose of the group was not to endorse any particular transition route, but parents spoke freely about the paths they had taken with their children whilst they languished on the NHS waitlist. There were private clinics in the UK that would see you once you turned eighteen, but under eighteen there was only one option: Gender GP, an organisation overseas, run by Helen Webberley, a British doctor. At the time, Dr Webberley was under investigation by the General Medical Council, following a series of complaints, but Gender GP was the only way that anyone under eighteen could legitimately get puberty blockers and hormone therapy. It all seemed a bit dodgy to me, but it was a lifeline, according to these parents, who had nothing but praise for Dr Webberley and her team.

Peter and I talked it over. I was worried about their ability to assess and treat our child remotely, but this was outweighed by my worry for Alice. The recent changes in her body were worsening her dysphoria. She had already tried to kill herself. I felt that if we did nothing, she would almost certainly try again, and when she was eighteen, in theory she'd be able to do whatever she liked regarding accessing medication. There seemed nothing to be gained from delaying and everything to be saved by getting started.

We agreed to approach Gender GP to see what they could offer. I put Peter in charge. Although I was the medic, I felt challenged enough managing Alice's mental health. I had no more experience of trans matters than he did, I reasoned, and I would be available to talk over anything he didn't understand. It was really the paperwork, the red tape that I needed his input with, I said. And crucially, I needed to feel the burden was not mine alone. This way, he could support me by taking on his share of responsibility for Alice's healthcare.

17 July 2022

Look what you've done, I hate you

The day after the beautiful ritual of washing the clothes, there's an incident. I don't recall how it starts ... we are due to eat at a friend's house; there will be good food (my friend's a chef) and pleasant company, a change of scene. But I can't leave the house and tension rises. My psychic pain cannot be contained. My brain is overloaded, a circuit board with too much energy powering through it, sparking and fizzing, about to go up in flames. I have Alice's relic stone in my hand. I am rubbing the special spot with my thumb. I am trying to feel her, be with her, but she is not in the stone, she is entirely gone and I cannot bear it. I am outside on the patio, down at ground level, not in a chair. I roll over into a huddle, knees tucked under me, child's pose, groaning. I am banging the stone over and over against the flag-stones, shouting out, make it stop, make it stop, I can't make it stop, make it stop, banging and banging the stone. Kate is crying, please stop, Mummy, stop, you're scaring me. And then a piece of the stone flies off and the smooth roundness of it, created by millennia in the ocean, is turned, in an instant, to a jagged, sharp edge and I am running my finger along it and howling, I've broken it. And Kate is berating me, look what you've done, shouting, stop it, stop it, look what you've done to Alice's stone, you've broken it, how could you?

In that moment, I may as well have pushed Alice off the cliff with my own hands. Look what you've done, reverberating in my ears.

It's mine, I'm screaming at her. It is, it is, it is. It's mine. And then I have the jagged edge and I am hitting myself over the head, bang, bang bang. To break me? To make the invisible seen, like the thin cuts on the forearms of countless young people? To punish me? To ask for help? One, some or all of these things? I cannot reliably answer.

Peter phones my medical-school friend Ali for advice. She tells him to call the acute home-care team's crisis line. They reinstate my olanzapine and I am put to bed.

I'm falling apart at the seams, a phrase my mother used when I was a child, something to be avoided at all costs: come on, now now, let's count our blessings, no point crying over spilled milk. That's it, good girl. As a child, I missed my father dreadfully, but talking about him was somewhat taboo. It was drummed into me that we shouldn't dwell on or wish for something we couldn't have. Let's dry those eyes.

But I don't want to stop crying about Alice. To stop crying means to stop feeling. I have no bones – I'm a rag doll, with nothing but stuffing to hold me up, stuffing that spills out where my stitches have come undone. I feel raw, each day lived as if without a skin, but deeper still, flesh cut through, eviscerated, so I feel pain, perhaps not literally physically, but a mental pain, so intense it is akin to a gaping wound, a severed limb. Alice has been torn from me and turned my insides out. But there is no visible wound and there are no simple remedies, no trips to accident and emergency for Steri Strips and bandages, to patch me back together. Just olanzapine to sedate me, to shut me up. But it's that or self-destruction.

The day after this, I write in my journal that being bereaved is boring, a relentless monotony of sameness. It is as if yesterday's drama is almost entirely erased. The only evidence a sore temple, a small bruise above one eye. I stay in bed half the day and when I get up, I walk around like a zombie, caught between life and death, my body moving but no one's home.

And the relentless heat is stifling. The thermometer climbs to 38 degrees. Harvey goes out on his bike, Peter is trapped – he must stay home to care for me, he must stay home because his hand is broken. Without exercise, he is suffocated, too, not by the heat, but by my tears. We fight again, something trivial but monumental, the way arguments can be. Harvey is not back when I expect him. What if something has happened to him? I say. Peter cannot show me that I have been heard. Instead, he texts Harvey to ask if he's all right. Engaged on his phone, like this, it looks like he's completely ignoring me, though the opposite is true. I hate you, I scream.

I have no parental boundaries. I tell Kate, and Harvey when he returns, that I can't be with their father, repeat, even though the heat of the moment has subsided, that I hate him. I love him, too, I add, but this grief, our differences within it, is breaking me. I've tolerated their father's odd little ways all my life, but right now, with no give, nothing spare, I can't take it. I just need to know he's listening, I wail.

September 2019

An assault, and an unusual Amazon order

Alice was finally being listened to, was under the care of a psychiatrist. School was going well, she denied any problems with staff or students regarding her transition and attended every day, smiling and bright.

In late September, the first of Alice's friends turned eighteen. Bea hosted a fancy-dress party at her house. The theme was a character named for the first letter of your name. Alice was very excited. She planned, of course, to go as the most famous Alice of all, Alice in Wonderland. She ordered a slightly slutty outfit from Amazon. She was so pleased with it; she went to the party full of adolescent joy.

In the small hours of the morning, around daybreak, I got a call. Please come and pick me up. Alice was dishevelled, her make-up a mess, she'd surely been crying. Her costume was covered in red and brown splodges. What's happened? I asked. Nothing, she said. She went to bed and slept off her hangover. When she came down again, she asked how to get the stains out of her outfit.

What is it? I asked.

Ketchup and brown sauce, she said.

How did that get there? I asked.

It doesn't matter.

It does, I said. What happened?

I fell asleep, and when I woke up, I was covered in it, she said.

Who did this to you?

I don't know, just leave it.

But Alice, this is awful, we can't let people treat you like this, I said.

I just want to get it out of my dress, she said. She buried any distress about the assault on her person, appeared only upset that her outfit was spoiled. And because she buried it, eventually I did, too. I did not try and find out who it was, to speak to a parent or the school. It was forgotten, but not forgotten.

After this incident, Alice's attendance at school started to slide and she began to withdraw again. This became a pattern: peaks and troughs, peaks and troughs. And when she entered a trough, you never knew how deep it would go, or how long it would last.

The assault at the party did cause a blip in her confidence, but a month later, Alice was on Amazon again, ordering fake breasts and a special pocket bra. She was delighted with how it changed her appearance. But the euphoria didn't last. Alice had been fully socially transitioned for four months, but progress accessing hormone treatment had stalled and she was despondent. Gender GP was overwhelmed. There'd been a huge upsurge in demand for their services due to the lack of adequate NHS care, they said, and they were also encountering problems introducing new computer software. Alice's school attendance dropped off again.

Jane messaged. She had been recently diagnosed with cancer. Could we meet up? Of course, I said, I'm so sorry. Jane continued to express her views, that trans women should not compete in women's sport or be imprisoned in women's prisons, should not be allowed to use women's loos. I think perhaps I let this happen because there was still a bit of me that hoped she'd eventually come up with a nugget of wisdom, something that would definitely help me change Alice's mind. She never did, she ploughed on with her whataboutery.

Finally, I saw sense. It only hurt me to hear my dearest friend say these things. Stop, I said, please, just stop. I can't listen to this from you. Alice isn't an elite athlete or a prisoner. Alice can't even use a public loo – can you imagine how that restricts her life?

But what about –

I cut Jane off. Alice is my daughter; I can't do this anymore. Can we get the bill?

July 2022

Someone else to worry over, where is Alice now?

Keith comes for dinner. Now I can't worry about Alice, I worry about Alice's housemate, for he was home when Alice left their house for the very last time. And if it is my fault, as I repeatedly insist it is, that Alice died, then any impact on Keith is my fault, too. How can I make it up to him? I ask myself. How can I make sure he's ok?

Kate takes me to task. You are not responsible for everything; she says, as she has said before. Keith is lucky, she says. You're kind to him.

What do you mean? I say. Of course I'm kind, he's just a child.

Well, plenty of parents wouldn't be, she says. You don't blame him, for a start.

Why on earth would I do that? I ask.

Well, you blame yourself and you weren't even there, she says.

This time, this reality repeated does help a little, eases some of my personal burden. But it doesn't ease my concerns for Keith. For whilst I was not there, he was, and I worry that if he carries even a fraction of my guilt, it may eat away at him. I feel very maternal towards him. I must check myself; I do not need a replacement child. He is not Alice. But I am very fond of Keith and worry about him, none the less.

We have a lovely evening. I drive him home at the end of the night and park up outside his mother's flat. If there's anything you want to say, or ask, any time, please know, I'm always here, I say.

There is one thing, he says. We're all wondering where Alice is now.

It floors me, the innocence of it. They are too young for death, funerals and cremations. And I'm a little embarrassed – it's eight weeks since the funeral and I really haven't given Alice's ashes a second thought. She's at the undertakers, I say. Her ashes, I add. Peter and I will bring her home and let you know what we decide to do with her.

October–December 2019

Looking forward to Christmas, a never-ending story

Alice's counsellor, Anne, decided Alice didn't meet the mystery criteria that would allow her sessions to continue. She'd engaged happily for sixty minutes once a week, so she seemed well, to Anne. But to us, she was still chronically unwell. We asked Anne if she would continue to see Alice privately, but she said she did not undertake private work. What's the point of so few sessions? I wailed to an empty room when her email reply came in.

We asked Alice to see the CAMHS psychotherapist privately. She didn't want to, but she agreed. It was a struggle to get her there. She didn't come out looking like she'd been treated to afternoon tea.

We got through the autumn term, but Alice attended less and less. To alleviate her anxiety, she dropped drama and then psychology. I was looking forward to the Christmas holidays when there would be no pressure to get Alice to school and I would have a two-week break from teaching. Kate and Harvey would be home and Alice was always more engaged when we were all together as a family. I was feeling more chilled than usual. Remember your CAMHS appointment with Dr S in the morning, I said to Alice, as I popped my head round her bedroom door to say night-night.

Peter and I were fast asleep when the landline on my bedside table rang. No one called the home phone except our mothers. Which one of them had fallen over and broken something? I wondered. But it wasn't one of our mothers. It was Lucy's mum.

Hi, I said, confused, looking at the clock.

Alice has taken an overdose, she said.

What? She's in bed, I said. Hang on. I hauled myself up and switched on the light. Peter rolled over and groaned.

She's taken ketamine, in the bath, and tried to drown.

What? How do you know?

She messaged Lucy when it didn't work, she said.

Peter, wake up, I said, shaking him. Alice has taken an overdose, she's trying to drown herself in the bath. He leaped up. The bathroom was just next door. He tried the handle, but it was locked.

Alice, Alice, open the door, he shouted.

Lucy's mum was detailing what had happened, why it was her breaking this news, all the way from County Durham, whilst we were in the room next door to the action, yet unaware.

I wanted to be in the bathroom, finding out what had happened to my daughter. Was she really alive? Could she soon be dead? Perhaps she had slit her wrists. Or hung herself from a rope or jumped out of a window. But instead, I'm hearing of the drama that has led us to this moment.

Alice messaged Lucy and Lucy woke me. She's so sensible, she added.

She is, I agreed.

She told me what I've just told you. I rang your mobile but didn't get an answer.

It's downstairs, I said, on charge.

So, I rang Peter, but he didn't answer either.

I felt like we were being told off.

I didn't know what to do, she went on. I was about to call the police, but for some reason, I had Kate's mobile number in my phone. I noticed it, in the list, under yours. I don't know why I had it, maybe from that trip to Durham, when the bus driver thought you and I were a couple.

Maybe, I said.

Anyway, I called Kate to get your home number.

176

So, Kate knows? I asked, still a little bleary.

Yes. She gave me your number. I can't think why I had Kate's number in my phone.

Kate knows, I thought. Poor Kate, I said out loud. What a fright, I must call her back.

Yes, she was pretty confused, but thank goodness I got hold of her.

Yes, thank you, I said.

I tried you first, but you didn't answer.

Ok. Thank you, I said, I have to go.

Is Alice all right? she asked.

I don't know, I said. *I don't know.* And then: how's Lucy? slipped out before I could stop myself. Lucy was not my concern.

She's pretty upset.

Of course, I said, cutting across her. I'm sorry, I have to go.

Let me know if there's anything I can do, she said.

Yes, yes, I have to go. I heard the noise of someone moving in the bath, a slosh of water and the dull squeaking sound of a body against the enamel. I have to go.

Alice was out of the bath and wrapped in a towel. She looked very pale, like she'd been or was about to be sick. Yes, she said, she'd taken ketamine.

Where did you get it? I asked.

I was offered it at parties but didn't take it. I stored it up. She was initially uncharacteristically forthcoming, told us she'd planned to k-hole in the bath, to pass out and drown. She was shivering and miserable and soon had nothing more to say on the matter. I did not push her to talk further. Experience had taught me that to do so would just amplify her silence. Let's make up a bed for you in our room, I suggested. Ok, she agreed.

Just like almost seven months previously, she slept under our watchful gaze. In the morning, we took her to the scheduled CAMHS appointment, but Dr S insisted she was seen at accident and emergency. If she needed medical treatment, she needed it last night, I said. She needs mental-health care right now, not medical. But Dr S insisted, to be on the safe side.

We were seen quite quickly. There was nothing medically wrong with her, they concluded, but she needed a psych referral. I rolled my eyes at Peter. We've just come from CAMHS outpatients, I said. They sent us here. Dr S will probably see us if we go back, tack us on to the end of her clinic, I suggested. It's what I'd have done, as the doctor, if the tables were turned, sacrificed my lunch break. But we were told to wait for the duty mental-health social worker or nurse, someone who'd never met Alice, to come and assess her. We went through her history from start to finish. It was all so hard, hurtful and pointless, so traumatic for Alice, as she was deadnamed and misgendered over and over again. Her name is Alice, I said, more than once. I regretted coming, but I hadn't wanted to be seen as non-compliant, or unconcerned. In the end, we were told to make another appointment with CAMHS, for a date in January. We returned home feeling as gloomy as the day.

July 2022

The heat, thick slices of Manchego, some nihilistic tendencies

The temperature outside continues to soar. Comparisons with the summer of '76 are everywhere. I can't bear for this summer to be remembered by the masses only for its heat, when for us it is memorable for something entirely different. Remember 2022, Caroline? The heat! Yes, I remember, I will say. Harvey says, don't fret, climate change will make this year just like any other, in terms of the weather at least.

We are able to enjoy some of the heat, have lunches under the fig tree, to evoke memories of Mediterranean villa lunches by a cool aquamarine pool. Prepare bowls of plump olives, red ripe tomatoes and cold cucumber with salty capers and red onion, marinated with garlic and lemon, all in the best olive oil. Tubs of aioli and loaves and loaves of crusty white sourdough. Platters of cured meats, oozing isosceles wedges of cambozola, thick slices of Manchego that never taste quite as good as they do under a Spanish sun, even when the temperature in the back garden is higher than in Grenada and Seville. Jugs of red wine and lemonade, infused with orange, cinnamon and clove. We recreate that last Spanish holiday we had with Alice, the summer after her first overdose. We play cards and reminisce. It was before she transitioned and had another name. But the person we miss is Alice.

My mental-health breakdown has been managed. I am no longer acutely suicidal, but my vague suicidal thoughts continue. If something bad were to happen to me, it wouldn't really matter. If I could only pluck up the energy to get out on my bike, I might fall off, be hit by an oncoming car. I have fanciful ideas that death is not far away – if my skin itches, I have liver disease, my nausea is stomach cancer. All these options seem preferable to the relentlessness of living without Alice. One night, I have severe abdominal pains. I will be rushed to hospital, they will find a growth and cut it out. This is what I want, for my grief to be cut out like a tumour. But it can't be, and the tummy pains subside, whilst my grief beds in and spreads.

I start to eat too much, the safer side of my nihilistic tendencies, better than drinking too much and driving my car into an oncoming lorry. I long to be a recovering alcoholic, so I can go to AA every day, twice a day. Bereaved people have their groups, but they only meet once a month. How can that be enough? But to go to AA I must become an alcoholic first and I do not want to be an alcoholic. I want to get my drive back, return to CrossFit, tone my muscles, get my body moving again, the way I used to, before Alice died, before she became quite so unwell.

December 2019–January 2020

A case study of one, a circular argument

After this overdose, Alice was buoyant again. Almost well. An article in the *Guardian* the very next day talked of the possibility of ketamine being a new breakthrough drug in the treatment of resistant depression. It could have enduring positive effects within hours of a single dose, it said. Look at this, I said, showing the article to Peter. Our case study of one supported the research.

Christmas came and went. We kept it quiet, just the five of us. Alice couldn't face a large family gathering with her cousins, though she seemed quite herself with us and her friends, with whom she spent New Year's Eve partying, as if nothing had happened. We too went out for the evening, to a speakeasy party. I bought a new flapper dress for the occasion.

But when Alice had to venture out into the wider world, with its inherent unpredictabilities, her mood deteriorated once more. She barely went back to school in January. We didn't have many conversations with staff about what support they could be providing when we discussed her lack of education. We are doing our best, they said, but she has mental-health problems that we're not qualified to deal with. School staff encouraged us to get her more mental-health treatment – that is the key to getting her back in, they said. The psychiatrist encouraged us to get her to school – that would improve her mental health, she said.

After five or so sessions of private psychotherapy with the CAMHS psychotherapist she refused to see him again. No amount of coaxing, bribery or threats could persuade her. And because she'd already nearly died once, had recently made a second attempt on her life, we were terrified of behaving in any way that might precipitate a third suicide bid, so we agreed. We looked for a different therapist, scoured the pages of online directories, read through dozens of bios, sized up multiple profile pictures looking for the right fit. We emailed a few about availability, were prepared to travel to central London where there were far more therapists who seemed to have the experience Alice needed. But Alice insisted she didn't want to talk to anyone. She'd had enough of talking to people who she felt didn't listen to her or seeing people who helped but then withdrew. She was disillusioned – why would the next person be any different?

Meanwhile, whilst we waited on Gender GP, I began to research private adult gender services in London, of which there were a couple. I tried to refer Alice myself, in anticipation of her eighteenth birthday, but this was not allowed. She would have to refer herself once she was eligible, they said. I was stuck.

July 2022

The mother of all arguments

Peter and I are stuck in an established pattern of behaviour that is ripping us apart. He resists his negative feelings; more than that, can't feel them himself. I am constantly on guard for any sense of being ignored, abandoned, unimportant. The arguments go something like this: he looks moody and I ask, what's wrong? Nothing, he replies. I press him, something's wrong. Nope, I'm fine, he insists. I start to feel attacked, what's he so mad about that he can't tell me? What have I done wrong this time? Alice's death amplifies this dynamic; his feelings are more painful than ever, so he reinforces his barriers. I feel even more guilty and responsible. All I hear in his silences and denials is *you* did this, *you* got it wrong, *you* must be punished. And I believe it. I have let my child die. Peter in these early days never expresses any self-doubt, any sense of responsibility for what has happened to Alice. It's not that I want him to feel as bad as I do, but I want him to feel something, acknowledge something. But he can't. A rage erupts from me once more. I can't do this anymore, I scream.

I stuff a few things in a bag and run to my mother's – for in that moment it feels easier to be without him, so he physically won't be there, than to be without him in the same room, in the same bed. It is the first time in twenty-seven years of marriage that Peter and I have spent the night under separate roofs out of anger and distress, out of my not wanting to be anywhere near him. My world has lost its shape. I'm untethered and adrift. Living is too difficult. I can't endure this with Peter; I can't do it without him. He's my world, yet he's not in my world and now I have abandoned him. He's alone – is he alone? – does he care? I want to hurt myself; I want it all to go away. I'm so alone, I'm all alone, I am nothing.

I text to let him know I've arrived at my mother's and I'm safe.

After a poor night's sleep, I text again: I'm coming home. On the way, I stop to fill the car tyres up with air, there is a slow leak.

Back at the house, we talk, calmly at first, but with increasing agitation. I am pushing him. I want to hear him express some personal if-onlys. I must go on and on about my feelings, about how he is so emotionally absent. Finally, he breaks. He's got empathy fatigue, he says. He's empty.

Empathy fatigue? I scream at him. Empathy fatigue? She's barely cold. If you've had enough of me already, we're done. You've no empathy at all, you're a monster.

No, he spits, no, *you* are the monster.

The tables are turned and Peter is leaving me, slamming the door and yelling he's had enough. Harvey follows him outside, talks him down, he can't drive with his hand in plaster, he can't run far, he's trapped. Harvey brings him home.

Don't leave me, don't leave me, I am sobbing into him. We are in a horrible mess. We need some couples counselling, I say.

But we don't get any. Alice has been dead two months.

February 2020

Turning eighteen and the changes that brings

Alice had been living as Alice for six months. For her eighteenth birthday, she asked to hold a party at the house. It wouldn't be a big affair – only close friends, a dozen or so in total, mostly from the LGBTQ+ gang at school and her Dungeons and Dragons group. She settled on a 1920s party. I hung a few garlands, banners and balloons – she didn't want much fuss. She borrowed my New Year's Eve dress. It fitted her very well. Six months later, it would not fit her at all.

Her eighteenth birthday brought new challenges. First, she was off-rolled from school. Peter and I acquiesced quite easily; she was smart, she could catch up later. It took the pressure off Alice and her mood rallied. And as her mood improved, so did mine, as I had one less battle to fight. I wasn't Sisyphus. I couldn't keep pushing a boulder up a hill. For this is what the last few years had felt like, trying to get my child's needs met. But the boulders kept rolling in.

When her birthday came and went, with no prescription from Gender GP in sight, I started to talk to Alice once more about alternative options. If she couldn't manage to make the referral herself, we could do it together, I said. But she was never available when I was. She always wanted to do it later, tomorrow, another time. She was in the middle of something, an online game, a chat, a sleep. Not now. When then? I asked, over and over. This is for you, not me, I shouted at her back as she disappeared upstairs.

A few weeks after her eighteenth, Alice and I attended the meeting to transfer her mental healthcare to adult mental health services, but the transfer never happened. Alice was assessed as not having a severe and enduring mental-health problem, even with two serious suicide bids, one only two months previously. Even though she was finally being seen six-weekly by the consultant child and adolescent psychiatrist. Now, just because of a date in the calendar, she was suddenly well and needed no support. It was unfathomable.

We were on our own. Alice was on her own. A grown-up. Her legal status had changed. I'd been pivotal in getting her seen and treated, but overnight I was silenced.

I'd been on the other side. I should have known how to navigate these waters, but I felt so at sea. How on earth was Alice expected to cope? And how on earth did it make her feel?

July 2022

Ricciarelli, chocolate eclairs and a pie

Now I'm medicated and 'coping better', Peter and I try to keep going, carrying on with the normal things people do. A friend recommends *Prima Facie*, National Theatre Live at the cinema. Is it triggering? I ask. No, it's grim, but no suicide. It's a one-woman play and it turns out Jodie Comer regularly refers to a character, her colleague Alice. Alice this, Alice that. I flinch each time I hear it. Alice, Alice, Alice. Did it bother you, Peter? No, he says.

The police come to take our statements for their investigation. They are here for the best part of the day; it harrows us all. I decide to bake some biscuits to cheer us up; it will connect me with Alice, it is something we used to do together. I choose a recipe for Ricciarelli; since we cannot be in Trieste, I will bring Italy to us. But I have not read the recipe properly, the biscuits need to rest for twenty-four hours before baking.

The next morning, the knowledge that Alice is dead hits me as if for the first time. My tablets and the kitchen knives may be locked up, but I still have the car keys. I will drive to Rottingdean and jump. Yes, that's what I'll do. Though it will be busy by the time I get there and the thought of landing on someone makes me hesitate. I remember that I have biscuits to bake, so I put the keys back in their bowl and switch the oven on.

I tell Peter of my thoughts and in the next breath ask him to stop being the gatekeeper to my medication. It's infantilising, I say. It makes me feel worse, not better, to not be trusted. There are other ways I will kill myself if I want to. He cannot agree, he is scared of course. In the end, it's decided Kate will manage my medication. It is a compromise we can all accept.

Kate is doing more and more for us; she is the adult, whilst Peter and I are the children. Our minds have recently turned to Alice's inquest, which is set for one day in August. This seems too soon and too short. Kate is planning on training to be a barrister, so Peter and I find we soon defer to her when it comes to all the legalities of Alice's death. She has been talking with Jolyon Maugham at the Good Law Project (GLP); if we are happy to go public, they will fund our legal team for the inquest. They see it as an opportunity to challenge the scandalous waitlists. We agree and he puts us in touch with a solicitor, whom Kate instructs. She is only twenty-five, it is a huge burden for her, but she takes on this task, for me and Peter, to reduce ours. It is her gift to us. Without the financial support of the GLP, we would probably have shrunk away and disappeared into our grief. Instead, we start to plan. We will make a noise about Alice's death, use it to increase awareness of the plight of trans people, particularly their lack of access to healthcare. We contact the coroner's office and let them know. The inquest is postponed.

The police have still not been able to access Alice's mobile or PC, but Kate has accessed her email. We find out that the day before she died Alice ordered a pie, the Kate and Sidney, for her lunch, then six chocolate eclairs from Bravo Patisserie for her last supper. Eclairs are a very particular treat that we only ever have at my mother's. Alice was thinking about her family, as I was thinking about her, on her final day. This knowledge, that we were both thinking of each other, without reaching out, that she was attempting to bring us close or simply saying goodbye, but without us there, sends me into a spin. My mental pain is so intense, so indescribable, it spills out. I flap my hands like the stimming of an autistic child, I beat my forehead over and over with the heel of my hand. I pick up a bag of Alice's personal items – eyeshadow, toothpaste, lip balm – and hug it close, as if it was

Alice herself, and rock back and forth. Peter offers me my relic stone, but Alice is not in the stone; she is in her toiletries, the things she used when she was alive, that she rubbed into her skin. Though she isn't here either, of course, and eventually I put the bag down and set about making lunch.

The next day Peter has a huge meltdown. He calls my name in a panic. He is sobbing and shaking and kicking his legs, as if there is a hoard of little critters snapping at them and he is trying to shake them off. I put my arms around him and hold him tight. I'm here, I say. I'm here. Mummy's here is on the tip of my tongue. It feels like I am soothing an overwhelmed child and I feel useful, for I am not required to comfort him often. Even today, he is unable to talk about any specifics of what he's actually been thinking to bring this on.

Could it be a delayed reaction to the eclairs? I ask.

I don't know, he says. I don't know.

March 2020

A trip to Girona and a nasty bug

In early 2016, when Alice was fourteen, an old school pal who I'd not seen for thirty years got in touch. We had been the closest of friends (I was taken into the fold of her family and included in their annual holidays and outings), but we lost touch. Sarah had recently moved out of London, back to the area where we grew up, where I still lived. She wanted to rekindle our friendship.

I'm a keen cyclist, she said, do you have a road bike?

I do, but I'm not a natural cyclist. I'm always at the back, behind Peter and Harvey, I replied.

Cycle with me, she said. I have a group of girls. It will be fun.

I loved being drawn into Sarah's cycling circle, though I was still at the back most of the time. Her friends were smart, funny and charming. I felt welcomed and accepted, despite differences in family background or wealth. They'd all succeeded in their fields: journalism, medicine, accountancy, banking and the diplomatic services, but aside from one, they had all taken time out to raise their families. They didn't seem to need to prove themselves, there was no sense of doubt or inferiority oozing from their pores, no mothering competitiveness. I felt so lucky to know them. We started cycling together once or twice a week. Started holidaying as a group: Majorca, France, Rimini and Girona, each time our bikes in tow, mountains to be conquered.

Our Girona trip was March 2020, a few days after Alice was discharged from psychiatric services. I was in low spirits, but the holiday was booked so I went, hoping to relax and clear my head. We'd booked a private guide. His name turned out to be Alice's deadname. I had to hear it over and over again, deadname this, deadname that. And none of the girls gave any sign that they'd made any connection, that this might in any way be bothering me. I'd gone to Girona to get away, to relax, but found myself increasingly agitated. In the end, I found the courage to tell our guide I was finding it difficult to ride with him. That I couldn't use his name because it was my trans daughter's old name. He was such a beautiful young man. In excellent English, he spoke so tenderly to me. He understood, he said. He could imagine life was very hard for her. It was a relief to have spoken so honestly and openly to him and been so nurtured in return. I kept hearing his name, but it didn't bother me so much after that.

Whilst we were away, a mystery virus that started in China and had gradually spread, was declared a global pandemic by the World Health Organization. Governments started to close their countries' borders. We joked that it would be lovely to be stuck in Girona for a few weeks, a month or two, as the weather turned warmer, leaving the dads to navigate family life alone for a change, unsupported and unprepared, whilst we cycled through the Catalan countryside. Thankfully, we made it home, for the reality of being stuck in Spain would have been far worse.

August 2022

A heated month in many ways

For Peter's birthday, I plan a picnic. We all go to Leith Hill, a place we went often as a family, and we imagine Poppy careering up and down 'the pit', our special place, Alice chasing after her.

A few days later, Peter is having beers at our local with a few mates. I go to pick him up, tell Kate I might stop for a quick one. The lads are in high spirits, Peter appears to be having fun and Kate and I have just had an awful afternoon at someone's house with copious cups of tea, dollops of sympathy and extra helpings of 'you're doing *so* well', all of which was well intentioned but utterly draining. One pint turns to two, then three, though I haven't forgotten about Kate waiting for me at home. I am drunk on beer and also the good humour of old friends. When we return there is a huge fight. It is entirely my fault; I have completely abandoned her.

The next day is our wedding anniversary. We have a theatre trip planned, *Jerusalem*. We've had the tickets since long before Alice died, it's a sell-out run. I do not want to go; the fight has drained me and I want to stay with Kate. Peter persuades me. We arrive early and head to a pub for a beer. After last night, I don't want a drink, but I have a half. When Peter wants another, I manage to say no, he got his evening out, this next decision is mine. I point out the fancy gelateria over the road and suggest an ice cream. I relish the coolness of the citrusy sorbet on my tongue. Alice would have loved this, I say.

We take our seats to enjoy the show, but a trans joke early on, which leaves the audience tittering, sends me sinking into my seat. I switch on my phone, order an ice-cream maker and wait for the play to end.

———————

Every time I do something I don't want to do I end up worse off than when I started. Yet my nurses tell me I must do these things, as steps in my recovery, and they are always pleased to hear what I have achieved. My antidepressants are increased, because whilst I'm now interacting with my world, I still need to enjoy it. I think that is their reasoning – that I am halfway there.

———————

That night, I dream I am in a relationship with a stranger, but for the relationship to work I must have some sort of body modification, something must be done to my genitals, a grafting of body parts to be undertaken; I am required to have both a penis and a vagina. The request seems odd yet entirely reasonable.

The antidepressants are giving me vivid dreams, I say. Today's nurse is not worried. I am discharged back to primary care. I must be getting better.

Peter, on the other hand, is worse; he is irritable and withdrawn. The limited home exercise he can cobble together is not enough. I take him to bed for afternoon cuddles, where we spoon and feel completely connected, like magnets stuck together, then something happens and we are far apart, opposite ends repelling one another.

It is not just me and Peter who are struggling. August is an intense month. We all fight with each other, in various combinations. In our grief, we say some of the meanest things to one another, make the most ridiculous claims. But we make up, we must never go to bed on an argument, I insist.

I *am* improving because I'm ready to start exercising again. I can't face going back to CrossFit, because people know me there and I crave anonymity. Kate loves swimming, so she suggests we join a local pool. The first time we go, we encounter humming woman. How dare this woman be so happy that she must announce it to everyone in earshot with her non-stop commentary of tuneless hum? I want to tell her to stop, to tell her that my daughter has just died. I think the only thing that stops me is that it is August and to say this would be a lie. Alice died three months ago. I'm afraid the passage of time is diminishing her death. People we know are not quite so interested in us as they were last month, so how can I expect a stranger to understand my pain is as fresh as if it were yesterday? But this cannot be true, for here I am in my swimming costume. I feel exposed in more ways than one, ready to be told I am a complete fraud.

We change our schedule to avoid a confrontation. Swimming becomes a soothing ritual. I'm not fast, but I'm methodical. I increase my stretches of unbroken front crawl from two lengths to fifty in under a month. It is mindful, meditative. I count my strokes, I count my lengths, I find a rhythm. It is doing wonders for my mental health. We start to swim outdoors, go to local lakes and the lido. One morning in late August, we bump into Ian, our neighbour who helped us out with the dog the day Alice died. He is with his new girlfriend, Tess. They're in love, you can tell – they hold hands like teenagers. And we don't think anyone has met her yet, we might be the first, we feel lucky. We have a coffee, a nice chat, we like her. On the way home, it hits me, as a moment of complete clarity: I am happy, life is normal. And the accompanying thought, inevitably (for how could it be anything else?): Alice is alive. It is impossible for her to be dead in a world where I can feel pleasure like this. But it lasts no time at all, this fantasy, this visit to a parallel universe, before reality hits me and I am gripping the steering wheel, crying and crying, and Kate is asking me, what's happened, what are you thinking? And I explain.

March–October 2020

Covid, long Covid, hormones and gin

One month after Alice's eighteenth, the UK went into lockdown. The skies were clear of flight trails, the noise from the M25 faded to almost nothing. Everyone was impacted, but not in the same way. Peter, as an office worker, moved seamlessly to Zoom. Working hours were slashed, since he no longer commuted, and it suited him fine. I, on the other hand, having spent the previous few months lurching from one rule to another to keep my face-to-face classes Covid compliant, now had to move them entirely online. Two-thirds of my income vanished overnight. I was run ragged with admin. Many of my older client base struggled with the technology. It was a demanding time and distracted me from Alice.

But conversations were had. Her prescription from Gender GP was almost ready and before she started treatment Peter wanted to talk one last time about the only thing that really troubled him about Alice's transition: her fertility. Trans women are offered, encouraged to store sperm for IVF, should they want to start a biological family in the future. Alice was adamant that she didn't want to, that she didn't want children, and if she changed her mind, there were other ways to have a family. Yet again, Peter and I disagreed. This time, I was with Alice, and it was Peter's turn to worry about regret. People can't have babies for all sorts of reasons, I said, this is just one more. In the end, Peter let it go.

Three weeks into lockdown I got Covid. I remember the date because it was 15 April, my birthday. It was in the days before routine testing but it was definitely *it*. I was so unwell, so tired. Fortunately, finding cover teachers was simple, now half the Pilates industry was unemployed. My clients welcomed their new teachers from Turkey and Northumberland. Gradually, I began to feel a little better and tried to return to work, but I was overcome with lethargy once more. Long Covid was not really a thing yet, although there were mutterings about it in the press. Was it real, or all in the head? A psychiatric manifestation of stress about the pandemic, not an actual physical thing, people were saying. Historically, psychiatry has often framed chronic fatigue as a mental-health disorder. This was what I was taught over the years, since so many of the symptoms ran parallel with depression: lethargy, low mood, lack of motivation. But now that I was experiencing it for myself, I began to change my mind. One day, out walking Pippin, I was so overcome by the need to sleep, I started to scan the hedgerows either side of the isolated downs path for a suitable spot to curl up and snooze. This was not depression, but several of my friends insisted it was.

You've been depressed before, they said. You've been through so much with Alice.

No, this is different, I said, without being able to make them understand exactly how.

But it wouldn't hurt, with your history, to go back on antidepressants, they said.

I'm not depressed, I repeated.

They muttered in a sort of agreement, which meant they didn't really believe me. And as I struggled to find the words to describe my experience and discovered that more and more people doubted me, I began to feel more empathy towards Alice. I saw how she was suffering mainly due to a society's, a profession's, inability to put themselves in her shoes and trust her.

It went on for months, this waxing and waning in my energy levels. At exactly the same time that Alice's hormone treatment finally started. After all the issues with Gender GP, plus an additional month of waiting due to an administrative cock-up at the online pharmacy, Alice received her first prescription in mid-April 2020 – two days after my illness began, eight weeks after her eighteenth birthday, seven months after our initial enquiry and a whole eighteen months after she first told her GP she thought she was trans. Alice's body had changed significantly in that time, a change that devastated her. And although the oestrogen had quite quick effects, producing some minor breast-bud development that thrilled her, there were no signs of her other puberty slowing down. I realised she wasn't on the gold-standard testosterone blocker because that was an injection and her GP wouldn't administer it, but all the bumf from Gender GP said finasteride was an effective alternative, so I trusted what I read. Alice felt she had been prescribed the medicines she needed, the best medicine available, and was happy. She didn't want to make a fuss and my ill health meant I didn't have the energy to make a fuss for her.

Luckily, with government announcements of financial help for the self-employed, I was able to make the decision to continue employing cover teachers for all my classes and take time out to recover. I can't know for sure, but I believe this opportunity to focus on my recovery prevented my post-Covid symptoms bedding in. I was able to rest as much as I needed and after about six months, I was completely well. I reopened negotiations with Alice about moving her care to a London-based private clinic. But one clinic had a long waitlist by now and the other wouldn't accept you if you'd started treatment elsewhere, which seemed harsh, given they didn't treat under-eighteens. I emailed the chief clinician at this private gender clinic, explaining Alice's situation, pressing my point of view, playing my I-used-to-be-an-NHS-psychiatrist card. I talked about continuity of care and a multidisciplinary approach. Alice must refer herself, they repeated. But Alice had seen how difficult the process of engaging Gender GP had been, so once her treatment with them had started she preferred to continue with them, rather than face the further battles she anticipated to get treatment somewhere new. Maybe, like many eighteen-year-olds, she simply didn't have much faith in her mother's judgement.

In her online meetings with Gender GP, they asked Alice if her medication was suiting her and it appears she said yes. But she was still very much a child and the person on the other end of the line was the boss. If she was unhappy with her medication, she wouldn't have been able to say. I wasn't there to lend a second opinion. I learned later that although finasteride was effective in most people, it sometimes wasn't in others. Whilst Alice was on it, the angular shoulders that she shared with all of us, got broader still. The oestrogel was also failing to live up to expectations, her breast development stopped and although she gained weight, it was in a general rather than a feminine way. Her initial delight seeped away as progress faltered and all that happened was her clothes became too tight and unflattering.

Alice was too shy to go to stores to buy anything new, so she ordered everything from ASOS. She had no idea what would suit her, and I tried to help, but on this also she doubted my judgement. Alice no longer wore much make-up and had swapped dresses and skirts for baggy jogging bottoms and hoodies from the women's department. She wanted to hide her body, but this just made her look larger, broader. This was what anorexics did, I thought – another ill-understood body-dysmorphic diagnosis that the psychiatric establishment has often struggled to treat well. It has a high death rate, from suicide and malnutrition. But people also get better from it. They stop thinking their body is one way, when really it is another. I couldn't help the odd doubt seeping in. We don't accept an anorexic's belief that they are fat and mustn't eat, so why do we validate trans people? Isn't something similar at play? I wondered. Shouldn't Alice's gender dysphoria first have been treated with psychotherapy before resorting to hormone treatment? But Alice had received counselling and psychotherapy, just not from those I perceived to be the experts at the tantalisingly out-of-reach gender-specialist services.

And in my anorexia argument I was clutching at straws, for the two situations are entirely different. If you agree with an anorexic, and do not intervene to help them eat, then they may well die, but if you agree with a trans person and enable them to be who they want to be, they are far more likely to flourish.

And Alice was flourishing, to a degree, for whilst for many, lockdown was an added pressure in their lives, for Alice, at least at first, it was a blessing. All of a sudden, the way she lived her life, often isolated and alone, was normal, as we were all forced online. Since being off-rolled from school in February, she'd kept in touch with school friends, still had her weekly Saturday-night Dungeons and Dragons sessions, which moved seamlessly online. We could hear Alice laughing and chatting in her room even more than usual.

I was worried about Alice being bored stuck at home with me, Peter and her dog, but we rubbed along ok. We had meals together, had moments of family fun. I helped her apply for Universal Credit, so she had some spending money to treat herself to a few things. Over the summer, Alice developed a penchant for a gin and tonic and the offer of a new gin to taste was regularly deployed to get her downstairs.

Still, Covid gradually began to lose its novelty and get in the way of Alice's care. She needed to be seen face to face, but telephone consultations were now the order of the day. I called the receptionists, told them Alice never had and never would answer her phone, that the GP should ring my mobile number and I'd put her on. But I was not the patient, so telephone appointments were made that went unanswered.

For the third time since Alice turned eighteen, I dropped a form at the GP practice to repeat that Alice was happy for me to be the access point for any communication about her healthcare. The truth was she couldn't do it without me.

July–November 2022

The hunt for a therapist, lucky number seven

In July, Peter goes to SoBS (Survivors of Bereavement by Suicide). I don't feel like it. More than that, we are so ill at ease with each other's way of grieving we are considering attending separate groups. We are both on the waitlist with Cruse. I decide I can't wait and email several private therapists via a reputable website. Each time, I mention that my child who died was trans, that they need to be trans aware and supportive. Not one turns me away.

The first one I see is in a chilly basement. I talk and talk about Alice, crying constantly. She says very little. I feel exquisitely vulnerable. Finally, she ventures, I'm picking up a lot about gender here. No shit, Sherlock, I think. I don't go back for a second appointment.

I like the next one I call to sound out, but she only does telephone sessions, so I hold her in reserve. I try someone else face to face. When she wells up at our first meeting, I feel she recognises the depth of my loss. But again, all I do is weep through my sessions and although this one says something rather than nothing, she often mumbles, puts forward her thoughts and ideas so quietly that I must keep asking her to repeat herself. We last five weeks before I have the confidence to leave.

I try again, another therapist who says yes, she can help. The session starts well, she seems confident. I am reassured, until she repeats two tropes that cis people use to talk about trans people. The first – perhaps Alice did not know what she really wanted, the implication being she was unsure, imbalanced, mentally unwell. Many transgender people, like Alice, do suffer with anxiety and depression, but this must be placed in the context of the increasingly hostile society they live within. Her second mistake is to venture: transition often isn't the answer trans people expect it to be. Another assumption, given away with the word 'often', that regret rates are high – worries I once had, but now know to be unfounded. Regret rates for gender-reassignment surgery are lower than for knee surgery, for example. I don't have the courage to argue with her in the room, but I send an email highlighting my concerns and the gaps in her knowledge and encourage her to read *The Transgender Issue* by Shon Faye. My experience with her has been traumatic and countertherapeutic. She takes my money and doesn't reply.

I book a taster session with a fifth therapist but change my mind. She's said over the phone: I don't think Alice's gender is relevant here, we need to focus on you. The first therapist thought gender was everything and this one thinks it's not significant at all, I say to Peter, to explain why I've cancelled. The dichotomy, the two extremes at either end of the spectrum, the parallels with 'the trans debate' – the attacked and traumatised trans community on one side and the gender-critical* community on the other, with their own fears and presumed traumas – are not lost on me. I just want to find some middle ground.

By now, I've reached the top of Cruse's waitlist. I'm scheduled for twelve sessions, but halfway through my therapist says she's sought permission to extend my therapy indefinitely – my complicated grief warrants it. I want to be pleased, if only because the counselling is free and neither Peter nor I are working, but I'm not getting on with this therapist either. She keeps telling me to be kind to myself.

Go out for a nice walk, she says, or for coffee and cake, that sort of thing.

---

* Those who are gender critical dismiss the concept of gender identity and see the human experience through the lens of sex at conception.

I don't want to do either of those things, I say, they make me feel ill.

Each time I see her, this is how we end:

What have you got planned for the rest of the day? Something nice?

Usually, my answer is, nothing, grieving is so exhausting, I might go back to bed. That is what I want to do, after all.

It's lovely and sunny outside, she urges, do try to go for a walk.

I tell Peter and he persuades me out of the house. I barely make it past the end of the drive. I can't do it, Peter, I can't. Physically, I don't have the strength to put one foot in front of the other.

One week I answer her question with: I'm going to put a wash on, then hoover.

That doesn't sound like much fun, she says.

It's not fun, I want to scream.

But it is progress. I haven't put a wash on or got the hoover out for five months. This deserves fanfares and party poppers, but she doesn't see it. I draw these sessions too to a close.

Will I ever find a therapist I trust? I am close to giving up. Then along comes Claudia. Therapist number seven. I've never had a lucky number, but if I were minded to pick one, seven might be it. Finally, I have what I need, someone who understands LGBTQ+ issues from lived experience and who I absolutely trust from the outset. It is the best fifty minutes of my week, because I am completely safe.

I'm so sad we didn't find an equally supportive and nourishing therapeutic relationship for Alice, but it was not for want of trying.

August 2020

A wedding anniversary, another little nail in her coffin?

Once Covid restrictions were eased, Alice started seeing a third face-to-face counsellor. It appeared to go well at first, but her enthusiasm soon dropped off. I was frustrated, though perhaps she'd encountered any manner of transphobia – either wilful or out of ignorance – to put her off, or to actually worsen things, just as I had.

Now we were allowed to have gatherings of up to thirty outside, Peter and I decided to have a party for our silver wedding anniversary. To narrow down the guest list we struck on a plan: we would ask those friends who'd been most supportive of Alice's transition and of us, on our journey with her. Transphobes were not invited.

Jane did not make the cut. We were still in touch, but on a very superficial level. Throughout 2020, we mostly texted about knitting. Jane is an excellent knitter and Kate had taken it up in lockdown and was showing real aptitude. It was safe to send each other photos of jumpers and socks, but we rarely ventured into in-depth conversations about Alice or about Jane's cancer.

The anniversary party was lovely, though Alice went out and missed most of it. I didn't mind at all. I was glad to see her socialising with her friends. Her first overdose had been fourteen months previously, seven months later she had tried again; and now, a further seven months down the line, she seemed ok – there was no talk of suicidal thoughts or any evidence that she was feeling that way. It was positive that she didn't want to spend the evening with us and a bunch of our friends.

Later in August, A-level results came in. Alice has not sat hers, but on my brother's advice, as a retired teacher, we'd asked for Alice's work in year 12 to be considered towards AS levels. When her certificates arrived, they were made out to Alice as requested – the school and the examining board had got that much right – but they had her original middle name emblazoned on them, too. I was furious, but in Alice's usual way she shrugged her shoulders and laughed. I wished she would allow herself what I considered to be a little bit of healthy annoyance or disappointment.

August 2022

The relentless irritation continues

Two years later, Kate and I are swimming at the local pool on A-level results day. There is much chatter amongst the older women. The conversation is so intense and competitive, grades and university places dissected, their own grandchildren picked apart like roadkill. I want to tell them to hush, that exam results are not the be-all and end-all, to get some perspective. Downstairs in the foyer I bump into one of my ex-Pilates teachers. She asks how I am and the floodgates open. I am struck by how open she is. Perhaps her not having children makes it easier for her to be with me. Most of my friends have children around Alice's age and I suspect many of them are, subconsciously at least, scared of me and what has happened to Alice. We serve to remind them of the frailty of life and how anything could happen to one of their children at any time. This is how I frame the inability of some of them to spend any time with me at all, especially one to one or as a couple. They invite us to ABBA nights and birthday parties, lads' nights and girls' nights, where we are diluted. I often decline.

I long for people to understand. I decide to go to the next SoBS meeting with Peter. Maybe it will help, if only to temper this relentless irritation I have with so many of my friends. But it reminds me of an NHS psychiatry in-patient group-therapy session. There is a lot of trauma in the room. I don't like it. I feel a sort of obligation, to be able to fix everyone, like I'm the doctor and it is not my place to speak of why I am here. It makes me feel unimportant again. I am not them, I say to Peter. This will not define me.

I don't go back, for now.

September 2020–June 2021

An online relationship, a job interview, ups and downs, ending on a high

Most of Alice's friends left for university in late September 2020. Alice didn't express any emotion about this huge rite of passage that she was not part of. Life was still continuing largely online, so her friends were available for banter most days. Alice had also formed a relationship with Megan, the best friend of Bea's Dutch boyfriend. They had never met in real life, but they became very close and talked to each other endlessly. This relationship lifted her spirits to extraordinary new levels.

After consulting her GP, Alice decided to reduce her antidepressants with a view to stopping them altogether. As she was doing so well, we discussed the possibility of her getting a job. I began to help her look for apprenticeships and was excited when I saw one advertised for a teaching assistant at a special-needs school near our house. It felt like an ideal job for Alice. Children with profound learning disabilities wouldn't judge or harass her for being trans. She filled out the application and overcame intense anxiety to attend the interview. She was required to come back and do a few trial days, to get to know the kids, and then the job was hers. But she just couldn't do it. The effort she'd put in to attend had left her completely drained. She felt a failure, though we tried to frame it as a success – she had done really well to get as far as she did.

In early December, unbeknown to us, Alice bought Megan tickets to fly over for Christmas. Megan's parents weren't having any of it. We had to mollify Alice when it became quite clear that Megan, although older than Alice, would not be allowed to come, but she seemed to recover from her disappointment relatively easily. We had another quiet but happy family Christmas.

Then, a few days later, there was a loud noise upstairs and a pained, bellowing sound. Peter and I raced up the stairs. Alice was in her room, throwing things, throwing herself about.

What's happened? we asked. Alice, sweetheart?

She was hyperventilating and could barely speak. Megan's blocked me on everything, she sobbed. They say they're a bad influence on me and I'd be better off without them. I'm so worried about them, she continued.

I was worried about both of them. I messaged Megan for Alice, to seek reassurance they were safe. Not too long after, they were back together. Alice relaxed once more and invited a few friends to the house for New Year.

In late January, Alice was suicidal again. She walked to the river in the middle of the night to throw herself in, but she'd taken Pippin with her and couldn't bear to leave him vulnerable and alone, so returned home. In the morning, she asked for all the kitchen knives to be locked away once more. Peter was overcome with self-reproach; he had heard footsteps on the gravel drive in the middle of the night but hadn't got up to investigate. I tried to soothe him, pointing out that I hadn't even woken up. But if you had, you would have got out of bed to take a look, he said.

I took Alice back to the GP. She registered for her appointment on the self-check-in screen, using her date of birth and her gender, but it wouldn't accept her. She tried again but still it didn't recognise her. Slowly it dawned on me – the system hadn't been updated to record her new gender, despite all our efforts to get the GP practice on board. I pressed M for her and her old name flashed on the screen. I burst into tears and ranted at the nearest receptionist. A woman came up to me in the waiting room a few moments later. I'm so sorry you and your daughter had to endure that, she said. It was a small comfort, there were respectful people out there. Alice attended a brief appointment and was restarted on antidepressants. No wonder you're fucking depressed, I said, as we left. I hate this place and how they treat you. I think it did her good to see how angry and upset I was.

The next month, I persuaded Peter we should put our house on the market. It had been extended to accommodate my Pilates classes, but one of our neighbours had put paid to my dream of working from home with a sustained campaign to the planning department. The house had lost its appeal. We'd been fortunate to benefit from the rising property market over the years. We could sell up and buy a suitable family home for half the price, have cash in the bank, Peter could resign from the job he wasn't enjoying. I wanted this, not just for him, but for me. Looking after Alice was taking its toll on me, on the both of us. Although we'd had a whole year with no actual acts of self-harm, we lived on tenterhooks, wondering if it might happen again, and this most recent incident had proved to us we were not out of the woods.

As Peter and I house hunted, Alice was always on our minds. How long would she need to live with us? Jane and I began to text less about jumpers and more about the various dream homes we wanted to escape to. I told her we'd put an offer in on a house with an annexe, so Alice could live semi-independently, with us on hand, for as long as it took to get her treatment, to get her through this. Jane reached out: 'I'm sorry it's so hard. I've been watching a trans YouTuber, who's making me think and open my mind a bit,' the text said. We tentatively started to message each other back and forth, about her views, about Alice, more than we had for the best part of a year. It felt promising.

We were gazumped. I was so disappointed, but the very next day a house came on to the market that we fell in love with – the house we live in now. It was across the road from Alice's old school, near the families of all her friends. It would help them keep in touch, we thought.

By June, Alice was in better health than I'd seen her for years. Harvey hosted his twenty-third birthday party in our garden. It was the first such gathering for so many of his friends since the first Covid lockdown over a year ago, and people had still been rationing their hugs, keeping a certain distance. Not today, though. From mid-afternoon, friends began to drift in. I thought Alice might retreat to her room, but she was there from the start, dressed up and as relaxed in the company of Harvey's friends as I'd ever seen her with her own. Later, I left to go to a party myself, so this one could go on without me. I returned around 2 a.m., with the party continuing in full swing. To my utter delight, Alice was still up, happily chatting away with Harvey's friends. This is a memory I cherish.

Alice appeared entirely well.

September 2022

A church service, a state funeral that gets me thinking, a girls' night

My own mental health is a mystery to me. Some days I feel sadder than when Alice first died, but I'm crying less. I am not happy; if anything, I struggle to feel much at all. I have an emotional blunting, which is a sign of depression, but I think it is an effect of the antidepressant. For a while, it's preferable to the intense displays of emotion that were such a feature of the previous month when I cried like an infant, demanding attention from any available parental figure, even my children, to console me. Now I am more like an orphan, a child without a parent to tend them, who has learned not to cry, or not to cry for long.

We attend SoBS' annual church service, at St Martin-in-the-Fields. I don't find much in it to soothe me. One of the things I've been hearing repeatedly, from friends, armchair therapists, is that there is no one way to grieve, that everyone's grief is different. Right now, this seems particularly true as, trapped in a long pew with no escape, I listen to an array of parents expressing their loss their way. One speaks passionately about all their child's accomplishments, their brilliance, in nothing but glowing terms. They still killed themselves, I think. The truth lies somewhere else. But am I just being cruel because I don't have an abundance of boasts for Alice, who achieved very little in the way of measurable successes in her short life? I surely would, if I could, talk about such things and how unfair it is that she is gone, since she offered so much. But all I have are clichés, she was lovely, gentle and kind. Platitudes any mother might say about her dead daughter. And with her gone there is no evidence.

Over time, I realise I don't need proof. I don't need certificates or medals to find ways to talk about Alice. Her attributes alone do her justice. Her kindness, wit and curiosity. Her contradictions, too. She could be quiet, earnest and often withdrawn, but also exuberant, sarcastic and playful. She was a conundrum. But however Alice presented, on any given day, those who knew her loved her completely.

The Queen has died at last and people are acting as we expected them to, as if it's a huge surprise and an enormous personal loss. It makes me feel more forlorn and alone. There will be a state funeral. Meanwhile, we still have to decide what to do with Alice's ashes. There's a natural burial site near us. Kate and I visit. The bells are peeling out from a local church, it's tranquil and we both feel this would be a good spot for Alice. But when we go back later with Harvey and Peter, it's blustery and rainy, which amplifies the traffic noise from the nearby dual carriageway. Kate still likes it, but I have changed my mind. I'm drawn back to the crematorium. The last place I physically stood with her body. Holding on to her coffin, arms outstretched crucifix-like along the lid, sinking my teeth into it, the final bars of Bronski Beat's 'Smalltown Boy' ringing in my ears. We decide nothing.

Decisions are so difficult to make. I think in part because I am so enmeshed in the idea that if I had just done something differently, Alice would still be alive. This prevents me making decisions now, for who knows what catastrophe they may predicate? Instead, Peter makes them for me. We book a holiday to Greece. I acquiesce, not because the decision is easy, but because it's not important to me. But with regard to where we inter our daughter's ashes, even in the depths of my despair, I cling on to the knowledge that I am allowed a say.

Around this time, I decide to stop taking my antidepressants. Peter is very concerned, but I can't tolerate the emotional blunting any longer.

I wake up one morning to several WhatsApp notifications on my phone. They all say the same thing: Alice left the group. I sit down to allow my jitters to pass, but I am glad to have felt them; unpleasant emotions are preferable to me than none at all.

———

I am reminded of the previous time 'Alice left the group'. It was shortly after her second suicide attempt. I came downstairs one morning, nothing was untoward. Peter was casually preparing his breakfast, scrolling the morning news on his phone. I made a cup of tea as we exchanged the usual pleasantries about the quality of our sleep.

Alice has left the family WhatsApp, he said. I wonder why?

What do you mean? I asked.

Look, he said, showing me his screen.

Have you been up to check on her? I asked.

No, he replied.

I flew up the stairs two at a time, knocked on her door, opening it without waiting for an answer. Alice was sat at her desk, firing away at some online opponent.

Are you all right? I asked.

Yeah, why? she replied.

You left the family WhatsApp, I said.

Oh yeah, that was an accident. She grinned at me, slantways.

Oh, ok. Are you sure? I ask.

Yeah, what do you mean?

I thought you might have done something, I said. I thought you might … I started to cry.

Nah, I'm fine, she said, getting up to give me a welcome hug. I'm fine, she repeated, before quickly resuming her game.

———————

Peter is planning a night out with his mates. I decide to ask my girl-friends over for dinner; everyone who has contributed to the now-defunct food rota is invited. I make a couple of giant lasagnes, in honour of all the lasagnes delivered to my door. I drink far too much red wine and behave as if nothing has happened at all. It is a release, to feel unburdened for a few hours, but it's a pretence. Peter comes home also drunk, and chats with the girls before they all start to head off, and we are left alone. Kate retreats to bed and so do we. Because we are drunk, we attempt sex. It is only the second time since Alice died. Once again, I burst into tears. I can't do it, I say. I'm sorry. Peter is kind and we spoon together. Maybe on holiday, I whisper, as I cry myself to sleep.

July 2021

A cycling trip, a run-in and a revelation

Whilst Alice was alive, we sought occasional breaks from worrying about her mental health. In early July, I went away with the cycling girls to one of the gang's Devon holiday homes. I hadn't cycled nearly as much as them over the preceding year, what with long Covid and ongoing concerns about Alice's transition and her withdrawal. The riding was hard and after the second day I was exhausted. I bowed out of the final ride. I'll rest and read my book, I said; you go without me. But the forecast was bad, so everyone decided on a walk instead.

One friend, Mon, arranged for someone she knew to join us. I was stuck behind them on the narrow coastal path when their conversation turned to trans women in sport. I didn't want to listen to two people on the same side, verbally backslapping each other, with their agreement of the injustice of it all for real women, that trans women must be stopped. I was on my holiday, my break from worrying about Alice. I didn't need this reminder of how hard her life was. I stepped off the path to let the others pass and joined the last person in the caterpillar who tried to calm me. It was ten minutes or so to the café, but I cried all the way and we fell behind. Everyone was sat on a wall by the time we arrived, drinking tea. The forecast had been completely wrong. It was sunny and hot, and we were all a bit over-heated and dehydrated. I had a monumental headache.

I turned to Mon. It was so hard for me to hear that conversation, I said.

Which one? she asked, and I had to spell it out. Aren't I entitled to an opinion? she asked.

214

Yes, of course you are, I said. Then: no, not really, not in front of me, anyway.

What am I supposed to say? she continued. Nothing?

No, I said. Then: yes, maybe, I don't know. It's just really difficult to hear.

I was finding it hard to speak, hard to think; I was gulping for air between words, wiping tears from my eyes so I could see. Alice isn't an elite athlete, I said. She's just a child, my child. I paused. I was shaking, biting my nails. All this debate about trans women in sport is very particular, very specific, but it filters down to the general and makes trans people's lives really hard, feeds the narrative that they're all a threat, I said, in all circumstances.

Although I didn't say it nearly as articulately as this because of the non-stop sobbing, tears streaming down my face, snot pouring from my nose, smearing it away with the back of my arm. Gasping. Pleading. Please listen to me, I said. It's so unkind, what you say, I can't bear to hear it.

Well, that's the trouble with you, she says. You're so demanding. It's your way or no way. I don't know how to talk to you about Alice. You're so controlling and difficult.

She went on like this, wouldn't relent, though I was in pieces. She wouldn't listen to my answer to the very question she had asked: what am I supposed to say? I stood and stared at her. I was an empty shell, the tears suddenly drying up with the shock of her attack. Here I was, her friend, baring my soul about my sadness and worry for my suicidal transgender teen and all she could come up with was that she had a right to speak.

Whilst she embraced this right, I gave up mine and walked away. Then, as we prepared to move on, Mon came back over. We're ok, aren't we? Yes, I said, although I should have said no. I didn't want to talk to her, be anywhere near her. I wanted to drive home that night, but I was too wrung out. In the morning, Mon and I crossed in the hall. I was civil. She was leaving early to get back for her child's birthday party. This is what I liked about her – she loved her child, she'd be there for his party, but she wasn't going to miss her cycling weekend. She had her needs, too, and got them met. I found her funny, charming and emotionally intelligent, until I dared to attempt to protect myself from a heated one-sided conversation about trans women in sport. We said goodbye. I haven't spoken to her since.

I drove home from that weekend sobbing all the way, shaking, longing for my family, for safety. And it dawned on me, in a moment of complete clarity: if I could feel like this, so unsafe in the company of friends, then what did Alice experience, living as a transgender woman, constantly under threat of attack from a society that challenged her very existence? I put my foot down. I couldn't wait to see Alice, to take her in my arms and ask for her forgiveness, to tell her I understood, that I would always support her, never doubt her again. I was her true ally now.

When I arrived home, I embraced Alice, told her of my epiphany, declared my allegiance. She was disappointingly underwhelmed. But I was galvanised. Kate pointed me towards Reclaim Pride being organised in London the following week. It was to be a return to the roots of the original Pride marches, not a corporate sponsored snaking street party, but a march of protest. I asked the rest of the family if they would like to go. Kate was busy and I couldn't persuade any of the others, so I went on my own. It was my first ever demo. I made not one, but two heavy placards – a rookie error. My heart and my arms were on fire that day. Of my two slogans, my favourite was, 'I love my LGBT kids (and you too, Harvey!)', though it was probably the one declaring Alice had been on the waitlist for 102 weeks that caught the eye of a photojournalist covering the march.

The rest of the month passed without much drama until Alice came down one morning with a declaration of her own: she was thinking of moving to Brighton, where Keith was at university. They were going to look at a house, could I drop them at the station?

Wow, ok, I said. They took the train together and met a man about a house share on Albion Hill.

We're going to take it, she said, when they returned. I might take an access-to-university course once I'm settled in, she said.

Peter and I were completely blindsided. It turned out Alice and Keith had been plotting for months; for them, it was a done deal. We wanted time to discuss it and weigh up the pros and cons, but as is the way with the rental market, a decision needed to be made. We agreed that on the whole, this was a really positive step and one we should support. We signed all the paperwork.

Now I was even more motivated to get Alice help. I'd learned that there was a GP surgery in Brighton with a trans GP, Dr J. We should get you registered there, I said, as soon as you move.

Ok, she said.

But it wouldn't prove so easy.

September 2022

More trips to Brighton and a place called Bridport

Kate announces she has entered the Brighton & Hove Triathlon and asks if I can take her down there for a trial sea swim. I look the start point up on a map. It's away from the part of Brighton I associate with Alice, so I agree.

The first time we go, the sea is millpond flat, but the next time, the breakers are rolling in. There's a sign for lifeguards on lookout, but maybe that's just at the weekend, because there's no one in sight. I refuse to enter the water and don't want Kate to either. I watch help-lessly from the beach as she bobs in and out of view.

I have a bad knee which stops me joining Kate on training runs, but I manage to take her out on a few road rides, even though cycling has become quite triggering for me, something I've not really enjoyed since Devon.

My mood is flat when the day of the triathlon arrives, but I muster enthusiasm, for Kate. Harvey comes down on the train to surprise her. She does well; we're all so proud of her and want to celebrate with a good lunch. Harvey has his heart set on a vegan restaurant somewhere or other. Bimini Bon-Boulash has recommended it on *Off Menu*. I'm exhausted and Harvey's vague about the location. It's ok, he says, looking at Google Maps, we can walk. It turns out to be on the far side of Brighton, quite close to where Alice used to live. As we walk, I become aware I'm on a familiar road. I'm not certain at first, but then I realise where I am. Trance-like, I press forward, even though there are roads to my left and right, down which I could escape. I'm compelled to follow this route. The route I took with

Alice, the last time I saw her. I don't tell anyone, until we get to the Krispy Kreme shack and I break down and cling to Harvey. You should have said, he says. Maybe part of me wanted to feel the pain, I say.

Not long after this I start to develop problems with my shoulder. It hurts when I move it beyond a certain range, which is becoming increasingly restricted. The swimming that has been helping me heal my wounded psyche has to stop.

Late in September I am on my laptop, distracting myself from grief by deleting several thousand unread emails when I hit upon one from the Bridport Prize. I have been on their mailing list since my Open University creative writing course when Alice was little. Once or twice, I've submitted a poem or a piece of flash fiction to one of their competitions, my short story about slimy sausage-finger Bob. This email is an invitation to submit to their inaugural memoir competition. They only need five to seven thousand words, the promo says. There are two days to the deadline. I can do that, I think. I sit down at the dining table and write a stream-of-consciousness dump of everything that's happened over the last few years, and press send.

July–October 2021

A couple of house moves

A few days after Alice's trip to Brighton with Keith, we moved house, a move made with Alice at the forefront of our minds.

That evening, Alice took a shower.

What's that noise? asked Harvey.

I told you 1960s houses have no soundproofing, I said, it's the pipes.

He went to get another beer from the fridge. Guys, he yelled, come quick. Water was pouring down the kitchen wall, the floor awash.

With a few beers in my belly I laughed and laughed, was uncharacteristically unfazed, but in the morning, when we discovered the oven and dishwasher no longer worked, that the kettle and toaster too would only function if plugged in at different sockets, the reality began to hit home. We'd been sold a pup. We lived through that summer with a hob and a microwave, and appliances connected via extension cables through an open window to a power supply in the garage, whilst we got quotes for the anticipated building work, plus these unexpected repairs. Alice was glad to move out two months later. Her grotty student house was better equipped than her parents' one.

We had no idea how she would cope, how we would cope. We were anxious, but it had been a pleasure to see her in such good spirits over the preceding few months as she'd planned this big step. Once Alice moved out, we were up and down the M23 to help her. A couple of times I had to ask Keith to check on her, because she'd stopped responding to texts. Once, I flew down in a panic when even Keith couldn't locate her. She answered the door bleary-eyed, what are you doing here?

Alice, I was worried, no one knew where you were.

I'm fine, she said, laughing a little at my expense. I was just asleep.

It was a challenge not to do this more often. Fear was never far away and now that Alice lived independently it became harder to manage. I started to explore Rightmove for a property in Brighton. If we sold up, we wouldn't have to go through another onslaught of renovations. It would be nice to live beside the sea, I said.

October 2022

Another injury, a sort of understanding

In mid-October Peter and I head off on our trip to Greece. It starts badly, with tears in the departure lounge. Then the weather's not great and my sore shoulder means I can't enjoy many of the sports on offer. Peter keeps himself busy and looks after me as best he can. I meet a retired doctor who has written a screenplay, has a film in production. I tell him a little of my writing dreams. Do it, he says.

I find some moments of serenity gently rowing out to the boundary of the water-sports area. The urge to keep paddling on is there, but not as strong as the desire to get back home. To do something with this life I have.

On our return, Peter decides his hand, which is taking longer than expected to heal, is strong enough for him to go back to CrossFit. In his second class, he cuts his shin open to the bone doing box jumps. It's hard for him to get around on the crutches he now needs, because they hurt his hand. He is bereft. He cries and cries, imagining months ahead when he may not be able to exercise at all. I feel so sorry for him. We manage to have a conversation about how we are managing our grief so differently. Peter finally comes to understand that he cannot expect me to need the things he needs, that to expect it is counterproductive somehow. I will get there at my own rate, I say. I don't afford him quite the same respect; his closing off from his feelings frustrates me enormously. He's started talking to a Cruse counsellor, which is something.

September–October 2021

Rekindled anxiety, our Brighton local, an impromptu haircut

Alice enrolled on a university access course to read humanities with social sciences, with cautious optimism. It wasn't ideal but it would do, and at just three days a week, it was a perfect springboard to the university path her brother and sister, her friends had all taken. With the college only a five-minute walk from her house, she got in easily at first, but her ability to attend didn't last long. We'd underestimated the demands of the course, fooled by the infrequent hours of face-to-face tuition time. The expectation for private study was huge; the course was designed for individuals with a high degree of motivation, something Alice lacked. She struggled and fell behind, which brought back familiar anxieties from her school days and she became withdrawn. I travelled up and down to attend meetings with tutors and support staff, but about halfway through term we agreed she would drop out and maybe try again next year when she was more settled and not having to cope with the new experience of living independently. She should focus on the day-to-day caring for herself for now, this was progress, maybe look for work.

In my day, I got work by word of mouth or answering handwritten adverts in shop windows, by popping my head around the door and asking, are there any jobs? Things are less like that now. Alice tried to apply for a job at Aldi, but the online form had boxes for which she hadn't got an answer. She got quite stuck, angry. The few times I ever saw her rage were at inanimate objects and unfathomable rules, not at people, rarely at me.

Perhaps you could get a job in a pub, I suggested, you can just ask at the bar. There was one not far from Alice's house that we'd started to visit, the Brighton Tavern, that I thought was ideal.

Peter and I had come down to see Alice one day, but she wasn't in the mood to see us for long, so after a quick cup of tea, we went looking for a place to eat. It was that awkward time between 5.30 and 6 – cafés were closing but restaurants weren't open yet or were empty and soulless. We decided a pub might fit the bill, but the first one we eyed up didn't serve food. Let's just stop for a pint, I said. It felt frivolous, light-hearted and spontaneous, words that weren't really in our vocabulary much at the time. Ok, said Peter, yes. We went inside and were immediately filled with positive energy. It was a Brighton pub, of course, so not surprising, but this one more than some of the others we'd been in seemed particularly queer. It had all the usual leaflets, flyers and phone numbers stuck to a noticeboard, for LGBTQ+ groups and activities, some of the staff had an androgynous look that was not easily pinned down and there was a particularly gorgeous Action Man above the optics, with a rainbow mermaid tail. Peter and I drank our beers with tears in our eyes. Alice could be ok here, we turned and said to each other. For the first time in almost two years, we believed.

The Brighton Tavern became our Brighton local, either with or without Alice. On one occasion, I asked them if they needed staff. We always need staff, the bartender replied, get your daughter to pop in. But she never did.

One day, I got a rare call from Alice. She'd attacked her long hair with kitchen scissors in a moment of acute stress. She wanted to come home, so I could help her sort it out. I did my best, but this needed a proper hairdresser. She wouldn't go.

Shave it off, she said.

Are you sure?

Yep, she said, do it.

Alice found Peter's clippers and plugged them in.

You look just like Kate, I said, once the job was done.

She skipped upstairs, happy with the result, and left me sweeping up clippings from the kitchen floor. As I unplugged the clippers, I realised they were plugged into one of the decommissioned sockets after the shower incident. I tried all the other out-of-action sockets and appliances. One by one they switched back on. Every cloud, I thought. The weather was turning cold and I could finally close my kitchen window.

Peter and I brought up Alice's impromptu haircut at the next Allsorts session. We were worried that she didn't have much resilience, no decent coping strategies if something was troubling her. A trans parent in the group reassured us. It's a thing, she said, a rite of passage. I'll put feelers out amongst the community to be kind to a young trans woman with a buzz cut. We'll look after her. But Alice never did, as far as we were aware, participate in the trans world that Brighton could have offered her.

November 2022

A film I don't watch, a remembrance service I don't attend

In early November we travel to see Ali and Elis. I'm afraid of seeing them, in case they think I'm better, but I cry on and off for the entire weekend, which is something of a relief. Ali suggests a movie afternoon, recommends a light-hearted family comedy, but within moments, I realise the lead role is played by Robin Williams. I can't watch it, this man who killed himself, blaring into the living room. It takes me a few minutes before I pluck up courage to ask for it to be turned off. I suppose this is the self-care I need to find. Being able to protect myself.

The next day, when we are trying to decide what to do, Peter asks, why did we stop watching that film yesterday?

You can't remember? I say.

No, he replies.

You're unbelievable, I say.

Driving home, we listen to Alice's playlist. I am able to do that now. I find myself feeling angry with Alice for the first time. She's fucked everything, I say. She's fucked us over. Our lives are fucked. Pleasure has become a dirty word. I can't enjoy anything, even a few days with a couple of my closest friends. But I can't feel angry with Alice for long, she was such a gentle person. The best part of the weekend, Ali saying that very thing, that her overriding memory of Alice is that she was just this, gentle.

Whilst we've been away, Mum's attended an annual remembrance service for the bereaved at our local church. I'd found out about it via a flyer that came through her door. Mum's not a churchgoer, but my brother and his family are devout Christians. I'd suggested they might like to take her. I ask Mum how it went.

Dr A (Alice's GP, who has been recently ordained) spoke at the service, she tells me. I'm so relieved I didn't go. My feelings are ambivalent towards Dr A. She's part of the institution that let Alice down. She let Alice down. Though she's adapted her practice now, is quite vocal in supporting trans patients, has taken herself off for training and is trying to set up better care pathways and guidelines. It shouldn't be this way, that personal contact with a trans person, especially one who dies, is needed to change your mind. But it is a story I hear over and over again from medics and trans people I know and meet.

It must have been nice to see her, I say.

It was, she says, and some of my friends were there.

That's nice, I say.

There was lovely cake.

What was the service like? I ask.

The church was decorated beautifully, she replies.

And how was the service? I ask again.

She hesitates …

It didn't do it for you, did it? I say.

No, she says. It just made me sad.

Isn't that the point, Mum? Why you were there – to remember those you've lost?

I prefer to remember the good times with Daddy, that's what got me through, she says. And the same with Alice.

I feel quite hostile towards my mother for a moment. I feel that her disapproval of the service is a disapproval of my grief. I am a leaky vessel, too emotional for my own good.

November is drawing to a close. For three days, I've been wearing the same floral, navy and orange grandad-style nightshirt over a pair of green camouflage joggers, with an oversized jumper in a bright electric blue. My slippers are purple and have holes in. And I smell. Yet if the doorbell rings, I answer with total disregard for how I look. Perhaps it is a statement. Look, everyone, look how damaged I am. I just want people to take me as they find me, to accept me, however different I may now seem. This grief that Alice has given me is certainly helping me see her life more clearly. But today the GLP are coming to interview us for a promotional video, so I shower and dress, pop on some make-up. These things that involve Alice some-how – visiting Brighton, the funeral, seeing her friends – are when I do my best, to put my face on and try. Not that you'd think so to look at me when the video comes out.

October 2021

A couple of coats and a sense of being heard

I went to Brighton again. Alice needed a winter coat. She tried loads on, was more engaged than she had been for ages, with strong opinions about what she did and didn't like. In the end, I bought her two. An impractical fake fur bomber jacket and a full-length khaki puffer coat. This will be great for long winter walks on the beach, I said. Yeah, yeah, she sighed. Can we go home now? I'm tired.

Back at her house, I popped upstairs to use the loo. As I came back down, I heard Alice talking to Keith in his bedroom. She was showing him her purchases. We got this one, which is a bit more fun, she said, and this one, which will be great for long winter walks on the beach. I smiled to myself; she did listen to a little of what I said, after all.

Maybe on this occasion, maybe another, when Alice was being chattier than usual, I asked about Megan. We've split up, she said, but we're still good friends. We thought it was better, with us in different countries and neither of us really able to travel by ourselves. To me, it sounded like a rational, adult decision had been reached and I was proud of her, of them both. I did not know Megan, but it was good to hear they were ok.

A few weeks later, Peter and I went to see Alice together. We'd been to a wedding near by, so it was convenient to drop in, we said. It was good to have a reason for our visit, so it didn't look like we were fussing over her too much. She was wearing a brown fake suede flying jacket that she'd bought in a local charity shop since my last visit. I never saw her wear her quilted khaki coat again.

November 2022

Dinner guests, divorce and distractions

Trevor and Julie are coming for dinner. For the first time in months, I'm genuinely looking forward to a social occasion beyond my immediate family. Trevor has been the best friend to Peter since Alice died. One of the few who can be both sincere and amusing in the same way he was before. And his wife, Julie, though I don't know her very well, is also someone I completely trust.

Tonight, we're having moules marinière followed by pasta puttanesca and panna cotta for dessert and I've prepared it all myself. The evening feels quite normal, until halfway through the starter, Peter asks if he can put some music on. That's fine, I say. It's thoughtful of him to ask. Other than Alice's playlist, I've rarely listened to music since she died. It is altogether too euphoric, or too sad. But present company permits me a little relaxation of my grief.

Hey, Google, he calls, play Bronski Beat. I freeze. I can't believe what he's done. The opening bars of 'Smalltown Boy' burst out of the speakers. A conundrum of a song, full of upbeat disco energy but with such a sad story at its core. A song from Alice's playlist and the final song we played at her funeral, as all the mourners filed past her coffin, which I have not heard since.

Turn this off, I snap.

What?

Turn it off, what the fuck?

Sorry. Sonos stop. Stop, he's shouting, stop.

It's hey, Google, stop, I spit at him. Turn it off.

Google stop, he says.

The music still blares. Make it stop. I say it very slowly. I am pushing back my chair.

Stop, he says, stop.

Jesus, it's hey, Google, I shout. Hey, Google, for fuck's sake. You
could have pressed the fucking knob by now.

Sorry, he says again. I wasn't thinking.

Well, no, I say.

Finally, it's quiet, which feels like minutes, but is only seconds. I
look down at my plate, no one says anything. Excuse me, I say, I need
a moment. I take to the stairs and Peter makes to follow me. Get
away from, me, I hiss, recoiling from him. Upstairs, I sit on our bed,
trying to control my breathing. I'm spinning. I feel so attacked, so
wounded. Nowhere, no one is safe, not even my own husband,
particularly him. A man of habit, who has become even more regi-
mented since Alice died, because he knows too well the pain of
unpredictability, simply wasn't thinking. I'm so angry. I want to run
away, but I am trapped, we have guests. I count to ten, slowly calm
myself down. I can do this. I won't run and hide, shout or scream.
After a couple more minutes, I head back downstairs.

Why did you do that? I ask.

I don't know, I didn't think, Peter says again. He gets up to clear
away the plates.

Sorry about that, I say.

That's ok, they say.

He's a dick, I say.

He's under a lot of pressure, too, says Trevor gently.

I know, I say. I forgive him.

I don't, says Julie, which breaks the ice.

In bed the next day, crying on my own, as I often am these days,
I practise telling Peter what I feel I need to say: I don't think I can
live with you anymore. It's very hard and the words come out falter-
ingly and soft. Don't think I can stay married to you. I don't know

231

that I love you. I don't feel loved by you. This last one makes me convulse in a sob. I want a divorce, I say, though this doesn't feel true, so I repeat, I don't want to be married to you, which is easier a second time. I don't want to be married to anyone who ignores me, exacerbates my feelings that I don't matter. But I can't imagine life without him.

But instead of saying anything, I distract myself with Wordle, Dordle, Quordle, Octordle, Sudoku and Solitaire, by searching Rightmove for a little house by the sea, or in a city for me to retreat to, by checking my inbox of 3,000 unread emails by now, scrolling through them aimlessly. I spot a message that I could so easily have missed; you're going to be busy, it says. My teeth begin to ache, deep in their roots, the dull, nagging pain that I've experienced so many times before in my life when I've felt I might have done some terrible, unknown wrong and am about to be found out, when I think there has been a dreadful mistake. It's such an unpleasant sensation, but this time it is accompanying good news. Why? Perhaps because Bridport themselves must have made a mistake. Because it couldn't possibly be true. I've done it. I've been longlisted for a prize, a writing prize, me: the half-hearted Pilates teacher, the failed psychiatrist, the mother who let her child die. Writing about that child. What bitter-sweet news. The pain of the night before is packed away. I have to submit a further 10,000 words in just under a week. I haven't given it a thought since my submission. I clear my diary and sit down to write. It doesn't come as easily as before. I try to garner inspiration from sitting in Alice's grotty desk chair, but in truth, I am beginning to hate it. For it serves to remind me of the countless hours she spent online, in some other dimension.

Christmas 2021

Our last Christmas

Alice came home from Brighton for Christmas. It would be the first one in the new house. We planned to have Shin Ah, my brother's family and my mother. Peter's mum, Gill, was too poorly to come. Twelve in all. We were all looking forward to it. Alice was in good spirits. But in the run-up to Christmas Day, Covid reared its ugly head once more. Whilst rules and laws weren't put in place, Rosie, my niece, who's a midwife, felt she should not mix at Christmas and put her patients and their unborn babies at risk. Her younger sister, Grace, did the decent thing and stayed home, too. They did not know this was the last time their brother, Michael, would see Alice, that they had both already seen her for the last time, at some unremembered family gathering in my mother's garden. We did not know that though it was not the last day, it was the last occasion that the five of us would all be together. It was a lovely day.

December 2022

Conventions are hard to break, whilst a hip breaks quite easily

Our first Christmas without Alice is approaching. Peter and I are strained with one another. He's enrolled on a personal-training course which will straddle Christmas and New Year. He'll be out of the house for twelve hours a day for a month in total. It doesn't feel like good timing to me, but Peter is quite determined.

Mum calls. She is writing her Christmas round robin. I've put: Alice committed suicide and everyone was shocked, especially Caroline and Peter. Is that ok? she asks.

No, I say. I hate committed suicide because it harks back to when suicide was a crime. Alice didn't commit a crime.

Ok, she says.

Can you say something like: Alice took her own life after four years struggling with her gender identity, abandoned by the NHS?

Yes, I will, she says, and she does try. But Alice is the youngest of six grandchildren, so when I'm sent the letter for my final approval, I must first read about the accomplishments of the other five, before this final detail is revealed. Alice is left until last because she is the youngest, out of convention, I am sure, but in that moment, it feels as though her death isn't very important, or is an embarrassment, to be minimised. But I don't say anything to Mum. I can't control everything. In next year's newsletter, she puts the inquest first.

Peter comes home in pieces from a pre-Christmas social event with ex-work colleagues. No one spoke about Alice at all, he said. No one asked me how I was. I wonder whether some of them even knew.

Of course, they did, I say. I'm furious on his behalf.

He cries and cries. He didn't feel safe crossing the Thames, he says. It's dark, swirling waters looked like an escape.

Perhaps you should see a doctor, I suggest.

He admits for the first time that he cries every day. I haven't known. I feel so sad for him. He's so cut off.

Our first Christmas card arrives. I'm away at a friend's, to escape the friction between me and Peter which simmers away. Peter takes a photo of it and sends it to me. Dear Caroline, Peter, Kate and Harvey, it says. The absence of Alice's name hits me like a punch to the stomach; I feel tears pricking behind my eyes. Once I've recovered myself, I pick up my mobile and read on. The card has the usual pre-printed Merry Christmas sentiment, the sender sends their love. It's not explicitly unkind, but in its failure to specifically mention Alice, to only acknowledge her absence by omitting her name, I feel her death is forgotten, a mere trifle, no need to draw attention: moving on, moving on. They did not really know her, perhaps that prevents them from knowing what to say? But they know us, well enough for us to be on their Christmas-card list, well enough to buy a card and a stamp, to send love and good wishes. Why take the trouble to do this, but not take a moment longer, to think? Dear Caroline, Peter, Kate and Harvey, thinking of you all, this first Christmas without your darling Alice – that would cover it.

A week before Christmas is Gill's ninety-fourth birthday. She is quite poorly. Peter and I go to bed after seeing her and have a lovely, long afternoon nap. We feel closer than we have done for months.

Christmas is somewhat overshadowed when Gill falls and breaks her hip. Going to see her in hospital on Christmas morning takes the sting out of any enforced celebrations and the actual day is not nearly as bad as the anticipation. It is a Sunday. We have been having Sunday dinners as a family for many months now, since Harvey moved out to live with Shin Ah's family in September. It's become a routine. This is just another Sunday. Alice is thoroughly ignored.

For New Year, we stay in and go to bed before midnight. There is nothing to celebrate in the passing of one year and the starting of the next.

New Year 2021–22

How beautiful you all are

Our last New Year was very different. Alice was home from Brighton and was hosting a party at the new house that many of her friends had not yet seen. Our house is built to the same basic template as others on our suburban street, but in a different stone, giving it a brutalist vibe. A neighbour we met in the pub one evening told us it's known locally as the Kellogg's house, because there's a rumour it was a prize on the back of a Cornflakes packet. And inside, it is anything but suburban, with its split levels, travertine floors, plaster friezes, spiral staircase, mezzanine and double-height ceilings. It's a perfect party house, but the only person who properly made use of it for this was Alice.

Peter and I were wanted out of the way, so we went round the corner to Ian's to celebrate. We staggered home in the wee small hours to find Alice's friends all gathered by the front door ready to leave. It was a moment of joy. Quite tipsy, I hugged them all, told them how beautiful they all were and how nice it was to see them. It was the last time they were all together.

In early January 2022, Alice returned to Brighton. Perhaps she would get a job. There was a new course in the pipeline at Brighton Met, a how-to-study course, an access-to-the-access course, if you will. Perhaps she would register for that.

January 2023

Beginning to know my brother, a new group, a very vulnerable moment

Peter travels up to London for the final fortnight of his course. I can't stop crying. I go to see my GP. Perhaps I was hasty coming off my antidepressants, I say. She starts me on some new ones.

My brother comes to see me. We enjoy a crisp winter walk together. It is the best two hours I've had for a long time. Back at the house, we sit together on the grief-couch and I rest my head on his shoulder. I am reminded of that strange day in 1979, when I snuggled up to him at the dining table. This is the beginning of a new stage in my relationship with my brother.

Can I come back and see you next week? he asks. Would that be ok?

I'd like that, I say, very much.

Over the years we have only ever met up at Mum's or as families, so have never really spoken intimately with one another. Our relationship opens up. Whilst my brother was away at boarding school, he did not see what went on between me and Mum. I tell him about the rows, the dreaded hairbrush, how I longed to get away. In my fantasies, boarding school was the answer to everything. I imagined myself at Mallory Towers, taking on wild adventures with friends who would never let me down. In reality, I had an insecure attachment to my mother, so that on nights away at girl-guide camp I would cry homesick tears into my sleeping bag. My brother, on the other hand, longed to be at home, hated being separated from us. This I already knew.

I talk to him about his reaction, when I rang, the day Alice died. Not just the 'you're joking', but that I had to push him, force him to drop some other commitments and take care of our mother.

I have a lot of regrets about that day, he says.

Wouldn't it have been better for both of us, I say, if you'd said sorry at the time?

Yes, I guess, he says.

It's not a guess, I say. You're telling me you've lived with shame for almost eight months, I've lived with a niggle of irritation. You must know both could have been entirely avoided if we'd discussed it at the time.

It has always mystified me that people find this word, sorry, so hard to say, when for me it's as simple as night-night at bedtime, as necessary as breakfast in the morning.

I think of Alice, the child who always owned up (until she didn't, about the knife); of me, in perpetual fear that I've said something wrong, asking Peter over and over, what have I done? Always looking for things to apologise for.

Anyway, I say to my brother, I don't want you to feel shame. I forgive you, I say, a little tongue-in-cheek. You made a mistake, it was the shock, you didn't mean to hurt me.

I didn't, he says, I love you.

I know, I say. I love you, too.

That Alice's death has gifted us this new relationship is profoundly special.

In mid-January, I knuckle down to write another 15,000 words when I learn I am down to the final five for the Bridport.

Peter and I start to attend The Compassionate Friends (TCF) meetings. There may be a few shandy drinkers in the group, but there's bourbon for breakfast, liquid lunches and drunk by dinner, too. As strategies for coping, they probably shouldn't be recommended beyond the short term, but they make me smile. These people feel human; they have seen into the abyss and pulled themselves back. They talk with a compelling freshness, an honesty and awareness that I find instantly soothing. It is a group only for parents who have lost children, at any stage in their parenting journey. It's a place I feel safe, until a member of Peter's SoBS group comes along.

At SoBS, which Peter still attends monthly, people have known Alice is trans from the outset. Here, at TCF, we haven't revealed this part of her. It's nice not to have to explain, not to feel people's curiosity. And although people in the group are exactly what it says on the tin, compassionate, I don't know their politics, their views on trans people. I can't face any negativity; I want Alice to be a daughter like any other daughter. I don't tell lies, but if I wanted to, I could. I could make up the ballet lessons and the party dresses and … here I get a little stuck, because there isn't much else to imagine. Little children have more in common than that which separates them. Right up until puberty there was no significant gender distinction between Alice and Lucy, just the convention of the clothes they wore, that and the style of their hair: short for Alice, longer for Lucy. I wish children's clothes were more gender neutral, that I could look back and see pictures of Alice in pale pink, raspberry and peach, or blues and greens, but floral or swirly, patterned and bright, not the grungy washed-out navys, khakis and browns of a boy's wardrobe. But all I have are pictures of her in combats and hoodies, t-shirts festooned with sharks or VW camper vans, Alice as surfer dude. It is difficult at first, when I look back on old photos. I feel such sadness. Obviously, Alice has died, but there is another layer, the clothes. I resent the gender stereotypes that we direct our children into, out of nothing more than convention. But slowly, I grow to love looking back at her old photos. I see past the clothes and see the child, my daughter. She is what matters. But will other people understand?

So, we keep Alice's trans identity secret for a while. It's not as if I really want to tell any complicated lies, about the girl childhood she never had; I think it's more that here, I can give Alice what she longed for, acceptance and trust. Here, Alice is absolutely 100 per cent the girl she begged her father to make her that morning, curled up on her bedroom floor, pleading and pleading, make me a girl. Here, she is, was and always will be Alice, and I don't want to let that go. But the arrival of someone who knows in the group, who may spill the beans, changes everything. I feel unsafe again, so we will tell them, I say. But for now, I ask Peter for one more month.

On 27 January 2023, we travel down to Brighton for Alice's pre-inquest review hearing. Despite over ten years working in mental health services, where I'd cared for several patients who took their own lives, or once, the life of another, I've never been involved in an inquest, have never been in a coroner's court. This one is small and grubby, quite Dickensian and depressing.

The clerk of the court asks us to identify ourselves.

Harvey goes first. Harvey Litman, he says.

And you're Alice's brother?

Yes, says Harvey.

Next, it's me. I'm Caroline, Alice's mother, I say, Litman, too.

May I offer my condolences, the clerk says.

Thank you, I say, then looking over his shoulder, to Harvey: you didn't get any!

Harvey laughs.

What? asks the clerk.

Condolences, I say. Are they only reserved for mums?

The clerk is embarrassed.

Sorry, I say. It was a joke.

The hearing is mostly procedural. Our barrister, who we have just met for the first time, engaging with the coroner about the scope of the inquest, whether something called Article 2 has been engaged, whether Alice's right to life has been breached by the state. The coroner doesn't think it has, but she leaves the door open for our counsel to argue it at the full inquest, which is booked for three days in September.

As we leave the court, our counsel turns to us and says, this may be the worst coroner's court she's ever sat in, but our coroner is the best of those she's met. We feel lucky, we would certainly rather have it this way round.

There has been some press interest at the pre-inquest review hearing and a few days later, a team from BBC South come to the house to interview us for a broadcast piece. An article is posted on the BBC News website. It is a top-ten news story for a while. This bodes well for the reach of the full inquest, we think. We are likely to make the news headlines. It is what we want. We just have to hope someone famous like Elton John doesn't die on the day and steal our thunder, I say.

January 2022

Jane's change of heart

Almost a year had passed since Jane reached out about her possible change of heart with regard to trans issues, but we still hadn't really discussed this in any depth. We'd both been busy – she with her various medical and surgical appointments, me with Alice in one way or another. We had one awkward dog walk when Jane found out she'd missed out on our silver-wedding bash. I'd mentioned the party, then seen her bristle before she said something about being unworthy of an invite. I was embarrassed because in the moment I'd forgotten she was not there and couldn't remember why I hadn't invited her.

Now, finally, we were both ready to talk.

Jane recalled the time I delivered my ultimatum: that she had to find a way to feel differently if she wanted to keep me and Alice in her life. I felt dreadful, she said, I wanted to support you, but I had no idea how to change the way I felt, or whether I even wanted to.

I didn't expect you to change, I said.

I didn't expect to either, she replied.

I was so angry, she said. I was a right little Millie Tant. All I could think was, how dare men tear down women's hard-won rights and invade their spaces. Women's rights seemed to be going backwards. And trans women were so reductive, in their high heels and blonde wigs. It was so demeaning to actual women, I was livid.

Alice doesn't dress that way, I said.

I know, said Jane. I just enjoyed being shouty and brave on Mumsnet, with people who agreed with me. She went on: I wanted to appear strong, smart and witty (which she always had, to me), but

I felt timid, stupid and dull. Joining the TERF* army made me feel all of the former and none of the latter. It made me feel safe.

I can see how that would happen, I said. How did things change?

It was Benedict, she said. (He is her eldest son.) I told him about Alice and he just said, well, if you think you're a woman, then you're a woman, and if you think you're a man, you're a man. It's not really complicated. I didn't agree, of course, she said. He sent me a link to a YouTuber – ContraPoints – to a particular video about JK Rowling, who had been embroiled in a TERF/trans Twitter storm at the time. The video was eighty-nine minutes long. I closed it straight down. I wasn't going to spend an hour and a half watching some pro-trans bullshit.

But you did?

Yes, a while later. To show good faith. To prove I was open to change, whilst believing nothing would change my mind, I decided to watch ten minutes.

How did that go?

I was completely drawn in. I watched it in one sitting.

When was this?

Probably about six months after we fell out about it.

So, well before our party, then?

Yes, but you were right not to invite me. I wasn't an ally when you really needed me.

Jane went on to tell me that Natalie Wynn – ContraPoints – was funny, clever and likeable,and that she was quite pissed off that it was really hard to argue with anything she said.

---

* TERF (trans-exclusionary radical feminist) was originally used to describe an advocate of radical feminism who did not recognise the legitimacy of transgender identities and opposed the inclusion of trans women in the feminist movement. It is now widely used to describe anyone with perceived transphobic views, especially those who ascribe to gender critical feminist beliefs.

I was floored, actually, she said. I watched more of her videos, different people's videos, I read and read. In not much time at all, I changed my mind.

Wow, I said.

I didn't mean to.

I've hardly read anything, I confessed.

Well, you're living it, aren't you, Jane replied. That's enough for now.

So, Jane and I healed our relationship. I was full of admiration and gratitude towards her. She'd bravely challenged her preconceptions and dared to be vulnerable, for me and for Alice.

February 2023

A murder, a vigil, a speech and Alice's twenty-first

I have been struggling for some time with the fact of Alice's cremation. As is my way, I am wishing I'd trusted my instincts and argued
my corner for a burial. Which is probably why, despite my promise to
Keith in July, Alice remains at the undertakers.

Peter is quite agitated that she still doesn't have a final resting
place. He needs this, a physical spot in order to commune with her.
We agree to sort it out before her birthday. We contact the crematorium and discover we can have a traditional full-size plot anyway,
amongst the graves of those who have been buried. This settles my
qualms; it will give the appearance of a burial, without a body decay-
ing under the ground.

We tell Kate our discovery. You can put us both with her once we
are gone, I say, as a selling point.

I don't care where I go, says Peter.

Well, I want to be with her when my time comes, I say. Do you
want to come with us this afternoon to choose a plot?

Kate looks at her nails, says she has a lot to do and goes to her
room. Perhaps it is too much, to have inserted my inevitable death
into the conversation.

Harvey and Shin Ah come for dinner. He senses an atmosphere.
What's up? he asks.

Kate's been a bit off, I say.

I'll come with you tomorrow, he assures me.

We choose a plot next to a bench, and as a bonus, there is a headstone near by that is top-to-toe Times New Roman, but halfway

down declares, *Jesus is Lord!* in Comic Sans. We think Alice would have honked like a goose.

Brianna Ghey, a fifteen-year-old transgender girl, is murdered in a park in Warrington. A few days later, Peter and I attend a vigil in Brighton, a stone's throw from where Alice lived. I turn to Peter: I was just thinking we should message Alice to come down and meet us. Me too, he confides. I am glad, momentarily, that she doesn't know the news, then feel sick, that she's not here.

The trans community is upset and angry. The first speaker rails against passive cis allies, that they are no use if they stay quiet and do nothing, that they are practically useless. I feel attacked, although I know he is not personally attacking me. Later, I take the open mike, but I have nothing prepared and feel I get it all wrong, do not say what I could have said. I am an interloper, out of my depth in a world I don't understand. I bump into my creative-writing tutor from my days at the Open University who is a staunch trans ally. He says I did ok. But I don't believe him. I can't sleep for days afterwards, ruminating about what I should and shouldn't have said. I am not cut out to be an activist.

Since Alice died, we've managed Harvey's, Peter's, Gill's and Kate's birthdays. There is one more to go before we face Alice's first birthday without her here. My mum is about to turn ninety-six. I'm supposed to be going to see her for lunch with my brother. On the day, as I'm wrapping a present for her, I break down. I will never be wrapping a present for Alice, who should be turning twenty-one in two days. Another spasm of grief assails me. I miss my mother's birthday and have to hope she makes it to ninety-seven.

––––––––

For Alice's twentieth birthday we visited her in Brighton, but Kate couldn't come, she was in Leeds. The four of us had a fabulous time, some cocktails and a burger, but we were not five. There would be other birthdays. Her next one would be a big one, her twenty-first. We would make sure everyone was available for that, we said. We'd have a proper party. In the event, of course, we didn't.

———————

I want Alice home for her birthday, with us, I say, with me. This is not just the day Alice was born, but the day I gave birth, though this last bit goes left unsaid. Peter and I go and collect her in plenty of time. It will be just four again, a different four this year. Kate stays over with friends the day before; she doesn't want to wake up in the house on Alice's birthday and find it impossible to leave us, for she has important lectures she doesn't want to miss. She will come home for dinner. Harvey arranges to work from home. We tell them both that we plan to visit Alice's spot we've booked at the crematorium, although she is not there yet – there is only a black stake, with a piece of laminated card stating LITMAN to mark the spot. We'll take cards we've written for her, flowers and a helium balloon.

We haven't been organised. It's hard to do anything that concretely reminds us Alice has gone. The day arrives and we head to the post office to buy a balloon. I don't want it to say Happy 21st; we aren't happy. I want it to be pink, not blue. There isn't a single one that fits the bill. These little things that aren't really important take on such huge significance; each time I fail to get it right is a reminder of every failure that came before. I run my fingers through the balloon stand one last time and I find it: 21 today, it says, in pink. No more, no less, no exclamation marks, no congratulations or happiness expressed.

In the car park, a preschooler walks by with their grandmother. Balloon! they say.

Yes, she replies, someone's having a birthday.

They're going to be twenty-one, the child continues.

Yes, says the gran.

Did you hear that? I ask Peter.

No, what?

Tears are streaming down my face and Peter doesn't know why, so I am obliged to repeat the exchange out loud.

No, I didn't hear, he says again.

And I cry a little more, I think because I feel quite alone.

Peter and I are close, then we are not. It takes very little for a huge void to open up between us. But we won't have a fight. Not today.

Harvey wants to come with us to the crematorium, so we pick him up from the station en route. It's a pleasure being there with him. He is so thoughtful. Where graves have football memorabilia on display, he stops for a moment to say how their team is doing.

Afterwards, Peter wants to eat cake, to remind him of Alice; our midnight baker who surprised us with fresh scones or chocolate fudge cake some mornings. Peter would never eat it, not for break-fast, whilst I could never resist, felt it rude not to. So, if Peter is saying he wants cake, then cake we must have. We head to Annaré, for the best carrot pistachio cake in the country.

Did you bring Alice here? asks Harvey.

No, I say. Sorry.

That's a shame, he replies.

She'd have liked it, we agree. We can pretend.

Whilst there, I buy fancy savoury aniseed snacks that I used to buy occasionally if we had guests. Once, Alice came down in the night and ate them all. She made no distinction between these 'grown-up' treats and Monster Munch or Hula Hoops. Whilst her siblings, espe-cially Harvey, always asked first, Alice never asked permission to take a biscuit from the tin, a packet from the cupboard – one of her few bad habits, that as the youngest, she got away with more than she should have done. Perhaps because my parenting style had changed and this transgression seemed less important somehow than it used to, or maybe it was just that she was so good about everything else.

When Kate arrives for dinner, the snacks are out on the counter. Why did you buy these? she asks.

They remind me of Alice, I say.

She didn't even like them, says Kate.

Yes, she did, I snap. My hackles rise.

I argue, after all, just not with Peter. I suppose Alice's twenty-first without her was always going to be difficult.

The next day, Alice's friends come for drinks and pizza. Bea and Iona fold Alice's clothes that we have left in a crumpled heap into neat piles. Keith pores over her Dungeons and Dragons plans; Iona says it is lovely to see Alice's face in ours. Says she knew Alice felt loved because of how she spoke about us, and that whilst we think Alice was an outsider in our family, they can see exactly how she fitted in.

After her birthday gathering, I begin to feel a bit better overall. Nine months have passed – the same time I carried Alice in my womb. It feels significant somehow, that I should start to feel better now. I can get up in the morning, I feel reborn. I start to drink my morning cup of tea again, a daily ritual, abandoned after Alice died, perhaps because the making of a cup of tea is that peculiarly British way of managing in a crisis, but it cannot fix this.

And each making of a cup of tea brings me pleasure, for as I squeeze the bag out between my fingers and thumb, I'm reminded of Alice. Of the Hedbanz game we used to play as a family. She was very young and struggling to guess what she was. You're something you use to take the teabag out of a cup of tea, I said. Cheating by saying tea, not once, but twice. Fingers! she proclaimed. The answer is teaspoon, of course, but for her, 'fingers' was the right answer. It was something she had seen me do, over and over again: take the teabag out of a cup of tea with my fingers. I'll let you have that, I said, laughing.

The Bridport result arrives. I do not win or come second but am highly commended. I am delighted, but conflicted, for I am only here because Alice has died. Better to have done this and feel some happiness, whilst impossibly sad, than feel only and always impossibly sad, says Peter. Thank you, I say.

I now have a goal. Perhaps I can get an agent. I mention my memoir to Jolyon Maugham from the Good Law Project, who has just published a book. He emails his agent about my prize. I begin to believe in possibilities. It gives me a reason to live.

Around this time, Gill's health deteriorates. She has recurrent chest infections and is prescribed several courses of antibiotics in quick succession. They work a little, but she really needs them intravenously. She is offered a hospital admission. We talk with her about whether this is what she wants. She decides against it, even though she knows what this might mean. I fully support her decision – I think it is the right one – but I cry and cry. I don't want her to die. Don't want anyone to die.

March–April 2022

Alice turns a corner

Alice was troubled on and off by anxiety for almost half her life, her adolescence characterised by episodes of very poor mental health, interspersed with periods of hope and positivity. Surprisingly, each suicide bid and the shaving of her head led to some temporary improvement; perhaps because in the aftermath, we were more attentive to her needs and things got done, or appeared to. And unsurprisingly, but strikingly, every moment when her transness was celebrated or embraced, when she was accepted as Alice, her mood soared, but it never lasted.

Until the spring of 2022, when she really did finally seem to be turning a corner.

In early March, Alice and Keith took a coach to Bath to see a friend at university there. Travelling on public transport was something she hadn't been able to do for a very long time. Her improvement was plain for all to see.

A month later, we went with Alice, together with another family we had met through Allsorts, to Eastbourne library for a Q&A with Shon Faye about her book. Alice uncharacteristically asked if we would buy her a copy, which we queued up for Shon to sign. The six of us went for pizza afterwards. It was unheard of, for Alice to meet happily with strangers in this way. It was another sign that she was doing well.

March 2023

Expectations, Mother's Day, a problematic professor

I manage a night out with Matt and Gareth, friends from school. They are both immensely kind, but don't dig too deeply into my inner world, and, perhaps because they are men, it doesn't bother me. In this sense, I think I am harsher on my women friends from whom I expect a more nuanced approach. But actually, this sex stereotype is a lazy one. Some men and some women are brilliant, some of each are rather rubbish. The ones who get it right, like Matt and Gareth, are the ones who seem to like spending time with the new me as much as they did with the old one. They have no expectation of me, are not constantly pushing to have old Caroline back. And because they are prepared to sit with the difficult new one, it is these people who are more likely to be rewarded with glimpses of the old me, who still exists but is less likely to come out to play these days, certainly not on demand.

I awake on Mother's Day feeling no worse than usual. A few friends message that they are thinking of me, on this, my first Mother's Day without Alice, which is kind and welcome. I go and see my own mum. She has a swollen leg and I'm worried it's a DVT. I feel panicky that my mother may die from a complication, but also about the prospect of a visit to accident and emergency. In the end, my fear of going back to hospital with her wins the day and I tell Mum to make a doctor's appointment in the morning, but if she gets breathless or develops chest pain in the middle of the night, to call an ambulance. I'm afraid she may die because I'm too afraid to get her seen, but my drive to go home is stronger. Mum does take herself off to the GP, who agrees with my provisional diagnosis, but the necessary scan is not available for three days, so I feel less guilty for doing nothing on Sunday. It turns out to be a ruptured Baker's cyst. Not everything is a tragedy in progress.

The last day of March is Transgender Day of Visibility. It is also tutorial day. A Zoom meeting with an English professor for the five finalists in the Bridport, part of our prize. I'm excited but nervous. I have imposter syndrome. Ahead of the day, we have each been sent the other's entries. One of the finalists, Patricia, has emailed me to say she too has a trans child. It is quite a remarkable coincidence, I think. Her email is full of warmth and intimacy that make me trust her, though not completely. She is a published writer and creative-writing tutor, so I feel insignificant and small.

The tutorial involves the professor talking to us all individually about our entries, in front of the others. I am the second to go. At first, I am amazed when he says he also has a trans child. Patricia unmutes her mic and tells everyone about her son. It is inexplicable good fortune, until the professor proceeds to misgender both Alice and his own child, so I'm unclear if he has a son or a daughter, in which direction the transition went. I'm aghast. I see Patricia's eyebrows rise. I find my voice. Please don't misgender my child, I say. Yes, well, he blusters; he has to ask what pronoun he should use, although he has supposedly read my entry. Her name is Alice, I say.

April 2022

A night out and another assault

Easter was approaching, and as Alice's friends would be home from university, she decided to move back in with us for a month or so, so she could hang out with them more easily. Her first night out was a trip to Wetherspoons. It did not end well. Around 11 p.m., I got a rare phone call.

Please come and get me. She was sobbing down the phone, please come now.

What's happened, darling? I asked.

Just come, she said.

Peter and I rushed out to find her. She was huddled, alone, in a bus stop away from the high street. She had grazes on her cheek and forehead and streaks of blood on her neck, from a cut ear. She was inconsolable. We couldn't do anything but hold her until she relaxed enough to speak.

Back in 2004, a BBC show awarded Leatherhead the title Worst High Street in the UK. Now, in 2022, it was once again making the news. A bar had opened up with a bizarre dress code. For ladies, bodycon dresses, sexy black heels and form-fitting tops were recommended to ensure entry. Alice found it hilarious but was also furious.

I was walking to the station and there were all these people queuing to get into Beluga, she said. I was so angry, all these women dressed up, and their boyfriends thinking it's ok, all of them thinking it's ok.

What did you do? I asked.

Nothing, I didn't do anything, she said.

Alice?

I just challenged them, that's all, on their thinking, that they should choose this sexist shithole for a night out. And they attacked me.

Who? The people in the queue?

No, the bouncers. I was on the ground and I couldn't breathe. She started crying again. They kept misgendering me and pinning me down and everyone was just standing there. She wriggled away from my embrace; you're hurting my shoulder, she said. She pulled her top down to reveal another pavement burn, weeping and raw.

This is wrong, I said to Peter, we should call the police.

No, said Alice. No! Anyway, they've been. They were nice, actually. I'm a bit pissed about that. She managed a smile, they didn't misgender me at all, they were quite kind.

So, if they were kind, we should report it, I said again.

No, she said, no. Let's go home.

Back at the house, we cleaned Alice up and I took photos of her wounds, in case she decided to take things further. But she didn't want to draw attention to herself, so we left it.

April–2 May 2023

Not dead, a good death, a traumatic death

In mid-April Peter and I go to see Elton John, tickets rescheduled from three years previously; he hasn't died yet. He sings 'Tiny Dancer', another song from Alice's playlist, and the tears flow. After the gig, we return to Gill's flat to spend the night with her. She's deteriorating. Peter's sister, Mary, who's visited often over the last year to care for Gill when we've been unable to, comes back up the next day and the three of us stay with her every night from now on.

On my birthday, Gill takes another turn for the worse. The antibiotics are giving her terrible diarrhoea and the constant trips up and down to the loo are exhausting. She decides to stop taking them. She's tired, she says. She's had enough and is ready to go. Kate, Harvey and Shin Ah come over to go out for dinner for my birthday, but instead we get fish and chips and sit and eat them on the floor of Gill's living room, apologising for the tantalising aroma, for Gill cannot eat. She doesn't mind, she says, she is happy to have us all there.

The next day, when Peter and Mary are out, I have Gill to myself. I talk to her about dying. She tells me about when her father died. I was devoted to him and never thought I'd recover, but I did, she says, and so will you. We both cry a little, which for Gill is a rare offering.

Do you have any thoughts about where you're heading? I ask.

I have no idea, she says, laughing once more. I'm not sure I believe in any of that sort of thing.

Me neither, I say.

I will have to wait and see, she says.

257

Wherever you end up, I choke, if you happen to bump into Alice, tell her we love her, that we miss her.

I will, she says, taking my hand, I will.

I put my head in her lap and she strokes my hair. Peter comes in and finds us like this.

We are comforting each other, she tells him.

I am hugging Gill, but I am also hugging Alice. It is a birthday gift from her to me, this intimate and loving conversation with my mother-in-law. It feels as if she is about to go, but she stays with us for another seventeen days.

Because neither Peter nor I have any responsibilities, we can devote ourselves to this period of saying goodbye. The palliative care team are called in and support Gill's deepest wish, to die at home. She watches from her bed as the trees turn from bare, to blossomed to bedecked with leaves, and we watch with her. But some days it becomes too much for me and I have to spend a day back at the house on my own. Gill is so settled, so peaceful, our goodbyes fully realised in these final weeks, and the contrast with Alice's death breaks me. The trauma of it, her aloneness.

For five days, Gill sleeps. We sit around her bedside doing crosswords and word games, for a book is too absorbing and distracts us from the changes in her breath that we are tuning into. We mop her brow and comb her hair, massage moisturiser into her hands. And then, quietly and peacefully, she's gone. I am out when it happens, but it does not matter, for I have been there and said goodbye.

I am happy to say that Gill has gone, that she has passed away, but if people say it about Alice, I feel irritated, annoyed. Some people express surprise that I'm able to say she died, that Alice died. It is as if they believe it somehow makes her death easier to bear if we say – or hear – that she's gone, lost or passed away. I don't agree, though I know other bereaved parents prefer it.

Am I mad? I ask Kate. Unreasonable?

No, she says. Grandma deteriorated gradually, over a period of months, spent the last three weeks in bed, getting weaker and weaker, for five days slept without waking. It was only after all that that she died. That is a passing, a slipping away. It feels ok in those circumstances, don't you think? It sounds soft, gentle and simple.

Yes, I say.

But Alice didn't pass away, she says. She jumped off a cliff.

Yes, I say, again. I picture her skull slammed against stone, her clothes ripped apart, her stomach split open, her femurs fractured right through.

She died a traumatic death, Kate continues. People shouldn't try and sanitise it with passings and moving-ons. It's not true.

April 2022

A kitchen disco, a reaching out and a warning

Whilst Alice was home for the holidays, she announced that she and Keith were going to Norwich, another university town, to see Bea, with a bunch of school friends. They were getting a lift.

Alice, like Kate, had not learned to drive. When asked if they wanted to, they both described it as too big a responsibility, this entitlement to sit behind the wheel of a weapon that can – does – kill people every day. It does me good to remember this; it serves to tell me I am not responsible for every character trait, every decision my children take. For driving, for me, is not responsibility, but freedom.

Alice returned from this trip in good spirits, but tired. She spent a few days quietly in her room, but soon rejoined me and Peter downstairs, helped by Kate's return from Leeds for the Easter break.

Peter and I took Alice and Kate to the National Theatre to see *The Corn Is Green*, for my birthday. It was the one and only time I witnessed Alice use the ladies' loos, with me to accompany her. I was hypervigilant, ready to protect Alice at the slightest hint of antagonism. No one said anything, no one stared; one person gave her a casual glance, which may not have been about her transness at all and more about her buzz cut, or her filthy boots.

The next day, the four of us went for a curry at our favourite Indian restaurant. Alice was in the best mood I'd seen her in for ages. We sang in the car to music from her phone. I realised I'd never heard Alice sing before. She was awful, tone-deaf, but she didn't know it or didn't care, she was unfettered. It was a treat. We came home and had an impromptu disco in the kitchen, dancing and more singing, to

Kate Bush, Marina and the Diamonds. Alice moved her body as if she didn't have a care in the world. Harvey had left for his travels by now and missed it.

But this isn't the whole truth about those remarkable few weeks. We did sit and talk about her mental health, she and I.

You seem so well, Alice. Is this the whole picture? Do you still feel suicidal?

And unlike the time almost five years earlier when I asked that question and she couldn't talk at all, Alice opened up. She felt that she was in a well, she told me. That she was on a ledge, which was secure for now, but she might easily slip, as she had so many times before. And each time she did, she went a little deeper, but was caught, saved by another ledge. I never know if there's another ledge, she said, or if the next time I'll hit the bottom?

That sounds really scary, I said. I think you need to see your GP.

Yes, she agreed.

Would you like me to help you? I asked.

Yes, she said. Her agreeing to our collaboration, another sign of progress.

Almost nine months after she moved to Brighton, Alice finally sat down with me and completed the forms to register with the local GP I'd researched. A few days later, she sent an e-consult. This is what she wrote:

I'm a transgender twenty-year-old woman and I'm struggling.

I need to sort out my hormones, I don't think I'm on the right ones.

I often feel hopeless, and helpless and that life is not worth living.

I helped her overcome her anxiety when a question seemed ambiguous, impossible to answer. Is this ok? she asked each time. Yes, I said, it's good.

To the questions that would have ensured a rapid response – have you made any plans to end your life soon? Are you contacting us to assess your low mood and depression, your anxiety? – she answered, no.

She pressed send and we waited for an appointment to be offered.

Over the intervening days, I carried on talking with her. I talked about taking her overseas for surgery. It would be a challenge to arrange, but if it was what she wanted, I would make enquiries. Ok, she said.

And I asked about her e-consult. You wrote that life isn't worth living. Are you suicidal? Do you have a plan? And now, as I write, I remember her reply: I've found on the internet a place to jump off the cliffs, she said. And in the writing of this sentence, my teeth ache, and the tears stream, and all the guilt and shame come pouring out. For she told me, she did have a plan of sorts, and to have a plan is a significant risk, yet I did nothing.

But what, practically, could I do? She wasn't actively suicidal right there and then; there was no crisis. If anything, she seemed rather well. Trying to make her an urgent appointment anywhere would have been a waste of time. She wouldn't have been accepted, or if she had, she wouldn't have gone, or if she'd gone, she wouldn't have got the treatment she really needed. A full and thorough assessment of her needs around her gender incongruence and associated dysphoria would remain entirely unaddressed. This was what she asked for on her e-consult. This was what got her down.

We just talked some more. About the last few years.

You were such a transphobe, she joked.

I was, I said. You know how sorry I am about that, don't you?

I forgive you, she said, with a twinkle in her eye.

Thanks, I said.

I'm proud of you, she added.

Thanks, I said again. I'm proud of you, too.

It was both a profound but quite light-hearted conversation. She told me she loved me, that I was not to feel guilty if she did end her life. But I will, Alice, I will, I said. The only way to ensure that is for you not to do anything. She smiled and shrugged. Ok, she said.

She'd had enough of talking and made to go upstairs. You've got that request in now, I said to her back as she retreated. You'll be seeing the doctor soon.

Help was just around the corner. Her new GP, himself trans, would understand. If anyone could help, it would be him. It was such a relief.

May 2023

The first anniversary and a miracle

My mother's leg remains swollen from her ruptured Baker's cyst. I can see she has an infection brewing and it's the King's Coronation bank holiday weekend approaching. I take her to the GP and have yet another panic attack, begging the receptionist for an appointment. The practice nurse agrees to see her, whilst the receptionist furnishes me with her opinion that my mother won't be prescribed antibiotics if I'm only 'anticipating' an infection. The nurse calls a doctor in and antibiotics are prescribed. I burst into tears, not for my mum, but out of relief that I have done the right thing and she is not going to die because of any failure, omission or mistake on my part. I've done everything that I could. That which I didn't or couldn't do for Alice. I've got her past the gatekeepers.

The one-year anniversary approaches. In the preceding weeks, I've been silencing my mind with a frenzy of uncharacteristic gardening, but not the nurturing kind: chopping, lopping, digging up and throwing away.

Little things keep happening to break through the distraction of the moment and send me back to the sofa, my bed, for a precious diazepam from my dwindling supply. The police turn up with Alice's laptop and mobile. No evidence had been procured from her PC and her mobile data remains behind an unbreakable password. We are not told any details of what she did or didn't look at in the days and hours leading up to her death. I let it go. The hunt for a specific trigger nags less intently in my ear now a year has nearly passed. She's done it, and is gone, no number of answers will bring her back. Alice is dead.

The anniversary arrives. Messages drift in from friends and acquaintances. Not many, not like when Alice died. Our message at the funeral – please don't forget us – has been largely forgotten. Rebecca, who understands, comes all the way from Yorkshire to see me for the day. And Jane delivers a blanket for the grief-couch that she has been secretly crocheting, square by square for the past year, as an act of remembrance, an act of love.

We've made plans to drive to Brighton and go to the undercliff path, to lay flowers. At the funeral, I said Brighton would always be a place of pilgrimage for me, but I was wrong. I've thought about driving down often enough, to lay a flower, to just sit, where she last was, but I find I can't. Sometimes the urge to go back was to join Alice in that leap into the unknown. So, the failure to return isn't necessarily a failing, but a positive thing. I didn't go back because it wasn't safe; through lack of action, I protected myself. But the anniversary seems appropriate. I'm ready. It feels akin to going to see Alice – the next best thing.

Kate and I pop to a local florist for flowers. They are low on stock and suggest we come back tomorrow. I only need a simple bunch, I say, something to lay – I stumble over my words – for my daughter … she died and it's the first anniversary. We're laying flowers. I do not need to say 'at the bottom of a cliff' – I am both wanting and not wanting to say it. Instead, I say, Alice was trans. I'd like them to be in the colours of the trans flag.

Without questioning, the florist starts to select different stems, then puts them back. That's not the right pink, she says. This will be lovely for the blue, she adds, pulling out a long, spindly, fluffy waft of a flower. Love-in-a-mist, she says, which is nice. It is, I say, it's lovely. And it is lovely, that this middle-aged, middle-England potential of a lady in a random florist is so gentle with us and so aware. We are lucky and the flowers remind me of the flowers on the coffin, 364 days ago. The first year is nearly done.

Peter suggests we take Pippin to see Alice too this time and we all agree. Over this last year, Pippin has changed. He's far more settled and comforts us more than he used to. Whilst we still can't train him to come back when called, he has tricks he can perform: paw, beg, dance, spin, roll over and so on. All of these were taught to him by Alice, so they are a way of connecting us to her; we sense her presence, carried in this series of learned responses in her little dog.

I'm going to take Alice a G and T, Peter adds. He decants some Mermaid gin into a little glass herb jar and pops it into the Cath Kidston insulated bag Kate used to use for her school packed lunches. We no longer have Alice's, it would have been black, grey or blue. I wonder whether she would have liked a floral one, I muse. Peter has prepared ice packs ahead of time – it has evidently been on his mind – and he fills the bag with these, plus a full ice-cube tray, a can of Fever-Tree and a tiny Tupperware with a slice of lemon. He's thought it all through; it is rather touching. It is his way to do something practical to show his love.

It's a beautiful day, sunny and bright, and my mood is very different from the first time we went back after her death. I'm almost relaxed. It isn't something I'm looking forward to exactly. It's a bit like a trip to a distant family member, but that isn't right, because it isn't a duty or a chore. I want to do it, but I'm a little nervous, as if I'm about to meet someone I've heard about but never met. I'm not sure what to expect. And when I'm nervous, I chatter, and this is what I'm doing, talking to everyone about this and that, in a carefree, superficial sort of a way.

We walk along the path, noting the way markers on the sea wall, counting off the distance to the marker near the spot. As we approach the right place, Pippin takes a particular interest in the cliffs and stops for a good sniff. Alice's scent is long gone, but it makes me happy, an imagined connection.

When we agree on the spot, I plonk myself down on the wall, where we sat and were comforted by that fluffy little dog back in June last year. Harvey and Kate sit next to me. I feel detached, I say to Harvey. Me too, he replies. But Peter, who is set apart, is not detached. His face is creasing, crumpling into tears, he is making connections. I send Harvey to embrace him. This is Peter's day to cry and feel a raw pain that is so often pushed away to make his living more tolerable. Here, today, it is on display and it fills me with love for him.

I'm not good at imagining like you are, he says, so it hits me harder.

Yes, I say. I've stood with her at the top of these cliffs and sat with her at the bottom, countless times.

I don't do that, he says.

I know, I reply.

We lay the flowers and Peter prepares the G and T in a large goblet glass. We all take a sip, as if we are sharing communion wine, then place the rest for Alice by the flowers. I pick up a piece of chalk and begin to write Alice's name on the wall, then the date she died. It's tricky, the wall is rough. I ask Kate to come and help me. We have to lick our fingers to smear the chalk into the gaps. We are engrossed in our task and don't notice a man pull up on a bicycle and stop a few metres away from us. Do we look up or does he start talking to draw our attention?

I'm the person who found Alice, he says.

I'm looking into his face and getting up to approach him.

Everyone has turned to him, this stranger, who says he was with Alice that morning. It's a miracle.

I introduce myself. I'm Caroline, Alice's mum, I say. I gesture towards my family, naming each of them and their relationship to me, to Alice. They are all staring wide-eyed at this man, astride his bike.

I'm Steven, he says, I found her.

I can't believe you're here, I say. I've thought of asking the police to put me in touch with you so many times and here you are.

I shouldn't be, he says. I'd finished work and was heading home, but I forgot my shopping so I'm heading back.

It's a miracle, I say again. Can you tell me a bit about it? I ask. He talks quite freely about how he found Alice, that he could see something from a distance and thought she was rubbish, bin bags, but when he got nearer, he could see it was a body, a young woman.

She was trans, I said.

I know, he replies. I thought it was a girl, he said. She was so young and pretty, but the cliffs had torn her clothes and she was exposed, so I realised she was trans straight away. I'm a gay man, Steven says. I notice he's wearing a wedding ring.

You're married, I say.

Yes, he replies, to Jon. The shopping's for him. It's only M & Ms but he does love them.

Who doesn't love an M & M? I say.

What a kind man, I am thinking, what a relief, that Alice was found by a gentle man, an ally, someone who cared.

Friend me on Facebook, he says, and anytime you want me to lay a flower for Alice, just message me and I will.

Thank you, I say, that's lovely.

He is crying a little now and we have a hug. It is a gift from the universe that makes me believe in something, but I don't know what it is. Possibility?

After Steven leaves, we walk down to the end of the groyne and sit to dip our toes in the cold sea, and we laugh as one of Peter's socks blows into the water. Then we have a drink in the Brighton Tavern, where we used to take Alice for a pint of Neck Oil. But it is not the same – the bar person is new and doesn't recognise us. It has lost its magic for me; Brighton didn't keep Alice safe, after all.

And it seems maybe this is the place to end, but there is more, there will always be more. To finish at a year implies that a year is all a person needs to come to terms with grief. One year. But that would be a lie, for now we must do it all over again.

Late April 2022

A rare and devastating argument

All too soon, Alice was ready to return to Brighton, even though there was nothing specifically to go back for, just independence. We'd had such a lovely month together, and it was sadness at losing this, rather than any fear of her being on her own in Brighton, that made it more challenging than usual to say goodbye.

The very next day, whilst I was at work, she texted the Team Alice WhatsApp chat she had with me and Peter. Jumping through the online hoops to request her repeat prescription from her new GP was sending her into a spin. When I finished teaching, I saw dozens of unread messages. Peter had been helping and reassuring her over the airwaves. I fucking hate this shit, she texted ... Every time I try to get something done it puts as many obstacles in the way as possible ... I think I need someone to pick me up. I can come right now, I replied. Yes please, she said, accompanied by a picture of her PC monitor on the floor with a caption: I might have got a little upset, lol.

I arrived to find her quite relaxed

I'm ok, now, she said. I think I'd rather stay.

Are you sure? I asked.

Yes, she said. I'm fine.

She didn't want me to stay, so there was nothing to do but turn around and drive back home.

I popped down to see her a few days later anyway. I needed reassurance. We had a rare and devastating argument. I vaguely remember how it started. Alice, please don't talk to me like that, I said. I've no recollection of what she said to elicit this remark – don't talk to me like that; not a particularly unusual phrase, but not one I used often. I'd driven from home and maybe I was tired and she'd forgotten I was coming. That had happened before. Or maybe she didn't seem to care I was there and had answered a friendly suggestion with a casual whatever.

Either way, it was a throwaway comment that could have been left unsaid and it hurt Alice. She flipped. It was such a shock. She'd never done anything like this before.

Get out of my house, she yelled. Get out. She was slamming doors.

What? I said. I haven't –

Just get out, get out, she continued.

But Alice, I said. What are you doing? What's –

This is my house, get out or I'll call the police.

Alice, please, I'm sorry, I didn't mean –

Get out.

No, I say. No! I can't leave you like this.

Get out.

I can't leave you.

I'll call the police. Get out, she screamed.

I could count on one hand the number of times Alice had ever lost her temper with me, raised her voice. This was so frightening and unfamiliar.

What's happened? I pleaded. What did I do? Please. Talk to me, I cried. I can't leave like this. Please.

She was in her bedroom now, behind a locked door. Just go away, she said.

The situation felt so unsafe. I told her through the door that I was going to leave the house but sit on the bench over the road. That I could not leave until I knew she was ok. Alice didn't reply. I sat down and sobbed. It started to rain. It had been mild and bright when I left home, now I was cold and wet, in a t-shirt with no coat. Several people passed by and appeared not to notice this shivering woman in crisis on the bench. Eventually, a young mother with three preschoolers stopped and asked me how I was, could she help? I was struck that someone with their hands entirely full was the only person to stop. I'm ok, I said, it's my daughter, she's not very well.

Eventually, I calmed down, texted Alice to ask if I could come back in. I'm cold, I said. Where are you? she asked. On the bench, I replied. I'll come out, she said.

She appeared a few minutes later with a couple of shopping bags. I need to go to Aldi, she said. Nothing more. Are you ok? I asked. Yes, she replied. Sorry, I said. Alice smiled. She didn't want to say another word about it.

We went to Aldi and she filled her trolley. At the checkout I paid.

If I'd known you were going to do that, I'd have treated myself, she said.

That's why I kept suggesting you had this or that, I said.

I didn't know, she said.

Kate and Harvey would have done, I replied. She shrugged. Do you want to go and get some more things now that you do?

Nah, she said. Let's go back.

Back at the house she was ready for me to leave. Are you sure you're going to be ok? I asked.

Yeah, I'm fine, she said.

I love you, I said.

Love you, too, she replied.

June 2023

Another funeral, a memorial tattoo

Harvey comes home for his birthday. It's a quiet affair; we will be cremating his grandmother the following afternoon. It will be my first funeral since Alice. Peter has attended a couple, though not at the same crematorium. Several of Peter's mates come to help us send Gill off. We behave badly, lobbing sausage rolls at Ginge. And later, Peter and I have sex. Kate has to put her headphones on! It's been a long time coming, and it doesn't mark a significant turn in our fortunes in this department, but it's a start. Perhaps it is very particularly because Alice is our child, and it's something about sex being tied with making babies that makes it so impossible, although it hasn't been about that for us for years. It's definitely too late for any of those sorts of ideas, even if I were to have them – about replacing Alice somehow, as if she were a dog.

Peter and I talk afterwards. I share that I am scared that our relationship may not survive, that I still find him unpredictable and that it is this, I think, that makes intimacy so difficult – for I need to feel entirely safe to allow myself to be so exquisitely vulnerable. I still have fantasies about running away and being alone and I share some of them with him, some of my rehearsed words. He goes very quiet.

C'mon, I say. Are you really going to tell me that it's never once crossed your mind, since Alice died, that life might be easier without me?

Fair enough, he says. Let's get that couples therapy.

A few days later, he takes himself off to the Lake District alone, to walk. It is the anniversary of Alice's funeral whilst he's away, and although this gave me cause to be angry with him when we discussed the dates, I completely forget about it on the day. I am worried about Peter, partly because I'm afraid he will get lost in the hills, but mostly because he's taken a bottle of whisky with him. I'm worried about what might happen whilst he's alone with his thoughts and alcohol, a long way from home.

I've decided to get a tattoo to remember Alice, to carry her with me always. Kate and Harvey already have identical ones of the handbag of Kate's that Alice used to play with as a toddler. Peter has one, from a selection Alice was considering, that the tattoo parlour sent us after she died. It's my turn. I choose the inscription from the 'fucking fuck' notebook. Alice had written on the preprinted lines within a lozenge, on the front page. Property of: Alice Litman, it says, in her spidery, childish scrawl. It speaks to me of a reversal. Whilst many parents treat their children like property, this was something I aways tried to avoid, but now, somehow, in her final act, I feel that Alice has taken more ownership of me than either of her siblings will ever demand. For Kate and Harvey will mature and change, and our relationships will do the same, but my relationship with Alice has been cut abruptly, frozen in time. Whilst she could not hold on to her life she has got her claws into me. The tattoo heats up, and throbs a little, at random times and I imagine Alice is saying hello.

Late April–early May 2022

Alice takes us to the beach

Our argument did not seem to set Alice back. She continued to be bright and communicative on the family WhatsApp. She messaged her opinion about stories in the news, sent a photo of her rearranged bedroom, organised and tidied, hoovered and dusted, simple things, but as I know myself, a sign of growth, of recovery. I posted a picture of a bedside table; did anyone want this before it went to the dump? Yes, said Alice, I need more storage, could you bring it down next time you come? Quite unremarkable to many, but for us, a huge change. Alice was beginning to look out for herself, make plans and decisions independently of me or Peter. She'd treated herself to a tattoo, was planning designs for another. Until recently, I'd been booking all of her speech-therapy sessions, liaising back and forth between Alice and her therapist – a complicated arrangement, given Alice was so bad at replying to messages and rarely answered her phone. Now Alice had become proactive, booking and paying for her own sessions, managing her own diary, without me as an intermediary.

Peter and I went down for another lunch, but this time a trip to the beach, somewhere she'd never wanted to go with us before. We passed Revenge. I might apply for a bar job there, she said.

We sat on the beach and watched the seagulls boldly scavenging. Alice laughed as she told us how once Keith's chips had been snatched out of his hands.

There was optimism in the air, not just for us, but for everyone. I had a sense that the finger had finally been lifted from the pause button of Covid and lives could now resume play. Alice took a photo of Peter and me on the beach, which I now cherish, because I am smiling broadly at the camera, smiling at my child, who I can no longer see.

July 2023

A small service of remembrance, some important news, an incredible find

In mid-July, we're interring Alice's ashes. At the last minute, I decide I can't put all of her in the ground, and that despite my initial thoughts that she shouldn't be divided up, this is what I would prefer, some of her kept back. Everyone agrees and we buy another urn.

We choose to keep this short service small. Just the four of us and Shin Ah, too, our new five, plus a few of Alice's friends. Lucy, who missed the funeral and Alice's birthday, comes to stay. It is so wonderful to see her. Whilst it was comforting to see so many people at the funeral, I sometimes wonder why some of the mourners were there. But her friends, I know why they were there, are here now, because they knew her and they loved her. They wrote such beautiful words about her that they read out on the day. And at the internment, Lucy speaks her words, for her dead friend, describes a friendship she hopes everyone has the privilege of experiencing, how Alice seemed to know her better than she knew herself and shaped who she has become today. How Alice lives on this way, in all of us.

Alice's friends have made a temporary headstone. It is pink, and floral, festooned with pictures from happy times. It is perfect. They adapt a Kae Tempest poem: 'You were the strongest one among us. Daring as you did to live wholly as you were'.

We finally receive the toxicology report from the coroner, a full fourteen months after Alice died. Our emotions are less intense, but Kate and I still have the same hope for the results. Peter doesn't express an opinion. Harvey wants the opposite, for her to have been really drunk, totally out of it, so she didn't suffer, feel any physical pain. Inevitably, someone is going to be disappointed.

No trace, it says, of any substances; no alcohol, no cannabis, no cocaine or benzodiazepines, nothing at all detected. I want to find the nurse who sneered at my child's lifestyle choices, shout: look, look, see. This is who she was.

The full post-mortem is attached to the email, too. The box for gender is left blank, but there is a description of her external genitalia. It is difficult to read. I have literally forgotten this detail of her life. What was between her legs is of no importance to me. Other details are recorded, the specifics of her injuries, plus things that seem irrelevant: the weight of her brain (larger than usual), her spleen (on the small side), her kidneys (not worthy of weighing). Kate and I picture her in bits on a slab, like offal at the butcher, before she was put back together for us.

We also receive a coroner's bundle, with a list of pdf files for our perusal. I worry that there will be photos of Alice's body at the inquest, because one file, named 'images', is not attached. Too graphic, then, to be shared over email, but available to the coroner. Will we be able to leave the court when they are shown? I ask. Yes, I imagine so, I'm told. Then I worry endlessly that I should stay and see them, for if Alice had the courage to end her life, the least I should do, as her mother, is have the courage to endure the physical consequences. In the end, there are no pictures at all, but no one thinks to tell us this months ahead of time and save unnecessary anguish.

A few days later, Peter and I go to see Royal Blood at On the Beach, in Brighton. I have bought the tickets for Peter for his birthday, emboldened because a dear friend is going too and I know I will be taken care of, if I find myself struggling in any way. We have a few beers, then join the queue to get in.

Shall we stop here or move a little nearer the front? Keep going. Here? No, a little further. Finally, we plonk ourselves down to sit and wait. Peter starts sifting through the pebbles. This one's nice, he says, I might take it home. I think about my precious contact relic and decide that I will choose another stone, too. A ritual beginning, one for every year that Alice isn't here. I pick up a simple, plain one and turn it over. On the other side is a perfect heart. Not just a vague heart that you can visualise by squinting at it sideways and pretending, but a full-on cartoon love heart, on this stone in the palm of my hand. How many stones do you think there are on this beach? I ask. I google it. One hundred billion, it says. And I sat here and picked up just this one.

7 May 2022

A very special day, a turn of fortunes?

In early May, I went down to see Alice at the weekend on my own because Peter was away mountain biking with the lads. She was in a buoyant mood, our fight of the previous week completely forgotten. She was dressed and ready when I arrived, had done her make-up.

You look lovely, I said.

I can't tell you how well I feel, she said.

We hugged. I'm so pleased, I said. You do look really well, really, really well.

And she did. She was a child restored, just as she had been after Lucy's visit almost four years before.

Has something happened to put you in such good spirits? I asked.

I don't think so, she said. Perhaps it's not taking the antidepressants.

Alice! When did you do that?

Ages ago, she said.

Can you be more specific?

Maybe about two months by now. I'd only been taking them randomly for ages anyway before then.

Have you had any problems with withdrawal?

Nah, I feel ok. I'm sleeping better, my weird dreams have stopped.

Well, that's good, I said. Let's see how things go.

We went shopping in The Lanes, browsed the second-hand clothes shops and the Emporium, but she didn't ask to try anything on, or hint that I might buy her something. Alice was not good at asking for anything. After lunch, I suggested taking her to buy some new clothes, since we hadn't found anything suitable in the vintage stores, but Alice had had enough, so we walked back to her house. Back in her bedroom, she showed me a new journal she'd treated herself to. I've decided I am allowed nice things, she said. She put the book up to her face and inhaled deeply. Don't you just love that new-book smell? she said.

I do, I agreed.

Later, when I recounted my day to Peter, he was sad to have missed it. She really did seem completely well, I said.

August 2023

More anniversaries, a relationship improving and another one ending

Peter celebrates another birthday. We celebrate another wedding anniversary. We go to a restaurant in London recommended by Harvey and order a bottle of red at random from their list. I read the label. Look at this, Peter, I say. Look who's made our wine: MarMot and Wii (born a transgender butterfly), it says. I am quite astonished at Alice's little habit of turning up unexpectedly.

But although I have a lovely day, as we stand on the platform to catch the train home, I have fleeting thoughts of how easy it would be to throw myself into the path of an oncoming train. Suicidal thoughts are still present, even today, on a thoroughly enjoyable day, our wedding anniversary. But I must not really want to, because I don't. Instead, I take a small step back and hold Peter's arm a little tighter. He smiles warmly at me.

Peter has always been able to feel and show happy, loving emotions. It's what drew me to him in my twenties. And lately, I've been discovering he's really good at reading and reacting to sad or bad emotions in other people, when I see him interact with others grieving at TCF. But doing the same for himself is quite new and a challenge. As we continue to attend our individual psychotherapy, we both learn and slowly draw closer in our grief. I can only speak for myself; I have stopped feeling responsible for him and his negative emotions.

Around this time, my school friend Matt suddenly becomes very unwell and is admitted to hospital for a barrage of tests. It soon becomes apparent that he's not going to get better. I'm invited up to

London to see him, to say goodbye. We hold hands, he drifts in and out of sleep, I feel at peace. I feel tranquil and safe in a way I don't in the company of many old friends. We talk, much as I did with Gill, about where he is going, about whether he might bump into Alice. Later, I tell his wife that my three hours with Matt have been the best of my life, since Alice died at any rate. The chance to say goodbye to Matt has been some small compensation for the goodbye I didn't have with Alice. She is glad. It crosses my mind to volunteer at a hospice as I seem to take comfort in being with people who are about to die.

A few days later, I'm due in Plymouth, but anxiety almost stops me going. I'm visiting a friend, meeting her new partner. The thought of small talk seems so banal after what has come before, though in the end, I do manage it, because I don't want to let her down.

Are you a barrister, too? someone asks. I try out my new job title for the first time: I'm a writer, I say. But I haven't prepared myself for the inevitable questions. What are you writing? A memoir. What's it about? My daughter. Is it funny? No, not really.

But I find on this occasion that I can cope with these questions and do not care if I've made my inquisitor uncomfortable. Earlier, we swam in the sea at Firestone Bay and it is like I've had a factory reset. I feel fully restored. And after that we took a trip on the Torpoint ferry to Whitsand Bay, where I sat and breathed in the air, took in the view, memories flooding back of summer breaks here with the children. I felt content, and this contentment lasts to buoy me through the evening.

Upon my return, Matt has taken a turn for the worse. I go to see him one final time. Like Gill, he's at home, surrounded by family. Before the month is out, he too is dead.

8–10 May 2022

Alice takes a slight turn for the worse

The joy that came from my most recent visit to Alice didn't last long. She woke the very next day with a nasty earache; it was stopping her sleeping and she didn't know what to do. If you have an infection, you might need antibiotics, I said. Can you make yourself a doctor's appointment?

I was due in Leeds to see Kate and Rebecca, but I cancelled, so I'd be around to help Alice if she needed me. We messaged back and forth. Alice did book herself an appointment and thought she would manage to get to it under her own steam or, if not, Keith would help her.

Alice became increasingly worried when dark gunge seeped from her ears. She wondered if it was blood. It's probably wax, I said; you need ear drops. I've already ordered some from Amazon, she replied. I was so delighted. This was another sign that she was doing well, was looking after herself, no longer required constant prompting and regular hand holding to get the smallest things done.

She sent me a photo of four slugs on her bedroom floor. She had emailed the landlord and put down salt. Even a story of slug-slime trails on the carpet was one of recovery.

But then Alice messaged the next day that she was feeling sick; she didn't know if it was her ear, or whether she was anxious. She was feeling down, she admitted. Her ear problem had knocked her back and her new-found confidence was seeping away.

She did need help to get to her appointment, after all.

September–October 2023

An empty nest, an inquest and a terrorist attack

On 1 September, Kate moves out, to a vast room in a third-floor Gray's Inn residential scholar's flat. It will be her home for the next eleven months. I drive through central London for the first time in my life to take her there. It is exciting to do something novel, something full of promise for my daughter.

Three days later, Peter goes away to the Lakes again, this time with his sister, Mary. There have been arguments about the timing of his trip. That he should plan to leave me entirely alone, now, when all my children have finally moved on, in one way or another. I tell Harvey I'm upset and, unprompted, he offers to come and stay with me whilst his dad's away. I accept gratefully. Over the last year, Harvey and I have taken to spending some mother-and-son time together every couple of months. Just the two of us up in town for a meal and a drink. We talk about Alice in a way that we don't when he comes back to the house and we're all together. On these occasions, Harvey takes on the role of jester, cheering us all up, but having him home to myself for a few days will be a treat.

Two weeks later, the inquest begins. We've booked an Airbnb. Harvey's been given time off work; Kate will miss the first full week of her bar course. Pippin comes, too. The inquest is set to last three days. My brother drives down with our mother for the first day, to hear me read my pen portrait, condensing Alice's life to a few words on a page to bring her to life for the coroner and the journalists that pack the courtroom. For it is as we wished and we have attracted the interest of the press.

Though it is not really a courtroom, the decrepit coroner's court has been upgraded to a room at the Sussex County Cricket ground. On the first morning, the room next door has been booked for another event. There is some sort of team-building exercise going on and whoops of laughter can be heard drifting in. No one else seems to be troubled, or aware, or mindful to intervene. I pop my head round the door and ask the bemused group, if they could please keep the noise down as my child's inquest is about to begin in the adjacent room.

But there is a problem that first morning. Every inquest must be recorded by law, and there is a missing cable or bit of equipment, and, after a wait of several hours, the hearing is adjourned until after lunch. Quite typical, we all mutter, when a prime focus of the inquest is on waiting times and delays.

PC Boris Becker is there. It is nice to see him again and revealing to me that he neither looks much like Becker nor sounds like a vicar who doesn't believe in God. He is perfectly charming. Dr J, Alice's Brighton GP who never met her in person, will give evidence, as will Dr Michael Webberley, Helen's husband. Although neither the GP practice nor Gender GP was entirely blameless, we choose not to pursue them at the inquest, for it seems wrong to criticise the few who struggle as they fight to treat the trans community in the face of the neglect of the many.

A senior nurse comes to represent Surrey and Borders Partnership NHS Foundation Trust. She ties herself up in knots. Ultimately, she says, Alice's needs were around her gender and they were not equipped to take care of that. Though on the other hand, Dr Barratt, lead clinician at the Tavistock GIC, won't accept any responsibility either, for it is not up to his department to take care of patients' mental-health problems whilst they sit on the waitlist.

It is hard to listen to people defending what to me feels indefensible – discharging a child from mental health services a few months after a serious suicide attempt just because they turn eighteen, deflecting responsibility.

Dr Barratt appears to be performing to an audience, forgetting who's in the front row. To answer a question about the records they keep of suicides of those on the waitlist, he gives an example of calling the GP of a patient he believes to have killed themselves. It turned out the GP had seen them in clinic that morning, they weren't even dead! he proclaimed. A punchline that sees me pushing back my chair and running for the nearest exit. But he does come up trumps in other respects. He states that the census data of 2021, which estimates 0.5 per cent of the population is trans, shows the need for care is 'way too frequent to be handled by specialist commissioning', as it currently is. He also asserts that 'statistically the thing that most lowers the risk of completed suicide and ... self-harm is actual treatment' and that 'the monitoring bit of all this isn't intrinsically particularly difficult ... treating something like diabetes is probably more challenging'. He says that he runs a one- to two-hour training session that leaves some GPs 'confident enough to prescribe bridging hormones (hormone treatment whilst people wait for a GIC appointment).' He continues, 'I can't think of any other condition, other than perhaps termination of pregnancy, where random people, who aren't themselves patients, feel they have an absolute right to have a view on what should and should not be provided, to people who aren't them, not even people they know ... and that view apparently, seemingly shaping services.'

We turn to each other and nod as he agrees with our counsel, that if you were referred to the GIC today, if nothing were to change, you might face a wait of close to twenty years. At last, we have it from the horse's mouth. Newspapers will have to start printing the truth about waitlists from now on: not the two years that's bandied around, so those who are opposed to trans healthcare can equate it with the wait for a hip replacement or a cataract, but a wait as long as Alice's life lived over. It is a frustrating day of evidence.

In the end, the coroner adjourns the inquest. She will sum up her findings at a later date to be arranged. Thirteenth October is pencilled in, pending availability of all involved. Kate sends out a press release. We are hopeful the final ruling will get extensive news coverage, that the plight of trans healthcare will be covered on television and on the front pages of all the national papers. This is what we have been working towards. We pray for a slow-news day. I repeat my joke that I do hope Elton John or some other national treasure doesn't die and steal our thunder.

I decide to start tapering my antidepressants. It is not as if my mood is particularly buoyant, but I am coping with all the challenges that keep coming my way.

On 7 October, Hamas launches an attack on Israel. Hundreds of hostages are taken, over a thousand Israelis are killed. Israel retaliates immediately, declaring a state of war. Thirteenth October arrives and we read a statement to the assembled press, but Alice's story is confined to a few sentences on the inside pages, if at all. Channel 4 News does carry our story; it is the only other one they cover that day. It feels wrong to express disappointment when such turmoil and tragedy are unfurling in front of our eyes, but for us personally, it is very bad timing indeed. It feels like there is nothing left to do.

11 May 2022

A trip to the doctor and an order for an americano that brings me joy

I drove down for Alice's GP appointment. Now that her ear was feeling a little better, she had the notion she'd be able to use the appointment to talk about her gender and hormone treatment instead. She was in such a buoyant mood, operating an internal logic that her most pressing issue would take precedence. It was difficult to burst her bubble.

This appointment isn't with Dr J, though, is it? I asked tentatively.

I don't know, she said.

I knew it wasn't. Dr J was in high demand because their practice accepted gender-non-conforming patients who were being denied healthcare by their local GP. Her appointment with them wasn't until 4 July. This appointment's about your ear, Alice, I said. But she didn't want to hear me.

We walked from her house to the surgery, a journey of about thirty minutes, chatting about this and that on the way. I sat in the waiting room whilst she went in. She wasn't long. Did you talk about your hormones, I asked? No, she said. He didn't even look in my ear.

We walked homeward, popped into the Co-op for a bottle of water. Do you want anything to eat? No, thanks, she said. She was definitely a little down. So was I. Alice had asked for an appointment about her mental health and hormones weeks ago but still had two months to wait, but when she'd had an earache, she'd been seen within days.

This discrepancy weighed heavily on my mind after Alice died. Had it weighed heavily on hers, too? Did it speak to her of priorities, importance and values? How much she mattered as a trans person?

———————

As we approached the bus station, she changed her mind. Could I have a doughnut? she asked.

We stopped at the Krispy Kreme outlet.

Do you want a coffee?

Yeah.

Which one?

An americano, please.

Milk?

No, black, like you.

Sophisticated, I said.

Yeah, I'm turning into a grown-up, she beamed.

We arrived back at her house. Would you like me to stay? Take you out for dinner later?

Nah. I'm tired, I think I need to go to bed, she said.

Ok, I said.

And I can't remember what I said next. I love you, see you again soon?

November–December 2023

Keeping busy and reflecting on the impact of trauma

I'm invited to speak on the healthcare panel at the inaugural Translucent Conference, a trans-led organisation campaigning for trans rights. Peter comes with me. Whilst we are glad to speak of our experience, I am uncomfortable, for we share a platform with Dr Helen Webberley from Gender GP. Helen comes across as passionate on her subject. She's been cleared of any wrongdoing by the GMC and her business is flourishing. I believe in her good intent with regard to trans healthcare, but I also believe Alice was let down. Just as she was by primary care at various stages.

We go to Shropshire to see Ali and Elis again. It's a year since we last saw them. It is clear to them how much better I am, and this helps me acknowledge that things have shifted, though some days I feel entirely back to square one. We see a friend of theirs who I've met several times before. Her daughter died in a drowning accident four years ago. It is reassuring to hear that she and her husband are still together, though I find out three months later that they have split up and I worry once more about the future for Peter and me.

In mid-December I travel to Norwich on my own to write, renting a little Airbnb on St Giles Street. I've never taken myself off like this before, have never been entirely on my own for so long in a strange place since my marriage. I'm on a reconnaissance trip; Norwich is on my list of running-away destinations. I explore the marketplace and the cobbled lanes, the cathedral square and the river, as much as my knee will allow. I meet Bea for lunch one day and find out we're both going home to Surrey on the same day. Bea's already booked her coach trip, but when she finds out she can come in the car with me she jumps at the chance. I'm overcome with affection and gratitude towards her, quite surprised that she would choose four hours in the car with me, rather than solitude on the coach. At her age, I wouldn't have done the same with any of my mother's friends. We chat, laugh and cry all the way home. Bea tells me about Alice's last trip to see her, that although Alice joined in and had fun, she seemed more tired than usual. They'd gone clubbing and Alice hadn't been able to enjoy it. She couldn't drink because she couldn't use either loo, even with her friends.

Her confidence had dropped, I think, since the last assault at Beluga, Bea says.

It must have been an effort, I say. She had to pretend to feel safe.

Yes, says Bea. I think it must have been exhausting, living with the fear that she might be abused at any moment.

This sounds like a truth, especially given what I now know of the effects of trauma on my own ability to interact with other people, be it an attempt at an anonymous shopping trip, hidden behind dark glasses and a baseball cap, or a planned coffee with friends. The constant feeling that most people simply don't understand me and my identity, that of a bereaved mother. The feeling that they would rather I behave as if none of this has happened, so they can, too, exhausts me in a similar way.

I miss Peter whilst I am away, so it is a comfort when I am home again.

12–18 May 2022

A quiet week

Alice and I kept chatting, privately and on the family WhatsApp. She was excited that Russell T. Davies was back as showrunner for the next series of *Dr Who* with Ncuti Gatwa in the title role. On 14 May, she messaged to ask who was watching Eurovision. We all replied, but none of us was. Was she reaching out? Would she have felt less alone if we'd arranged a Zoom Eurovision night and got drunk together over the internet? Alice didn't engage on the family WhatsApp after that, but I still messaged her the odd little thing. On 16 May, I asked if she was ok. Yeah, she said, I'm ok. Two days later, I found her laptop charger; it had been left behind at Easter – I asked if she had any thoughts on when she'd like me to bring it down? She didn't mind, she said; it wasn't very urgent.

December 2023–January 2024

Christmas is nearly here and this year I find myself looking forward to it. With Kate and Harvey both now living independently, Christmas is a time for reunion. It will be good to have them home again for a few days.

I find I can't go to my Christmas meeting of my TCF bereavement-support group; I don't want to hear them all say how difficult Christmas is. I don't want to be boxed in by Alice's death. Though I am, frequently. It affects everything.

Alice's friends come round to the house, as they did last year, and for her twenty-first. The holidays pass quite pleasurably, except for a choking experience on Christmas Day, when Harvey and Kate make me laugh so hard that the Ferrero Rocher I'm indulging in gets lodged in my windpipe. Peter enacts the Heimlich manoeuvre to good effect and I live to tell the tale. Contrary to what I keep saying to myself, it turns out I don't want to die and am glad to be alive.

I work flat out for the first two weeks of the New Year, finalising the first draft of this manuscript. I barely leave the house. I become quite disturbed. It's rubbish, it's unintelligible jibberish, no one will want to read it. If I had a paper manuscript and an open fire, the whole lot could have gone up in flames. Harvey arrives for dinner and calms me down. My big lad, who used to be such a tearaway, so impossible to negotiate with, has become a kind and thoughtful young man, who cares for and reassures me. I settle down to eat.

But later, a low mood descends. My knee pain is quite disabling. I am on the waitlist for a small op to fix it. I grow roots out of my backside into the grief-couch, where I have sat and done most of my writing. I feel destined to stay here forever, getting more and more entwined in this relentless grief. Alice's office chair sitting unused and discarded in the corner of the study sends me into a spiral of gloom. Does anyone mind if we throw it away? I ask. No one wants it, so I take it to the dump and launch it into a skip.

At the end of January, a reporter from BBC *Newsnight* comes to do an interview with me. He is here for hours and although he is incredibly kind and thoughtful, it saps any remaining energy. I am tearful and lethargic for weeks after. Peter is worried; I am continuing to taper my antidepressants and am on a very low dose. He thinks I should restart them, but I'm determined not to. I've recently learned that there's a syndrome of permanent post-SSRI sexual dysfunction, PSSD, that tens of thousands of people in the UK suffer from. It fills me with rage and despair. I'd flagged up sexual side effects to the psychiatric team as a reason why I might not want to take an SSRI and now I'd found out they can be permanent. PSSD wasn't known about whilst I was a psychiatrist, but a quick google shows it's well documented now. Why wasn't I told? And it's not just my own sexual health that concerns me. One argument against prescribing cross-sex hormones for trans people is sexual dysfunction as a possible side effect. It makes a mockery of this argument, I rant at anyone I can corner, when psychiatrists and family doctors are quite happy to risk rendering so many cis people sexually inert, prescribing SSRIs like Smarties.

I want to stay off the medication and hope my libido returns. And anyway, I argue, as I've argued before, I shouldn't be medicated to treat extrinsic factors. I simply need to rest, to heal, just as I believe time to rest prevented long Covid from taking a grip on me. I'm exhausted after my writing marathon, after the interview. My mental wound is just like a physical wound, and I need time for my edges to knit together. I can't be hurried. I will continue to weep if repeatedly picked at. I have a few weeks now, with no expectations. I will ride it out, I decide. And I do.

18–25 May 2022

A week in which I did not do that which I wish I had done

Although Alice was being generally unresponsive on the family chat, she engaged with Peter about his next trip to see her. Peter took Pippin with him. It was something we had always talked about doing, but the plan had never been executed until now. They walked with the dog first, then went for something to eat. How was she? I asked when he got back. Great, he said. We had a lovely time.

Much later, Peter asks me, in a very quiet voice, do you think it was me, taking her for a walk on the downs that last time that gave her the idea? No, I reply. Of course not, no. Though I've sometimes thought, if only Peter hadn't taken Pippin on that walk, maybe then Alice would still be here. Not blaming Peter – for it had been my idea, the location and the dog. She'd love to see Pippin, I'd urged. Go for a walk at Jack and Jill Windmills. Treat her to a pub lunch. It's just we'd never taken Pippin with us before. His presence at home a lure to bring her back to us. But on this day that spell was broken.

The photos of Alice after her assault kept popping up as memories on my phone. I found them distressing. They felt like my wounds, too, a reminder of what had and could happen to my trans child. I wanted to delete them, but I didn't want anyone to think I was deleting them because I didn't care. I didn't want Alice to ask me for them later, perhaps if she changed her mind about making a complaint, only for me to be forced to admit I no longer had them. On Sunday, 22 May I messaged her to ask if it was ok for me to delete them. Yeah, she said. I didn't explain why, as I have just done here. I can only imagine what Alice made of this request. It was the last thing she replied to.

Are you sure she was ok when you last saw her, Peter? I asked. She's gone quiet again on the chat.

She was fine, he said.

I need to go and see her, I told him. To check in.

She's fine, he repeated. She's always going quiet. Remember the last time you drove down there in a panic?

Yeah, I said. I know.

On Monday and Tuesday, I had busy days at work. I'll go down on Wednesday, I said.

We're going to iFLY on Wednesday, Peter reminded me.

Damn, of course. Our Christmas gift from Harvey. Perhaps we could rearrange? But the expiry date was rapidly approaching and to not go would disappoint him. It was such a lovely gift and I posted a picture to the family chat of me and Peter smiling happily as we ventured off on our trip. Another of us flying in the magic column of air that stimulates flight. Alice saw the pictures but didn't reply. Kate and Harvey did, just a quick 'have fun', nothing more, but a reaction, none the less. I noticed, felt a little unease, as I always had, over the years when Alice became more withdrawn. But I didn't message her to say that I needed her to reply or I'd call Keith to check in on her, or that I'd call the police if she couldn't let me know she was safe, as I had done in the past to elicit a response. Two and a half years had passed since her last attempt and she had recently been feeling on top of the world.

I would go and see her in the morning.

February–March 2024

Trauma shifting and something else bedding in

My mother has made it to her ninety-seventh birthday. This year, I am able to spend it with her, enjoy the miracle that is another year lived independently by my remarkable mum.

Two days later is Alice's twenty-second birthday. Peter and I go to the crematorium, but in truth, after all the agonising about burial or cremation, about this plot or that, I don't feel much connection to that space at all. I rarely go to see her the way Peter does. We spend the evening with Harvey, meet him in a pub between our home and his, have a bite to eat. It's a quiet evening. Alice is not talked about a great deal; she is skirted around. I feel skirted around. I carried Alice in my belly for nine months, laboured and delivered her, fed her at my breast for a whole year. I feel particularly sensitive to the tradition of birthdays being solely about the child that is born rather than the mother who did the birthing, especially now this is all I have left.

Jane rings. She has been thinking of me at this difficult time. She has a favour to ask. Could she borrow Alice's desk chair? She wants to paint it for her art project on grief and transition. Twenty years after our catering misadventure, she, like me, is finally answering the call of her heart.

I've thrown it away, I whimper.

Well, if it was making you unhappy, that was the right thing to do, she says.

A few weeks after Alice's birthday is Mothering Sunday. On Saturday, Kate runs 44km from Holborn to our home in the Surrey Hills to deliver her card. Despite being overwhelmed with the bar course and pupillage applications, she is training for an ultra-marathon. On the second anniversary of Alice's death, she will run 100km, from London to Brighton, in memory of her sister. Harvey takes me and Peter out for lunch to mark the day. He books it and pays for it himself. It's a first; he is growing up. Seeing them both fills me with joy and the opposite: despair. Hearing the usual platitudes, you're such a good mum, catches at my wound and aggravates its edges. And the words Kate has written in her card are so intense and profound, not platitudes at all. If I am this good for Kate, despite all the things I ruminate over in my relationship with her, too, then perhaps it is true, I am not to blame for Alice, I am good enough.

Peter and I go to see my own mum. It is his first Mother's Day without his mum, but he isn't focused on this; he is focused on me as a mother. He has learned since Alice's birthday, when I felt a little forgotten.

A few days later, I have my knee arthroscopy to trim away my torn meniscus. Within a few weeks, my knee is improving and I'm able to walk the dog again, enjoy the simple pleasure of the rustle of the leaves in the wind and the spring sun on my skin. For I've really been experiencing a kind of semi-hibernation for the last three months, barely going outdoors at all unless I absolutely have to. Now, at last, I get up off the sofa and venture out – because I want to.

Peter gets a virus and is confined to bed. We are due to attend another wedding and he's too ill to go. I decide to go on my own. This is a shift in me that feels welcome and necessary.

A few days later, I'm at my mother's. You won't believe what happened last night, she exclaims. I fell out of bed!

Mum! Are you ok?

Yes, I just found myself on the floor and thought, how on earth did I get here?

She is quite amused at herself. We are both laughing.

You've strong bones, I say.

I must have, she agrees.

But seriously, I say. You could have broken something, your hip. I think it's time for that fall alarm we've been discussing.

Yes, she says.

She is ready, realises she is getting older and older, that one day she might take a tumble and not be able to get up again. She has cut herself in several places and patched herself up in the middle of the night. She has an appointment with the nurse in the morning, so I leave all the dressings in place. There is nothing practical I need to do, no trip to accident and emergency.

When I leave, I reverse the car off the hardstanding and swing up the road, looking in the rear-view mirror as I do my usual toot toot on the horn to say goodbye, as she cannot see me wave. Normally, Mum is stood on her doorstep waving me off, but today she has popped across the road to chat to her neighbour who is unloading his golf clubs, always curious, a little nosy she'll admit, to know what everyone is up to. I am overwhelmed with love for her. I know that I will not be able to run away, run from what has happened to Alice, that I need to stay – want to stay – to take care of my mother as she gets even older. I am grateful for the long life she has lived, and the fact that although over the years we have struggled on and off with our shared and individual traumas, time has given us the opportunity for our relationship to change, to grow and deepen. I think of Alice, how our relationship, and her relationship with the world she lived in, has been arrested, that we do not have a future to grow forward into together. I feel sad, but not hopeless. The future is there for the living and I'm beginning to feel that I am ready to act in my world, rather than react to whatever it throws at me. I honk the horn again and drive away, thinking, as I do more often these days, that this time might be the last. And when that time comes, I will be sad, but I won't be broken, for I will be glad of our time together. And this realisation gives me hope that one day I will be able to see my relationship with Alice in the same way, simply grateful for the fact that we knew each other at all.

Epilogue

People ask me if writing has been cathartic. Has it helped me process my grief? In short, no. It has felt like a drive, not a choice, something that must be done but in the end, my grief remains. I still have days where paroxysms of despair mean I cancel everything and reach for the medicines kept close at hand to quieten my mind and still my body. For Alice will always be dead and some days that fact hits me afresh, just as it did in my mother's garden not long after she died and will hit me again at any moment for as far as my mind can see.

But the drive remains. Why? I hope the answer is clear. Alice took her own life in the fledgling years of a decade that I believe may come to be recognised as the most hostile one in the history of modern trans existence, at least in the UK.

Alice's story is of a fight to be understood, by me, her doctors, the media, our politicians and the public. In telling it, I hope to show Alice as someone who was repeatedly let down, disregarded and abused out of fear, ignorance and prejudice. That the society she lived in ultimately made living intolerable for her. That it is a testament to trans people's resilience that so many can fight and thrive in spite of the way they are treated.

Alice's withdrawal into an online world, which I first saw as a place to distrust, full of groomers and ne'er-do-wells, had a purpose: it insulated her to some extent from the world around her, an important and necessary self-defence. I wonder whether the sense of optimism and new beginnings I felt as the Covid mindset finally seemed to lift in the months before Alice died was something she noticed, too – but for others, not for herself. Instead, she saw the Everest that lay ahead and the years she would spend in the foothills. Whilst her friends, her siblings, forged their own paths, she would be stuck. Alice didn't want, nor should she have been expected, to climb a mountain but that is surely how it felt. There was nothing to do but wait. She'd been on the Gender Identity Clinic (GIC) waitlist 1,023 days at the time of her death; if she were still alive, she would still be waiting now. For trans people like Alice waiting has become a super-power. This is not care, not a service – it is a holding cell, a type of torture. And it breaks people – Alice broke.

At her funeral, whilst I took the opportunity to reminisce and amuse the congregation with her sleeping and rugby skills, I also found a different voice, one I rarely found whilst she lived. Alice's eulogy was my first opportunity to speak to a captive audience about her transness and the impact society had on her life. It was the start of my campaign.

I described the first few days after Alice's death when I told myself and anyone who would listen that Alice was happy now. We even played Marina and the Diamonds' 'Happy' as a moment of reflection during the service. In a way, her death was the natural outcome of a resistant depressive illness, I said. We could compare her first suicide attempt on 1 June 2019 with the day a child is first diagnosed with cancer and the ensuing three years with a period of treatment, recovery and relapse that might be familiar to those who have experience of unsuccessful cancer treatment. The difference, of course, for Alice, I went on, is that her medical treatment was woefully inadequate and no child with cancer would be expected to wait over five years or more for their first appointment with an oncologist or rely on private prescriptions for basic medicines that may save their life.

Now I would add more, assert that there would be an outcry if whole cohorts of children (and adults for that matter) became so depressed because they were denied basic healthcare for their needs that the only answer was to battle to be seen for mental-health support. That depression, rather than the underlying issue, somehow became their primary diagnosis but it is what Alice and I had to hear about her gender incongruence on repeat.

The cycling girls came to the funeral, except Mon, who was on holiday. They sat in a pew – just as I did a few months later at St Martin-in-the-Fields – and listened as I told the story of my Devon trip, my epiphany. I didn't tell it to hurt or embarrass them, though I knew it might. I told it to illustrate the impact of speaking out concerning something you know very little about. I wasn't even that angry with Mon. She'd accidentally done me an enormous favour, crystallising the fight Alice was up against. After the funeral, my relationship with them fizzled out. I miss them and don't miss them. It's complicated.

Complicated ... a word you hear often about trans people. More broadly about their very existence – she'll never really be a woman, will she? said one friend about Alice after too many glasses of Prosecco – to more specifically how they take up space in our world, in toilets and prisons, and, specifically for me, in the healthcare system.

But it's not complicated. We have the Equality Act 2010 which, if applied correctly, can easily accommodate trans people's rights alongside the rights of cis people. The complication arises when gender-critical people make unevidenced statements and decisions, which diminish trans people. By talking of them only in terms of the risk they pose, the lies they embody, in suggesting that trans people, contrary to the rest of us, are all insane and that today's world would be better with fewer trans people living in it. This sort of speech seems designed to stoke fear and encourage division. And it's working. Trans discrimination is rife, both at street level, as evidenced by the assaults on Alice (neither of which she reported, suggesting the 2023 Office for National Statistics hate crime statistics, which show a

186 per cent increase in trans hate crime over the preceding five years, are most likely a huge underestimate) and at the very heart of government. Nowhere is this seen more clearly than in a trans person's inability to access appropriate healthcare.

Although Alice was never formally on the GIDS waiting list, it is worth explaining a little of the general situation in trans healthcare for young people around the time of her transition. In December 2020 in Bell v Tavistock, the High Court ruled under-sixteens could not consent to puberty blockers. This led to NHS England immediately stopping the Tavistock Clinic, the UK's only gender-identity development service for children and young people, from accepting any new referrals. The clinic was also instructed to cease any new prescribing of puberty blockers for under-sixteens already on its books.

Around the same time in autumn 2020 NHS England commissioned Dr Hilary Cass, a paediatrician with no experience in gender services, to undertake an independent review of gender identity services for children and young people. Whilst Dr Cass and her team began their work, Tavistock and Portman NHS Foundation Trust challenged the Bell ruling at the Court of Appeal. Almost a year later, in September 2021, the original High Court ruling was overturned. However, NHS England did not subsequently reverse their referral and prescribing decisions. The following year, February 2022, Cass published an interim report in which she wrote as if speaking directly to trans youth, saying, 'I think that more services are needed for you, closer to where you live.' She concluded that a 'single specialist provider model was not a safe or viable long-term option.' As a result, NHS England decided to close the Tavistock Clinic. Trans youth and their parents were naturally devastated by this turn of events: the only clinic in the country, already prevented from prescribing and accepting new referrals, was earmarked for closure without any alternative provision in place. All this took place in the period of relative stability in Alice's mental health, after her discharge from Child and

Adolescent Mental Health Services (CAMHS) and whilst her care with Gender GP seemed to be suiting her. I was aware of the issues, but to engage with them too deeply was distressing; knowing that other young people and their families were being denied support was no comfort.

In the run-up to the inquest I started to engage more, making enquiries into the current state of trans healthcare that might help our legal team. My bed-breaking pal, Andy, put me in touch with the head of the Royal College of General Practitioners (RCGP). We spoke 'off the record', my main focus being to establish the amount of trans healthcare training available for their members. Not a lot, it seemed. Similarly at medical school, practically none, which was confirmed by my nephew Michael and Emma's daughter (both junior doctors), who told me they had just one or two hours of lectures on LGBTQ+ healthcare. Although Ali's son, who trained in Sheffield, told me some clinical students had an opportunity to work for a week at the local gender identity clinic as part of their psychiatry block. Odd, when gender incongruence is no longer considered a mental-health disorder.

This makes me appear proactive and organised when really, I was floundering in a sea of grief and clutching at any opportunity to feel like we were doing something rather than nothing. And what did we hope to achieve? We hoped that going public with Alice's inquest would see a tidal change in opinion, raising awareness of the lamentable wait and the lack of mental-health support and promote a discussion about how best to move forward. We had bold ideas to upend gender specialist services and reduce NHS waitlists by despecialising and placing more responsibility on primary care, uncomplicating the treatment pathways trans people in England are forced to follow. Dr Barratt himself agreed at Alice's inquest that the medical care of trans patients is not complicated.

Another medical-school contact put me in touch with Dr Sophie Quinney, Clinical Director of the Welsh Gender Service, herself an ex-GP. She got into gender care because she saw how her trans patients were being let down and now leads a national service that has GPs at the heart of caring for their trans patients. The Welsh service is a beacon of good practice. This is what trans people want, need and deserve: timely, appropriate assessment treatment and follow-up, in the same way anyone would hope to be treated for any issue that required medical intervention. But in England, the service remains highly specialised, with GPs often afraid of, or worse, refusing to treat their trans patients. Waitlists grow and grow. Lives on hold.

And what about those questions that dominate the headlines: trans women in sport, prisons and public loos? Alice's story is not about that, but I'll address it briefly, and to do so, let's return to Jane. She watched videos and read and read. She learned that trans women were far more likely to exclude themselves from sport than ever participate at any level, let alone competitively. We saw this with Alice, an active young person withdrawing from the activities she loved. Jane read that there are policies in place to accommodate trans people in prisons that are completely reasonable, but the general public just aren't aware of them. They're only aware of the times when things go wrong, as they often do in prison, with no trans person involved at all, yet nobody makes a song and dance about it then. She recognised she was being sold a narrative by the mainstream media, whose main aim is to sell papers, and advertising space, to make money. Sensible policies and insignificant risk aren't interesting, are they? she said. I've never even encountered a trans person in a public toilet.

Ironically, any successful bid to secure and police women's toilets as single-sex spaces will see gender non-conforming cis women, in their failure to meet society's expectations of how women should present, at risk from anti-trans interrogators. Trans exclusionary politics are regressive and anti-feminist, but have captured the imagination of a few determined and angry women, including some with an apparent licence to write whatever they like about trans women and the 'threat' they pose.

Our media has a lot to answer for. I can only conclude that there are lots of staunchly gender-critical people in charge of editorial decisions since media coverage is relentlessly hostile. In 2012, just sixty articles about transgender issues appeared across the whole of UK media.* Ten years later, in 2022, the year of Alice's death, this had risen to 7,525. An increase of 12,400 per cent. Most of this rise has occurred since 2021, a year that saw some anti-trans activists gain media attention and political influence. In May 2022, the month Alice died, the *Daily Mail* alone published 163 articles on trans topics, mostly negative.

Alice's inquest did garner media interest. The coroner understood clearly, with wisdom and compassion, the problems Alice faced and issued a narrative verdict that concluded that Alice's wait for gender-identity services contributed to a decline in her mental health. Specifically, she issued a Regulation 28 report to Prevent Future Deaths, raising five main Matters of Concern. To paraphrase, these were:

- the knowledge and training for those in mental-health settings to care for those in the transgender community
- the delays in access to gender-affirming care
- the lack of mental-health care whilst on the waitlist
- the lack of clarity for clinicians in primary care and
- the lack of clarity for clinicians in mental-health settings as to how to support young transgender individuals.

---

* http://committees.parliament.uk/writtenevidence/128369/pdf/ for the figures from 2012 to 2022

Several sympathetic journalists reported our story, our call to arms, but no momentum was sustained. And our family's collective grief left us ill equipped to push, just as we struggled to push whilst Alice was alive.

We waited three months for the four organisations – NHS England, the Tavistock and Portman NHS Foundation Trust, the RCGP and Surrey and Borders Partnership NHS Foundation Trust – to respond. The latter was the only body we felt genuinely took on board their mistakes and reached out to meet with Peter and me to discuss how they could improve their care of young LGBTQ+ people accessing their service.

We are involved in developing LGBTQ+ training, to be made mandatory for all their staff, but government policy on the care of trans youth is a rapidly changing area and although the chief executive has committed to his promise, how this initiative will progress in the current climate remains to be seen. And what is the current climate? In April 2024 two new clinics for children (now called Gender Dysphoria Clinics) opened in the UK. All children from the Tavistock waitlist were moved to one or the other. This hardly counts as 'more services … closer to where you live'. In the same month The Cass Review final report was published. At 388 pages, this is not the place to dig deeply into what it said. For me it is enough to point out that in her foreword Cass wrote, 'this Review is not about rolling back on people's rights to healthcare.' Yet within months of its publication the Conservative health secretary used emergency legislative powers to impose a total ban on prescribing puberty blockers for trans youth (but not for cis youth with other medical issues) despite no call for a blanket ban in the report.

As I write, in July 2024, the Conservative administration has been replaced by a Labour government. In his first speech as our new prime minister, Sir Keir Starmer stood on the steps of Number 10 Downing Street and said, your government should treat every single person in this country with respect. The trans community and their allies will be watching closely to ensure trans people aren't left out of this commitment. Forgive me for finding politicians hard to trust.

The head of the RCGP is not a politician, but she is in a position of power and influence. I respected her request that our pre-inquest phone call be off the record, but when approached by ITV News for comment after the inquest, she changed her terms. She issued a statement that sent 'condolences ... to ... the Litman family' and used our off-the-record phone call to say, 'we have spoken to them at length.' The implication being we had all met after the inquest and discussed the findings when in fact we did not, we'd only had that one phone call between the two of us. It felt like a betrayal, a using of me to protect herself. It made me think of the complicated dynamics of doctoring.

The NHS is currently staffed by around 130,000 doctors: skilled, dedicated, caring people. But taking a psychodynamic perspective for a moment, whilst people get into the caring profession for all sorts of reasons, sometimes it's an unconscious way to have their own unmet care needs fulfilled. When they find themselves in the spotlight, with any possibility that they may have made a mistake, not been an ideal carer, they can't bear the pain this causes them so they deflect and deny. It is someone else, not they, who have got this wrong. A complete failure to recognise any darkness within. The great projection.

Nowhere do I see this more clearly than on Twitter/X, where the hate extended towards trans people and their allies is off the scale. I repeatedly hear that gender dysphoria is a mental-health problem and that is the only care Alice should have received. It is my fault, people say, that I couldn't see this and encourage her down another path. I am a murderer.

I've not been arrested yet, I say, whilst pointing out that homosexuality was listed as a psychiatric disorder until 1990 when it was removed from ICD-10. That whilst gender-identity disorder *was* recorded as a psychiatric disorder in ICD-10, this has been superseded by ICD-11, where, according to a vast body of medical and scientific opinion, gender-identity disorder is now recorded as gender incongruence, a condition related to sexual health, and *not* in the mental and behavioural disorders section at all. As with homosexuality, change and progress happen, I say. Pervert, they retaliate.

I am criticised for weaponising Alice's death and for using her as a shield to hide behind. She cannot be both, I say. They come back with something else, about my grooming, paedophilic ways. I soon realise my fight is not with those of gender-critical persuasion on Twitter/X. This is not where trans rights will be won or lost. Rather, I need to reach out to the wider public. My book is a call to arms. Just like the speaker at Brianna Ghey's vigil, I want trans allies to stand up and be counted. To speak out against what they see. The trans debate is steeped in language from the 1980s. Towards the end of that decade, we were in the midst of the AIDS crisis, Section 28 and a media campaign that portrayed homosexuality as a sin, an aberration, a fetish and something it was totally legitimate to discriminate against. Homophobia was rife. Now history repeats itself. The same 'legitimate' concerns that kids are too young, they'll grow out of it, they've been indoctrinated, it's not natural, but with a different group under attack.

In 2015, the UK was placed top on the Rainbow Map (rainbowmap. ilga-europe.org), an annual benchmarking tool ranking forty-nine European countries on their LGBTQ+ equality law and policies. In 2024, it sits at fifteenth. With the recent deterioration in healthcare for trans youth I can't see us maintaining even that position in 2025 unless there is some major sea change in attitudes to trans people within our new government. Within the general public, the British Social Attitudes survey 2024 shows approval ratings for trans people declining, in line with the ramping up of media animosity. And according to the IPSOS Pride 2023 global survey, the UK is now an outlier, positioned twenty-eighth out of thirty countries for positive attitudes to youth trans healthcare.

The few with the power to make decisions about how trans people are represented embolden the masses, creating hostile environments in homes up and down the land, where young trans people feel alienated from the families and within the communities who should be supporting them.

When Kate came out as a lesbian at thirteen, I thought nothing of it, but when Alice came out as trans ten years later, I didn't afford her the same level of respect. I'll never know if Alice would have survived if she'd grown up in a household where trans people were talked about with ease and grace. Might she have spoken to me aged fourteen, been referred and seen in a timely manner as my friend's daughter was? How different things might be.

I'll experience this self-recrimination, with varying degrees of conviction, until the day I die, but it will never bring Alice back. If, by way of her death, my experience can help another family, help a young person thrive, that is all I can hope for. But I cannot just hope. I must act. But I need help; I am ill equipped. And here, Twitter/X comes into its own: I find a community of trans people who are forgiving, supportive and insightful. They reach out to tell me my voice is heard and important to their community and this buoys me up when I am down and motivates me to continue. They do not blame me for one minute, the way I blame myself, for Alice's death. They recognise my experience, and hers, and it is a comfort, to feel understood.

And this is surely key. Are we not all seeking to feel comfortable in our bodies, our minds, our worlds? And for that to happen, we desire to be understood and seen, for who we are, not who others want us to be.

For a long time trans people have lived amongst us without the sky falling in, but in recent times, they have been othered, cast out and denigrated, portrayed as dangerous and mocked for their difference. The majority of women, a group who have historically been similarly sidelined, but for other things: their weakness, their feeblemindedness, their hysteria, support trans rights. But a very vocal minority choose to side with the oppressor rather than the oppressed in the matter of trans people. It feels safer, I suppose. Easier. Women have battled for so long against the patriarchy and achieved relatively little. I guess the easy wins some are now achieving over trans people boost their self-esteem.

Jane agrees. As a woman, I felt so vulnerable, she said. I saw danger in absolutely everything. Uniting with other women against trans people made me feel safe. My judgement became so skewed, I couldn't even see how skewed it was. But in the end, she said, I finally understood that trans women are as vulnerable as cis women, on the whole, and way more vulnerable in most cases.

But others doggedly continue with their moral policing and lives are blighted, cut short because of it. Recent revelations from two whistleblowers who worked at the now-defunct Tavistock Clinic have told Jolyon Maugham at the Good Law Project that in the seven years before the Bell v Tavistock case, there was just one suicide of a patient whilst on the waitlist. In the four years since the case, with the subsequent restrictions on access to treatment, there have been sixteen suicides that they are aware of. It's extremely distressing, a feeling exacerbated by the fact that no mainstream media outlet carries the story.

Just hours before I'm due to submit my final revisions of this book to my publisher, I make another disturbing discovery. I'm already aware of a well-known video, in which prominent gender-critical activist Helen Joyce, head of advocacy at Sex Matters, talks of reducing or keeping down the number of people who transition, because every one of those people is a huge problem to a sane world. What I have not realised until now is that this video was released less than twenty-four hours before Alice died. It sends me into another spiral of what ifs? I am beside myself at the thought that Alice might have seen it. Was this the very particular trigger I have ruminated and worried over? Certainly, it is something far more sinister than an empty jar of Nutella. I will never know. But it is another thread in Alice's story. And the story continues to unfold. Hilary Cass, in her final report, notes, the toxicity of the debate is exceptional, and goes on to write, polarisation and stifling of debate do nothing to help young people. Yet the outcome of the Review has been more polarisation, not less. We have a situation where one side, those with gender-critical views are lauding the Review and the decisions already made on the back of it, whereas the other, trans people, are in despair.

Can you imagine if a review of women's reproductive healthcare was undertaken by a man with no experience in that field and when the findings were reproduced, all men were happy with what it said whilst all women were up in arms? Would that feel ok? Would we expect women to roll over and take it lying down? Yet the Cass Review feels like just that. Trans people have effectively been told they need to get in line and accept the 'facts'. But the validity of the Cass Review has been challenged by many, not least and most recently (June 2024) in a report co-authored by a professor of law at Yale Law School, a doctor from Yale School of Medicine and their team of international experts. No wonder actor David Tennant, as the father of a non-binary child, when speaking at a recent LGBT awards ceremony, spoke of wishing the then Minister for Women and Equalities, Kemi Badenoch, would shut up. Earlier the same month, whilst still in government Badenoch tweeted that one of the reasons the UK had achieved a blanket ban on puberty blockers for children was, having gender critical men and women in the UK government, holding the positions that mattered most in Equalities and Health. It feels like a stitch up. The election of a new Labour government brings change, but whether this will be a positive change for trans people remains to be seen. The future remains so uncertain. What will happen next? I do not know.

Which is why it's so hard for me to end. Finishing this book feels like another loss, the pressure to hand over a perfect manuscript and not see ways, or find out things later, where I could have done it differently and ended with a different result. It is as though if only I could just keep on writing, I might be able to write my happy ending. Or if not my happy ending, at least a happy ending for all the trans people who need one so badly. But life is not like that, not neat and tidy. I must trust the book has done what it can, even as the story keeps on changing. Let me leave you with the final words from my eulogy as an example, so far removed from where I am now, still with something to say:

> What I try to take from Alice's death is that ultimately, whatever chain of events led her to take that final journey from her home in Brighton to the cliffs at Rottingdean, it was a path she took with fortitude, determination and certainty. That this was something she had agency over, her own destiny, and for that we should be grateful.

Again, with the passage of time, I've more to add. I am not grateful. I am perpetually on the edge of broken, that choosing death was all the agency she had.

Acknowledgements

This book's first incarnation was an entry to the Bridport Prize 2022, submitted as *My Fourth Child*. I thank everyone on the judging panel for seeing the potential in my unpolished submission.

To my daughter Kate, and the trans readers I reached out to regarding the original title, particularly Hugo, thank you for your advice on changing it.

Thank you to Jolyon Maugham at The Good Law Project, for recommending me to Antony Topping at Greene & Heaton and thank you, Antony, for trusting that introduction and taking a chance on me. Thank you to Imogen Gordon Clark, my editor at HarperCollins, for your trust, for giving me so much freedom, but invaluable direction when I was losing my way, and to Anne Newman and Georgina Atsiaris for your meticulous attention to detail. Thank you to Rachel Saunders for reading the manuscript from a trans perspective and for your reassurances.

Thank you to those in the LGBTQ+ community who have embraced me wholeheartedly. Your encouragement and compassion mean so much. Thank you to Claudia, therapist number seven, for the safe space you offer me. And thank you to Iva and Martin: though you are long gone from our lives, you are the au pairs the children, especially Alice, felt safe with and loved by.

Thank you to my friends, especially Ali, Elis, Chris, Caroline, Ingrid, Viv, Sarah and Dru, who have supported me unerringly since the day Alice died and continue to do so, and to Patricia, a new friend but one of immense importance to me. I will never forget the love you have all shown me through the worst of days. Thank you to Paul (Ginge) and Trevor, Peter's closest friends, and friends to all of us.

To Alice's friends, it is a joy to know you, though a great sadness that it is Alice's death that has brought us closer. My door is always open to you, as much for me as for you, for the stories of Alice you share are a precious gift. Thank you.

And finally, thank you to my family, my mum and my brother, and my husband, Peter, and our children, Kate and Harvey. Thank you all for understanding how much writing this book has meant to me. Thank you for accepting that in the sharing of our flaws, our love for one another and our mutual love for Alice shine from the page more brightly.